Sociology, Gender and Educational Aspirations

D0875015

Also available from Continuum

Analysing Underachievement in Schools, Emma Smith
Educational Attainment and Society, Nigel Kettley
Social Realism, Knowledge and the Sociology of Education, Karl Maton and
    Rob Moore
Identities and Practices of High Achieving Pupils, Becky Francis,
    Christine Skelton and Barbara Read

Sociology, Gender and Educational Aspirations

Girls and Their Ambitions

Carol Fuller

continuum

Continuum International Publishing Group

The Tower Building
11 York Road
London SE1 7NX

80 Maiden Lane
Suite 704
New York, NY 10038

www.continuumbooks.com

© Carol Fuller 2009

First published 2009
This paperback edition published 2011

British Library Cataloguing-in-Publication Data
A catalogue record for this book is available from the British Library.

ISBN: 978-1-4411-5207-7 (paperback)

Library of Congress Cataloging-in-Publication Data
A catalog record for this book is available from the Library of Congress.

Typeset by Newgen Imaging Systems Pvt Ltd, Chennai, India

To my aunty Hazel Page and to all the staff and girls at 'Southwell'.

Contents

Acknowledgements

In carrying out this research, special acknowledgement goes to Tony Walter and Paul Croll for all their patience, academic motivation and feedback they gave me. In addition, I would like to say a special thank you to Paul Croll for his encouragement and support and also to both Paul and Gaynor Attwood for providing me with the opportunity that enabled me to complete this study and thus realize my own aspirations. Thanks too to the Harold Hyman Wingate foundation for demonstrating confidence in me and funding a small part of this work.

Having never expected to go to university myself, I would like to thank the academic staff I met who engaged me with a desire to learn and enthused in me a passion for academic enquiry. Particular thanks go to Roberto Franzosi and Jeff Hass. In addition, it goes without saying that desiring to pursue knowledge is irrelevant unless those you are interested in exploring permit it. It is therefore most heartfelt thanks I offer to the head and the staff at 'Southwell'. In particular, thanks go to the head of sociology who went far beyond any expectation with the help and assistance she gave me. To the girls included in this study saying thank you seems hardly enough. Many of those included shared much of themselves with me and were excited by the prospect that someone may one day read about them. I thank them all for the time and the trust they gave me and can only hope I do them justice.

Finally, I would like to thank all my family and friends for their encouragement and support but, more important than that, their patience and understanding. In this respect no one deserves thanks more than my friend Sam, for her practical assistance in the earlier years, my mother for her words of wisdom or my father for helping out financially. Loving and special thanks go to my husband Kevin and to Alessandro, Megan and Georgina. Without them I know for sure I could not have undertaken the journey that I did nor have got to the end in one piece.

Chapter 1

Introduction

Introduction

A dominate concern and issue faced by government ministers and policy makers in UK today is how to raise the higher education participation rates amongst students from families not traditionally associated with going to university, principally the numbers of students attending from the working class. In attempting to devise strategies and schemes that promote both the individual and social benefits of higher education the question as to how and why educational aspirations are shaped is therefore relevant. In an increasingly globally driven market place, skills and credentials have become particularly important. As a result the government has introduced a number of policies that encourage and promote a wider skills base to ensure the UK's competitive edge and central place on the economic global stage. In light of a wealth of research linking social deprivation and poor educational attainment, Every Child Matters (2003) was one such initiative introduced with the specific aim of raising both the attainment and the educational aspirations of socially disadvantaged students; the aim being that through the collaborative efforts of professionals, communities, schools and families, all children, regardless of their background, can and do achieve their full potential. The concept of class is clearly central to this particular white paper and by utilizing concepts such as social and cultural capital associated with class, government initiatives aim to target and compensate for class shortfall with a number of different schemes, such as, Aim Higher, Sure Start, Educational Action Zones and Educational Maintenance Allowance. However, despite achieving some success, research suggests that government initiatives are yet to achieve any real progress and the targets of 50 per cent of all 18–30 years old in higher education by 2010 is highly unlikely.

Part of this failure may well be explained by the ambiguous nature of class itself; academics fail to achieve consensus as to a standardized conceptualization and whilst some research strongly supports the causal relationship between class and educational outcomes, other research suggests a more complex relationship. Applying macro theory to individual actors is also inherently difficult; particularly as an approach that assumes shared values and norms within a class has difficulty accounting for individual experiences of the class. In light of this, this book explores differences in the educational aspirations of a small group of girls. In particular, it investigates differences in the aspirations of three groups of girls from working class backgrounds.

Fieldwork

To address the question of aspirations I opted to conduct longitudinal research using the case study method, a popular method within educational sociological research (e.g. Hargreaves, 1967; Willis, 1977; Ball, 1981). Furthermore, I adopted the deviant case approach (Patton, 2002) whereby I chose to focus on a setting where certain outcomes would be expected: an underperforming school on special measures where low academic achievements and consequently aspirations would be the expected norm,[1] and looked for deviations, that is, students with high aspirations within the case.

'Southwell' is a single sex girls' state secondary school located in an economically thriving town in the south east of England. However, the area of the town which the school serves is, as OfSTED (Office for Standards in Education) notes an, 'area of high social deprivation' (2006), one of the 20 per cent nationally most deprived and locally the most deprived. In addition, the area is in the top 5 per cent of areas nationally most deprived for education, skills and training and crime as well in the top 10 per cent of areas for income deprivation affecting children, according to the English Indices of Deprivation, 2004. The area in which 'Southwell' is situated is part of the Excellence in Cities programme and is home to the Sure Start scheme, schemes designed to tackle raising educational attainment and social exclusion. Most students who attend live close to the school although a small number travel a greater distance as a response to parental preference for single sex education. The school is smaller than average with 703 students, ranging from Year 7 to Year 13 of the secondary school curriculum and struggles with consistently low academic achievement rates (some 20 per cent lower than the national average for General Certificate of Secondary Education (GCSE) at the time of commencing the study).

Standards on entry to Year 7 are below average, as are standards on entry to sixth form when compared to national standards and within the Local Authority (LA). From September 2004 until the end of the academic year in July 2005 there were 94 fixed term and four permanent exclusions. In addition, truanting and poor levels of attendance were noted by OfSTED inspectors as significant. 'Southwell' has a high proportion of ethnic minority students (50 per cent) that the OfSTED report noted reflects the surrounding area. The report also noted that the number of students for whom English was not the first language was also higher than average. The school has five streams. Stream One is selective and requires students to pass an entrance exam. Other students are sorted by ability into streams; two through five, based on Key Stage 2 SATS results, where five is for those with particular educational needs. Streaming is fluid however, and students can go up and down the streams during the period of their school lives. Just after commencing field work 'Southwell' was placed on special measures.

At 'Southwell' school, I focused on Year 10 and Year 12 students. Year 10 students were selected as they had just begun their GCSEs and their careers advisory sessions and were thus beginning to consider their futures. Year 12 students, having already made the decisions to remain in education, were beginning to consider their future careers. These students were followed for a period of two years, until several months after the results of their GCSE and A Level exams and relied upon a variety of data collection methods that include participant observation, focus groups, structured and semi-structured interviews. This multi-method approach was adopted with the view that it would provide much richer data than using one method alone. Participant observation in school was used to explore, at first hand, the school practices of students and staff, and was carried out in a variety of settings: Year 12 student common area, staff room and main areas of the school, for example, during assemblies, lunch area and tutor group times. This permitted observations to be made during both structured and unstructured periods of the school day. Focus groups were used to explore students' perceptions of education and attitudes to schooling and to get an initial sense of students' expectations and aspirations. Focus groups also proved useful in another way in that it gave students an opportunity to get to know me within a group setting prior to one to one interviews and enabled students to feel more confident and comfortable to meet with me alone. The information collected from the focus groups was used to direct in-depth, semi-structured interviews with students and were used to identify the value placed on education, students' expectations for themselves in terms of achievement and their life course, and how these views impact on students' perception of themselves. Students participated in a minimum of two focus groups and most students were interviewed formally between one and three times. Data is drawn from unstructured conversations also.

Structure of the Book

Chapter Two offers an overview of some of the important current theoretical contributions used to understand and explain the reproduction of class within education. The sociology of education is as broad as it is rich; therefore, theories presented in this chapter are those which address mechanisms and processes that are most currently used to account for the concerns of this book, that is, class and educational aspirations. As well as class theory that addresses how class shaped dispositions and culture as well as economic resources impact on aspirations, I also address some alternative theoretical perspectives. Primarily, alternatives such as individualization theory are presented that challenge the dominance and over reliance of class as an explanatory tool to explain different educational outcomes, suggesting instead an approach to understanding and exploring aspirations that is much more individualized (Beck, 2001). In this chapter I also explore some of the literature relating to the role of gender and ethnicity within education and aspirations and offer a short overview of some of the ways in which the most important theoretical contributions are adopted and used by policy makers as they strive to raise attainment alongside further and higher educational participation rates.

Chapters Three to Five are the empirical chapters of the book. These chapters present the results of my findings and are organized into three chapters that reflect the different educational attitudes and aspirations of the students included: Chapter Three addresses low aspirers (i.e. those who intend to leave education at 16), Chapter Four the middle aspirers (i.e. those who intend to pursue further but not higher education) and Chapter Five the high aspirers (i.e. those who intend to go on to higher education). These chapters explore students' aspirations and attempt to situate these ambitions within the context of their relationships with family and friends and their experiences and relationships with school. Issues of self identification and how these impact on attitudes, values and future aspirations are also explored, as is the role of gender and ethnicity. Using students' narrative, findings are then considered in relationship to theoretical explanations that help explain them.

In Chapter Six I discuss the main findings that emerge from the data and address these in relationship to key theoretical ideas that relate to class and education, in particularly aspirations. Some of the evidence presented support current academic understandings whilst others question popular assumptions concerning the dominance of class in shaping aspirations. For example, some evidence is offered that suggests that cultural values and dispositions towards education do not present as class specific for the students in this study, suggesting that, despite demonstrating outcomes in terms of a 'collective pattern', more individual factors also appear significant to students' evaluations of future choices. The role of self-identification is discussed, particularly in terms of how structural messages received from both family and school impact on a student's attitudes, degree of attachment and trust in meritocracy and how this in turn impacts on aspirations. The apparent link between emotional support and aspirations is also explored. Finally, I also discuss some of the findings that relate to the role of gender and ethnicity in aspirations. In considering future educational pathways, some evidence is offered that what matters for the students included in this study is the interaction of structure and individual factors, which are reflected on by students in terms of their suitability for the different options they could pursue, suggesting that class does not determine outcomes independent of other important and significant individual factors that interact to shape educational identities.

Chapter Seven is a summary of the main findings. I conclude by questioning the relevance of class as a variable of analysis at the micro level when considering educational aspirations because of the variability in ambitions within the class for the students included. Whilst this research is a small scale qualitative study and so no generalizability can be claimed, I suggest that it is possible that the changing cultural context in which young people and their families live means that it now appears to be increasingly difficult to continue to use terms such as class to understand individual experiences. For the students included in this study at least, class background alone did not explain mixed levels of aspirations. However, that inequality exists is without doubt. Unequal access to resources and ambitions is inherent in every aspect of social life as is gender and racial discrimination. For the students included here, understanding and explaining inequality in a way that reflects the social processes that shape the experiences of the individuals is clearly complex. Whilst this book is a case study and therefore specific to the students within it, it is hoped that the voices of the young women included may still contribute in some way to our understanding of the processes shaping educational aspirations.

Note

[1] This is an assumption of course, but is primarily based on low rates of academic attainment at GCSE.

Chapter 2

Class and Education

Introduction

A central issue within sociology is the persistence of class in determining the life course. Of particular concern within the sociology of education is the cross generational persistence of differences in both the educational achievements and higher educational aspirations of young people from different class background. In this chapter some of the ways that academics make sense of the role of class within education are explored and some of the ways that these ideas are taken up by policy makers as they strive to raise both educational attainment and aspirations are addressed.

Class is a term used to denote hierarchal distinctions between people, distinctions that are founded on economic differences, that is, occupation and income. Income and wealth remain at the very heart of conceptualizations of class because income mediates so many other important aspects of everyday life, for example, where one lives, the food one eats, leisure pursuits and social relationships and so on. On a more subjective level, class is also considered important in shaping opportunities, values and attitudes. Different socio-economic groups are situated within social networks that are predominantly composed of individuals sharing similar social backgrounds and experiences. This 'herding together' of individuals bonded by strong social similarities generates a shared culture that is legitimized through practice. Class imposes its own boundaries and horizons which, when applied to education, can be viewed as highly influential in the shaping and influencing of a students ambitions and aspirations for themselves.

Whilst class can be considered a somewhat abstract term, its importance with respect to educational outcomes becomes much more tangible when looking at data on attainment. To illustrate, in 2002 Government statistics reveal that 77 per cent of children in Year 11 in England with parents in higher professional occupations gained five or more A* to C grade GCSEs.

Only 32 per cent of children with parents in routine occupations achieved the same (Office for National Statistics – ONS, 2006). Government sources also show a link between class background and participation rates in further and higher education. Statistics reveal that in 2002, 87 per cent of 16-year-olds with parents in higher professional occupations were in full-time education compared with 60 per cent with parents in routine occupations. The important influence of class on aspirations for higher education is also illustrated when looking at university admissions. Statistics for admission rates of students from different class backgrounds appear to clearly illustrate the 'poverty of aspiration' that working class students are claimed to suffer from. In 2005 the proportion of students from the bottom three socio-economic classifications accepted into an undergraduate degree course was 19 per cent compared against 52 per cent of students from the middle and upper classes (The University and Colleges Admission Service – UCAS, 2007). As the labour market is so competitive and qualifications link so clearly with employment prospects and earnings, this correlation between class and educational attainment is significant. The reproductive nature of class and outcomes becomes clearer still when considering the relationship between higher qualifications and higher earnings. Government data show that the average gross weekly income of full-time employees in the UK with a degree was £632 in spring 2003. This was more than double the weekly income of £298 for those with no qualifications. The likelihood of being employed is also higher for those with higher qualifications. In spring 2003, 88 per cent of working-age adults with a degree were in full-time employment compared with 50 per cent of those with no qualifications (ONS). However, whilst the data clearly illustrates the link between class background and educational outcomes, understanding the mechanisms within class that underpin these outcomes is far from straight forward.

Cultural Capital and Habitus

For Bourdieu, education is one of the primary institutions in which the power of class can most readily be observed, most notably in terms of differences in the academic performance and attainment of children from different class backgrounds and, consequently, in life-course outcomes. For Bourdieu, economic resources associated with class underpins one of his most academically influential class concepts, that of cultural capital. Cultural capital refers to general cultural background, that is, dispositions and skills possessed by an individual, like linguistic ability, cultural knowledge of art, taste and shared norms and values, acquired in childhood. Cultural background is classed because it is economically determined, first because finance is a pre-requisite of many lifestyle choices; for example, taste and leisure pursuits will be determined by expendable income. Secondly, as cultural knowledge and linguistic abilities and the like link so strongly to educational attainment and resultant employment opportunities, the transformation of cultural capital into economic capital can be observed. Cultural capital works within education and educational attainment on a number of levels. For example, the elaborate linguistic codes of the middle class are expressed in the language of teachers, text books and examinations (Bernstein, 1971).[1] If a student using restricted language codes does not understand the language of the teacher or the text book, then learning is impaired. This then effects examination performance, educational attainment and consequently employment opportunities. Class and cultural capital is therefore very important within education because it serves to reinforce and reproduce class boundaries.

As already noted, the educational system for Bourdieu is of primary importance and influence in reinforcing and reproducing class differentials. By evoking the metaphor that physicist James Clerk Maxwell devised to explain the Second Law of Thermodynamics, Bourdieu graphically illustrates how the institution of education serves as a site of social reproduction:

> [A] demon sorts moving particles passing before him, some being warmer, therefore moving faster, others cooler, therefore slower moving; the demon sends the faster particles into one container, whose temperature rises, and the slowest into another, whose temperature falls. He thereby maintains the difference and order that would otherwise tend to be annihilated. The educational system acts like Maxwell's Demon . . . it maintains the pre-existing order, that is, the gap between pupils with unequal amounts of cultural capital. (Bourdieu, 1998: 20)

Cultural capital is central to Bourdieu's argument of class reproduction within education. This is because education, essentially viewed as a middle-class institution, engages in the 'sorting' that Bourdieu refers to by rewarding the cultural capital of the middle classes with higher grades and with better set placements. For example, recent research commissioned by the Department of Children, Schools and Families found that many working-class children are being placed in lower ability school sets despite having above average test results. The study also found that pupils from middle-class backgrounds were more likely to be allocated higher set placements, irrespective of their prior attainment (British Educational Research Association Press Release, 2007). As research also highlights a link between setting and attainment (see Hargreaves, 1967; Ball, 1981), this would appear to support Bourdieu's contention that it is the middle class who are rewarded in school, most notably with educational credentials. In these terms cultural capital in education does appear then, as Devine notes, 'to capture important class processes' (2004: 93) and appears to illustrate a link between education and class reproduction.

The cultural capital of families is also important with research illustrating a link between the cultural capital of parents and educational achievement. Because of the significance of parents in education, government policies now directly target the encouragement and promotion of parental involvement in schooling (e.g. the Excellence in Schools (DfES, 1997), white paper introduced the Home/School contract designed to promote the idea of co-operation between school and parents as well as ensuring parental support of children's learning). As Reay (2004a) notes, parental involvement in education is no longer optional; parents are considered of primary importance in the attainment of their children and are now viewed as 'co-educators alongside their children's teachers' (Reay, 2004a: 76). However, whilst parental involvement is emphasized as crucial to the educational attainment of students, parental class and cultural capital have an impact on both the ability and confidence of parents to be actively involved.

When considering parental involvement within education, research suggests that it is the middle class that most actively engage (Ball, 2003; Devine, 2004a) which is explained as resulting from their greater levels of cultural capital. For example, middle-class parents are more likely to challenge schools if their children are not doing well (Gillies, 2005), question and ask for clarification on school homework, be physically involved, for example, by coming in to school to assist in literacy reading hour, by serving as members of the Parents and Teachers Association (PTA) and the like. The shared cultural capital of middle-class parents and schools means they are less likely to feel intimated empowering them with a confidence that encourages pro-activity in their children's education. Lareau (1997) illustrates disparity in confidence of parents from different classes in an ethnographic study of parental involvement in schooling. Based on a series of interviews with both middle and working-class parents of primary-aged children, Lareau concluded that whilst both groups of parents valued educational success, the ways in which they promoted educational achievement differed. For the working class, responsibility for educating their children was largely viewed as the domain of the school whilst for the middle class it was a collaborative effort that was constantly scrutinized and monitored. These differing approaches were explained as the result of differing social and cultural skills. When it came to explaining their reluctance to assist with school work at home or attend parent information evenings at school, the working-class parents in the study, for example, cited a lack of confidence in their own educational abilities and skills. This finding is similar to Reay's (2005) study on parental support, which also found that, among other things, cultural capital was particularly important to a parent's ability to support their children's learning, again impacting on ability to feel confidence in engaging in their children's education.

Research clearly illustrates the important link between class and the cultural abilities and skills of families to assist their children. The economic resources of families also have an important role to play in the way that cultural capital impacts on attainment. The connection between money and education relates to funds available to invest in goods and activities that compliment and support schooling. For example, access to external resources such as the internet is particularly necessary for students doing course work at GCSE. The internet is also a useful way for parents to access information important to decisions regarding their children, for example, when considering secondary school placement. The internet allows parents to review OfSTED reports and compare attainment results, through published league tables, for example. (Knowledge to do this type of research is of course also cultural knowledge, an element of cultural capital.) Finally, economic resources are useful for the accumulation of cultural capital through extra-curricular activities such as music lessons and cultural visits to museums and theatres that both compliment and support the curriculum.

The families of working-class students are clearly at a distinct disadvantage within education, which is further exacerbated by the fact that teachers and schools implicitly view parental involvement and responsibility as an implied measure of the value they place on their child's education. In this sense, despite valuing the educational success of their children as much as the middle class, working-class parents essentially appear to be caught between a rock and hard place, where increasing educational demands on parents results in them feeling 'frozen out of their children's education' (Connell et al., 1982: 53).

As illustrated, the social background of a child will have a direct impact on levels of attainment due to the cultural resources that result from class background. Educational attainment is thus largely understood as determined by the cultural skills endowed on a child by their family, alongside families' ability to engage with their children's education and provide the additional resources necessary to support and encourage children's learning. However, research also suggests that class and family are also important in shaping attitudes towards education. Class imposes sub-conscious dispositions that pre-dispose children from different social backgrounds to value education differently. This impacts on the educational ambitions and aspirations they have for themselves in terms of further and higher education. Therefore, whether a student chooses to stay on or drop out of schooling will be the result of 'structurally determined products of parents and other reference groups' educational experience and cultural life . . . [which shape] their practical expectation of the likelihood that people of their social class will succeed academically' (Swartz, 1997: 197). In terms of aspirations for higher education, working class students do not aspire highly because, according to Bourdieu, they have internalized and reconciled themselves to 'the limited opportunities that exist for those without much cultural capital' (Swartz, 1997: 197). To illustrate, focus group research by Archer and Hutchings (2000) found that amongst working-class non-participants of higher education, the view of university as 'an unattractive or uncertain option for people like them' (2000: 570) was offered as an explanation for non-attendance. Additional research by the same authors (2001) also found that non-attendance was often a consequence of students not being encouraged to aspire to higher education by teaching staff, lacking knowledge about university and that achieving the necessary entry requirements required skills they considered as being 'higher than Einstein' (2001: 77). Indeed, even when working-class students do aspire to higher education, class still constrains and restricts options open to them. For example, Reay (1998a) found in a small study of students who had completed UCAS applications for university, that class limited knowledge about university institutions, such as where and what best to study. Class also imposed geographical constraints in decision making as did the desire that the university be a place were they felt they would fit in.

Underpinning the idea of class shaped dispositions is the concept of habitus, another theoretical contribution of Bourdieu, used to explain differentials in educational aspirations that bridges the gap between the objective and subjective. Habitus refers to a 'cultural tool kit' (Swidler,

1986) 'a universalising mediation which causes an individual agent's prac-
tises, without either explicit reason or signifying intent, to be none the
less "sensible" and "reasonable"' (Bourdieu, 1977: 79). Essentially, habitus
is a set of fixed and sub-conscious ideas about how society works, that is,
shaped and common to the experience of class. Through this experience,
one is disposed to make certain choices. For example, knowledge of the
desirability of higher education as a route to potential future success is
acquired through the accumulation of information from those who have
experienced university. If middle-class parents have studied at degree
level, it is highly probable that they will encourage their children to aspire
for the same. Conversely, a lack of knowledge means that it is quite logical
to suppose that higher educational institutions are perceived as mysteri-
ous and alien, as well as places that incur a great deal of risky cost. As a
result, university will not feature in the construction of future aspirations.
Habitus in one sense then, is the accumulation of a set of knowledge on
which one draws to determine actions, a tool kit that provides a range of
strategies for action and a foundation on which to build choices.

Cultural capital and habitus are theoretical concepts that are drawn
upon to make sense of and understand the lack of students from poorer
socio-economic backgrounds attending university, despite targeted efforts
to widen participation. In light of data that supports a lack of participation
of students from working-class backgrounds, class, cultural capital and
habitus would appear to present as highly useful constructs, providing a
great deal of explanatory power and weight in understanding and explaining differential aspirations.

Some critics, however, caution against an over-reliance on these theoretical tools. DiMaggio (1982), for example, concludes that cultural capital
and parental background were not as strongly linked to school success as
Bourdieu's theory might predict. He found that whilst cultural skills are
undoubtedly important, these concepts could not explain all the variation
in educational choice he found. Bogenschneider (1997) also concluded
that children with parents involved in their education performed better in school regardless of class. Modood (2004) adds that cultural capital is not helpful either, in explaining in-class variation in educational
success between different groups, that is, students from different ethnic
backgrounds.

Jenkins (1992) challenges what he views as the somewhat deterministic
and over-stated nature of the concept of habitus. He argues that the idea
of class based strategies that shape and pre-dispose action are merely pre-
sumed to exist, asserting that many of Bourdieu's assumptions concerning

habitus are structurally functional and simply used as a safety net to capture what cannot be readily explained:

> [W]hat goes on in people's heads' is confused and conflated with its putative consequences. In the case of, for example, Kabyle or Béarnais kinship and marriage patterns, since the 'official accounts' of ideal behavior match up with so little observed reality, another set of explanations-neither causes nor reasons-is produced, in the shape of unarticulated or inexplicit strategies, to explain what remains. Strategies, in Bourdieu's sense are presumed to exist because, for explanatory purposes, they *must* exist. To use Bourdieu's own expression, we are slipping . . . from a model of reality to the reality of the model. (Jenkins, 1992: 84)

Goldthorpe (2007a) also adds that the idea that habitus is formed by family and class and 'may be subject to confirmation by the school but not, other than quite exceptionally, to any kind of reconstitution' can be directly challenged by research. For example, Goldthorpe cites research by Halsey et al. (1980) which showed how children from working-class backgrounds attending selective secondary schools were able to acquire cultural capital not present in the home. Goldthorpe suggests that evidence such as this seriously challenge the view that the family is the only site for the transmission of cultural capital and implicitly, one may presume, values. Therefore, as Halsey et al. notes, whilst cultural capital may be a useful umbrella term for a set of mechanisms within education it is not 'an exclusive means of cultural reproduction of social classes . . . [nor is] the working class family [the sole] transmitter of attitudes and aspirations towards education' (1980: 88).

Whilst Jenkin's criticism is somewhat scathing, it is probably fair to say that 'habitus' is something of a theoretical Pandora's box in that it cannot be opened and explored, that is, in a sense it is a theoretical 'catch all'. Empirically, one could assume that cultural capital has a much greater utility because it can be operationalized and captured. Research by Sullivan (2001) aimed to test Bourdieu's theory of cultural capital and its link with educational attainment via a survey of Year 11 students. She concludes that whilst cultural capital provides neither evidence nor support for a grand theory of cultural reproduction it does, however, work well as an explanatory concept – in this case in explaining GCSE results – and is therefore a useful tool. Indeed, in this study the concept of cultural capital does indeed appear relevant in a number of ways to the students included in this study. For example, some students with limited knowledge about university admissions and so on sent UCAS applications that were doomed to fail. A lack of cultural capital or the cultural capital of others on whom to draw led to disappointment and the eventual death of an aspiration for higher education. Despite this, however, I also suggest that cultural capital and cultural reproduction theories are not overly useful in explaining variation in educational aspirations, particularly amongst those students of similar social background.

Class and Rationality

Critics of theories of a culture of class prefer instead to consider the role of class on aspirations in more economic terms, that is, in terms of the risks, costs and benefits associated with different post-16 options. Goldthorpe (1996), for example, advocates that understanding macro process, in this case persisting class differentials in education, can only be achieved by 'methodological individualism' (1996: 485), by adopting an approach that focuses on the evaluations that individuals from different class backgrounds make in relation to the different options open to them, that is, through the rationalization of choice. Whilst Goldthorpe does not assume that all students have clear goals or perfect information as to how to achieve them, what he does state is that students are able to evaluate the options open to them and therefore finds contentious the notion that young people merely follow social norms and cultural values without thinking. In a significant departure from cultural reproduction theory, Goldthorpe argues that students do have some capacity for acting autonomously in their educational choice processes, assuming that the educational system excludes working class students through arbitrarily defined concepts of cultural capital is simply wrong. He adds that far from encouraging students 'to collude in their own disadvantage' (1996: 488), post-war educational expansion has increased the opportunities available to children from less advantaged backgrounds. In developing a theoretical approach that considers the rational action behind aspirations, Goldthorpe develops and expands on the contributions of Boudon (1974). Whilst Boudon's work is somewhat dated it is still worth considering in light of the theoretical ideas that emerge and build on it.

Boudon (1974) suggests that regardless of how meritocratic a society is, it will not necessarily reward those who have reached a high level of education, despite the increasing level demanded by society. For Boudon this appears as a paradox that can be understood in two ways.

1. Those who generally achieve a higher level of education often also have a high social status and work much harder to climb the social ladder to avoid 'social demotion' (1974: 14).
2. Despite higher degrees of meritocracy, individuals with the same level of education still reach different levels of social status because education has no impact on social mobility. Primarily, this is because of the increasing number of individuals seeking the same level of education.

For Boudon this explains why, as levels of inequality of educational opportunity appear to decrease, inequality in social opportunity does not and why students from different socio-economic backgrounds choose to continue into higher education, or not. Thus, working-class students' aspirations are understood as being the result of expected returns rationalized in terms of reward relative to their middle-class counterparts.

Goldthorpe and Breen (2000) build on Boudon and claim that notions of class values and norms have little relevance for explaining educational differences. What is important is an individual's position in the social order, that is, their economic 'class' location. For Goldthorpe and Breen cultural explanations are unsatisfactory because they do not explain the 'temporal stability' of culture or how culture has maintained its differentiating force, virtually undiminished, over generations. Culture is therefore a circular argument that lacks parsimony and explanatory power in explaining why educational differences persist. For Goldthorpe (1996), difference can be understood simply. Class based differences remain despite educational expansion and reform, because the general costs and benefits of higher education in terms of economic reward, 'from the standpoint of different classes' (1996: 492) has not altered. Educational choices and aspirations are thus the result of a rational calculation 'determined via the evaluations that children and their parents make of the costs and benefits of, and the chances of success in, the different options they might pursue' (Goldthorpe, 1996: 490). Calculations and costs are economically determined, that is, in terms of the cost of the education itself and that incurred through lost earnings and on the basis of the parameters determined by their position in the stratification system (Boudon, 1974; Goldthorpe, 2000). Students therefore calculate the cost of achieving a higher education, relative to their economic security needs, and choose based on the likelihood of material reward for effort. It is implicit that higher education is not an entirely rational choice for those from less advantageous backgrounds when the distance to travel is far greater, when rewards may be fewer and where there is economic pressure (in terms of immediate needs and the problem of student debt). Research by Archer and Hutchings (2000) offers strong support for this view, with financial issues cited by a large majority of respondents as a reason for not going to university. In these terms, the distance for children and parents from less advantaged backgrounds and thus costs, are greater than those of more advantaged children. The introduction of the Educational Maintenance Allowance (EMA), as well as grants for higher education, in some respects attempts to address the very real costs associated with pursing further education. By offering financial incentive, the EMA, for example, aims to offset some of the costs connected with remaining in schooling thus making it a more attractive option to consider. It is therefore under this principle that Goldthorpe's focus is on the secondary, rather than the primary effects of class on educational aspirations; 'the effects of choice under constraints' (2007b: 6).

In summary then, the rational action theorists' focus, when exploring educational inequality, is not on the impact that class has on educational attainment (i.e. the primary effects of socio-cultural factors) but the specific role that class plays in determining educational aspirations (i.e. the secondary effects of economic resources). In a nut shell, rational action theory seeks to understand and explain why, even when academic performance is held constant, students from less advantaged backgrounds still make less ambitious choices. It is worth clarifying at this point one of the critiques often levelled at this approach. Rational action does not discount, as some critics claim, the important role that cultural factors have within education, it is merely that values are considered as having less of an impact on aspirations than the resources 'cultural or other, that children and their parents have in pursuing values that are . . . largely shared' (Goldthorpe, 2007b: 6).[2]

In exploring the role of cultural capital versus rational choice on educational aspirations, Van de Werfhorst et al. (2007) found that whilst cultural capital strongly influenced the primary effects of class on educational outcomes, that is, attainment, it had little impact on educational aspirations. Drawing on data collected from a survey of 621 secondary school pupils, the authors concluded that the aspirations for higher education of those in their study were best understood as resulting from a calculation of risk,[3] most notably the risk of downward mobility. However, whilst it is undoubtedly true that individuals do act intentionally and on the basis of a cost benefits analysis, what the rational approach fails to do is account for why people choose to pursue alternative routes. For example, why does a student who recognizes the financial constraints associated with higher educational still aspire to follow that particular trajectory? As Gambetta (1984) points out, the rational choice theorist is more likely to ask which course of action an individual is likely to choose among those open to her, rather than how or when individuals will take action for changing the available alternatives. In addition, the rational choice approach fails to address how preferences are shaped in the first instance, whether, and what, external forces help shape them. Probably the best critique of the rationalized approach is summed up when J. S. Mill accuses Jeremy Bentham (the founding father of utilitarianism) of 'knowing so little . . . of human feelings, [and] still less of the influences by which those feelings are formed: all the more subtle workings of the mind upon itself, and the external things upon the mind escaped him' (in Gambetta, 1987: 20). So, whilst individuals are no doubt rational, it is important to address also the limits of that rationality. As Devine (1998) notes, an overly materialistic view on educational choices, one that ignores the role of values, norms and the institutional context in shaping aspirations, has serious limitations.

Social Capital

Cultural reproduction and rational choice theories offer different explanations for the ways in which the economic foundation of class limits and constrains educational outcomes (in the case of cultural reproduction theory) and shapes educational aspirations. Whether the result of class shaped dispositions or calculated risks, class is presented as an explanatory tool to understand and explain why children from different class background have different aspirations. Alongside these popular theories another aspect of class, that is, social capital, is now receiving attention and is increasingly the focus of educational policy, with a particular emphasis on the role that families have to play in terms of the educational success of their children. Social capital however is a slippery concept in that, just as with cultural capital, it is defined in a number of ways. Essentially, social capital refers to 'sociability, social networks and social support, trust, reciprocity and community and civic engagement' (Morrow, 1999: 744), that is, social relationships between individuals and communities. These relationships are important because they promote shared objectives and enable communities to be cohesive. A positive consequence of cohesive neighbourhoods is, for example, that social issues such as crime and drug problems decrease

(Gerwirtz et al., 2005). However, social capital also has individual benefits. In relationship to education, research suggests that families with high levels of social capital promote success thus educational attainment is viewed as casually related to the social capital of a student's family. This is because families with strong relationships with community, in this case with school for example, are more likely to promote and reinforce the attitudes and values relevant to their children's education. For example, if a parent is involved in their children's school it is probable that they will value the work carried out there. Indeed research suggests that children are less likely to drop out of school, truant or perform badly academically if their parents are involved in their education in some way.

For Coleman (1988) social capital is defined by its function and, like other capitals, is productive because it creates outcomes that would not be possible otherwise. For example, Coleman explored the role that frequency of religious attendance had on school drop out rates and found that drop out rates were more than double for students who rarely attended religious institutions as opposed to students who did. For Coleman, social capital is thus about the resources provided by community relationships. For example, strong relationships, in this case with religious institutions, provide obligations, expectations and trust which then serve as influential determinants of action. In terms of education, social capital within families 'promotes attitudes, efforts and conception of self' (Coleman, 1987: 38) which collude with schools to promote educational attainment. Implicit in Coleman is the possible explanation that social capital provides in understanding and explaining why, despite educational expansion and reform, educational differentials remain. His view is captured in his somewhat pessimistic stance that it is the declining levels of family social capital, symptomatic of modern western society, which is responsible. For example, geographic mobility and financial pressures that require that both parents work are but two of the factors that account for increasing isolation between families and communities. Isolation, alongside an over-reliance on the state to provide some of the roles traditionally carried out by the family, for example, extended child care through breakfast and after school clubs, has had a negative impact on students and education. Implicit in this, one could assume, is that this has a negative impact on educational aspirations also.

Putnam (2000), in contrast, focuses on the role of social networks and trust in his understanding of social capital. Social capital for Putnam is a capital acquired through social networks (and the relationships within them) that emerges through civic engagement. Civic engagement promotes knowledge and shared norms, underpinned by trust which is highly beneficial for society, particularly in terms of democracy. Civic engagement refers to activities such as voting, membership of different groups and voluntary work. Civic engagement for Putnam is, as Edwards and Foley (2001) point out, not just an indicator of social capital it *is* social capital. Thus, when considering education, civic engagement would refer to parental involvement within school whether formally, for example, by serving as parent governors; as members of Parents and Teachers Associations and the like, or informally by, for example, coming into school to help with school trips, literacy hour and other activities. Engagement of this nature encourages and promotes trusting relationship between parent and institution and supports the transference of the ethos of school to home. Understandably, the consequence in terms of educational aspirations for children from families with greater levels of social capital would be positive.

Whereas Coleman's indicators of social capital are centred within the family and Putnam's are external (Croll, 2004), both acknowledge the importance of social networks within the concept of social capital. However, Boride offers an alternative framework for understanding social capital which is conceptualized as a structural resource determined by class. For Bourdieu, membership of a network provides access to the collectively owned capital available within it which can be mobilized to an individual's advantage. The size and value of the capital available within the network however, is determined by both size of the network and the structural location of those with in it. Therefore, accessibility to and accumulation of social capital is not open to all. Social capital is not independent of economic or cultural capital; membership of a group and a network requires 'a minimum of objective homogeneity' (1997: 51). Thus, social capital is structured and classed and serves symbolically to promote social closure whilst reinforcing class boundaries. In terms of education, social capital can be seen as important when attempting to negotiate the field of education, (Ball, 2003), for example, when making secondary schooling decisions. Social capital is therefore intrinsically linked to career, and thus educational, ambitions and aspirations because of the interconnection between economic, cultural and social capital (Grenfell et al., 1997).

For some theorists then, social capital is a useful theoretical tool because, as Coleman states, 'by identifying certain aspects of the social structure, the concept of social capital constitutes both an aid in accounting for different outcomes at the level of individual actors and an aid toward making the micro-to-macro transitions' (Coleman, 1988: 101). Thus, social capital provides an explanatory means by which to explain differences in individual educational aspirations as well as broader class differences. However, critics are concerned that the arbitrary nature of social capital creates problems in applying and testing the concept empirically. In addition, Morrow (1999) suggests that Coleman's development of social capital is not adequately contextualized in terms of socio-economic history and that, along with Putnam, is a concept that is 'gender blind and ethnocentric . . . imported from the USA without . . . attention to cross and inter-cultural differences' (1999: 749). This is a very relevant critique. If strong community relationships have positive consequences educationally, as Coleman suggests, then how can social capital adequately explain the disparity in terms of educational attainment in the UK amongst students from different ethnic backgrounds, particularly Pakistani and Bangladeshi students? Students from Pakistani and Bangladeshi backgrounds consistently underachieve at GCSE yet are a group who could be considered as high in social capital because of typically strong family and community ties. Morrow also notes that Coleman appears to implicitly advocate a theoretical model that is founded on assumptions associated with the nature of family structure, that is the 'norm' of the nuclear family. Such a theoretical stance essentially demonizes single mothers and other family types, that is, as not being conducive to social capital and, therefore, implicitly lays the blame for declining social capital and ensuing poor educational achievement, indeed all social ills, at their door. In terms of social capital and class, research by Croll (2004) suggests that whilst social and economic influences do constrain the resources families have available to use on behalf of their children, they are not solely determined by them. Finally, an over-emphasis on the family and the influence of parents' social capital on their children ignores the important point that children are autonomous individuals in their own right, capable of not only utilizing the social capital of their parents but also of acquiring their own (this view is also expressed by Morrow, 1999). High aspiring students in this study did indeed act autonomously and are able to generate and create their own social capital and, whilst not necessarily illustrating a causally related connection between this and their aspirations for higher education, they appear to demonstrate that there is indeed a link that does appear to underpin those aspirations.

Individualization and the Death of Class

The literature presented so far illustrates the important role that class has to play in shaping and influencing the educational aspirations and achievement of young people from different backgrounds. However, whilst academics agree that there is marked inequality in the attainment and ambitions of different members of society, not all theorists agree that class is the best way to understand it. Beck (2001) for example, dislikes the term 'class' and believes that the changing nature of society has rendered it a 'zombie category' (2001: 203), that is, a term that is kept alive through use whilst being empirically obsolete. For Beck, class is a term that is conceptualized and defined on the basis of the head of a household, in terms of their income and profession. Yet he believes that empirical definitions assumed in this way are no longer relevant because a specific feature of modern society is that there are now no clear definitions of what constitutes a household or a family, either in social or in economic terms. What Beck finds particularly contentious is that by objectifying society through class categories academics then attempt to offer collective images of how different people from different classes think and live, that is, how they organize their lives, what they value and so forth, and he believes that this is misleading. For example, Beck states that terms such as 'poverty' are unreliable; we cannot know what lies behind the term; a measure of material deprivation tells us someone is poor but not what kind of life they lead, what they value or what path the rest of their life will take. Essentially, Beck is objecting to a universalizing 'culture of class' that dominates much theorizing of class and inequality. The idea that people from different class backgrounds have different values and norms and that differential life course outcomes can be predicted on the basis of a structural location is considered simply wrong. For Beck, individuals respond differently to different situations based on their own reflexive understanding of that situation. Therefore, the most appropriate way to understand what is going on in peoples lives and minds is to understand the different cultures of individualization and the different reactions to it. By doing this, Beck suggests, it is then possible to identify a variety of different collective life situations.

For Beck, individualization is the 'historically contradictory process of socialization' (2001: 31), that is, a process where historical changes in the labour market and increased competition mean an individual's survival is dependant on them making themselves the centre of their own life plans; ties to occupations, families, neighbourhoods and cultures are no longer significant. Essentially, changes in the labour market have resulted in a society now atomized rather than stratified and is a view supported by the work of Pakulski and Waters (1996). Thus, when evaluating different options, it is the risks and benefits associated with labour market changes that shape choices and aspirations and not past traditions associated with class, that is, an individual will decide what course of action is needed to ensure survival; the influence of class and status group sub-cultures in shaping their decision has dissolved and disappeared. Thus for Beck, individuals are removed from traditional ties to class and are tied instead to 'the labour market and as a consumer, with all the standardizations and controls they contain' (1992: 131).

In terms of understanding the choice making process then, implicit in Beck (and in this one respect similar to Goldthorpe) is the notion that individuals rationalize and evaluate their choices. This is done on the basis of knowledge of the labour market; a market defined by its competition and demand for skills. Therefore, according to Beck, to understand social inequality one must understand how an individual's reflexive understanding of their own life situation shapes their responses to these broader social changes. Education is central to the skills drive that defines the labour market so understanding differential educational aspirations in Beck's terms means exploring to what degree educational aspirations are shaped by an understanding of market place competition, as well as understanding perceptions of the risks associated with the choices students make for themselves.

Education is a fundamental dimension of labour market changes and links so significantly with the competition that Beck refers to. Competition requires people to advertise their 'individuality . . . uniqueness of their work and of their accomplishments' (2001: 33) and educational credentials thus become an important means by which people can do this. Whilst Beck asserts that educational accomplishment can only ever protect against downward mobility, the belief that upward mobility is possible is what leads students to construct and pursue individualized career opportunities, whereby 'planning one's own educational life course . . . [means a student] . . . becomes the producer of his or her own labour situation, and in this way, his or her social biography' (1992: 93). The idea that students must decide for themselves their future identities rather than follow in the footsteps of past tradition is expressed in the work of Du Bois-Reymond (1998). In a longitudinal study of adolescents in the Netherlands Du Bois-Reymond explored some of the processes involved in the planning surrounding the future aspirations of young people. The study highlighted the anxiety and complexity that often accompanies the choice making process; usually a result of tensions arising due to changing labour market demands as well as personal issues and ambitions. Du Bois-Reymond identified two types of decision making that illustrate how students' future aspirations are very much bound up in their individual expectation of their future identities. Future goals are thus understood as reflecting either a 'normal biography' or a 'choice biography'.

Normal biographies refer to traditional life trajectories associated with class and gender. Typically in the domain of the working class, normal biographies refer to aspirations and ambitions that are gender and class specific, for example, males in breadwinner, blue collar manual worker jobs, roles as wives and mothers for females. Choice biography, primarily associated with the middle classes, refers to an individual's ability to decide autonomously on a course of action to follow, that is, they decide for themselves what they want to be. However, options must be evaluated against each other, justified whilst, at the same time, a preferred course of action may be closed or simply unavailable to an individual. Du Bois-Reymond suggests that as the possibility of opting for 'normal' biographies in modernity disappears, some students struggle with the array of choices presented to them which creates issues and anxiety for young people. In his work Du-Bois Reymond draws attention to what he considers a paradox facing young people today. In line with Beck's view, Du Bois-Reymond suggests that societal changes that have resulted in the rapid modernization of both the educational and cultural fields, alongside the disappearance of the option to follow traditional 'normal' pathways, meaning that young people's life choices no longer follow linear patterns, for example, school, work, marriage, and family. Instead future life courses have become negotiable. For example, a student may decide to leave school for work, with the intention of returning to their education at a later date. They can decide to have children and not work, or have children and work. The point that Du Bois-Reymond is trying to make is that frequently students find themselves overwhelmed with both the opportunities and the choices presented to them. A consequence of this is that some young people simply decide to defer committing themselves to any particular choice (Du Bois-Reymond, 1998). This issue of pressure is a valid one. As we will see, many of the middle aspiring students did take this option and decided to remain on in further education simply because they did not know what else to do. Staying on gave them time to decide.

Beck's theoretical contribution, in terms of understanding educational aspirations, is that he offers a bold and significant deviation from current main stream thinking. Essentially, Beck is challenging the somewhat deterministic nature of class by proposing a fairly dramatic alternative to cultural reproduction theory. In a sense, theory of individualization throws down a theoretical gauntlet through the presentation of ideas that challenge popular academic opinion. Using Beck's framework, educational aspirations and life course outcomes are understood as being reflexively constructed by the individual rather than structurally pre-determined.

However, critics of Beck argue that there is a lot of ambiguity and contradiction in his theorizing. For example, Atkinson (2007) illustrates how Beck offers no clear picture as to what class is before rejecting class as 'dead'. In addition, he adds that many of his ideas are inconsistent and contradictory. In one example Atkinson discusses how, on the one hand, Beck advocates an end to analysing 'collectives' whilst, at the same time, suggests a focus on 'cultures of individualizations' and 'collective life situations' (2007: 356). Implicit in Atkinson critique is that ignoring class in an analysis of educational choice making processes by adopting Beck's framework is problematic. This is because, whilst he does not say why, even Beck concedes that not all students leave education 'equally reflexive' (Atkinson, 2007: 361) despite education being a 'class free institution experienced in a uniform manner regardless of one's background' (Atkinson, 2007: 361). In addition Ball (2003) suggests that understanding choices as resulting from a risk analysis fails to account for social differences in these risk evaluations or differences in the strategic planning undertaken to counter risks.

As Beck claims, whether class is dead or whether it is very much alive is difficult to ascertain. However, there can be no question that debate on the issue will continue to dominate. Reay for example, is but one of the many voices advocating the need to 'reclaim class as a central concern within education' (2006: 288), whilst others such as Ball believe that 'no analysis of social advantage or social reproduction is possible without attending to class' (2003: 174). For proponents of class, it is the belief that class remains intrinsically bound up in individual identities that underpin their stance. For Ball class can most readily be observed through practice and this is important. This is because it is through practice that individuals show an awareness of themselves, most notably when negotiating fields of competition. Practices, when applied to educational aspirations, demonstrate then, an understanding of who you are as well as showing 'who you are not' (2003: 176) through the process of deciding who and what you want to be. The suggestion that class identities matter is an important point. This is because, as Savage (2000) states, whatever the theoretical problems of class analysis, if class identities matter to people, then this is reason enough to defend its use. However, Savage also adds that in his own research class was not part of deeply held personal identities, nor did 'class belonging appear to invoke strong senses of group or collective allegiance' (2000: 37). Savage further notes that this is also true in terms of class consciousness and collective group memberships, with neither presenting as developed as theory and research tends to suggest. However, Savage is not saying that class no longer matters; simply that class analysis needs now to be re-thought.

In addressing the theoretical debate that surrounds understanding social inequality in class terms, Savage claims that the biggest difficulty is posed when analysis draws upon ideas that class cultures are naturally collective. As he notes, an understanding of class in a collective sense will automatically give credence to any sign of individuality as indicative of class demise. Savage suggests instead, that class cultures should be considered as 'contingently embodying forms of individualized identities which operate relationally' (2000: 150). He adds that achievements, in the labour market and incomes, for example, should be understood as the accomplishment of individuals rather than as the result of a broad class structure. For Savage then, 'while old models of collective class cultures are . . . dead and buried, we should not leap to the other extreme of positing thoroughly individualized beings who fly completely free from class' (2000: 101). As Savage notes, whilst individuals no longer belong to static groups but must work to achieve their class positions and future identities, individual inequalities persist. Inequalities between men and women would be one example. In terms of educational aspirations then, one must consider how individual identities shape aspirations whilst at the same time understanding how these identities and aspirations are understood in relation to experience.

Gender

Whilst the role of class in terms of identity and, consequently aspirations, is subject to debate, the role of gender is much more salient. A plethora of research illustrates well the ways that gender still retains a significant impact on the career choices students make, despite a considerable cultural shift in ideology around gender and equality. As Tinklin et al. (2005) note, whilst attitudes towards gender amongst students have changed, their behaviour has not and differences remain both in subject choices for further study and in the occupational and career aspirations of males and females. Class, therefore, cannot be considered in isolation of other important aspects of identity.

For working-class girls, marriage and motherhood were once seen as the only viable future career option (McRobbie, 1978). But, as Connell et al. (1982) note, changing patterns of women's employment as well as the integration of feminist ideas has resulted in working-class girls attracted to a new set of values. Indeed, research by Francis et al. (2003) supports the idea that girls are generally much more educationally ambitious and focused than 20 years ago. In addition, their results also highlighted the fact that a majority of girls in their study were now aspiring to professional careers, careers traditionally pursued by men. Whilst this is encouraging news, research also suggests however, that this is more likely to be true for girls who are achieving educationally. In a survey of 190 young people, Tinklin et al. (2005) found that it was the lower attaining students who were most likely to be influenced by gender in their future occupational choices, that is, aspiring to jobs seen as caring ones. As a wealth of literature links socio-economic background to levels of educational attainment, implicit then, is the idea that less advantaged students are more likely to be influenced by gender in their future career choices.

Arnot (1999) suggests that many working-class girls are still frustrated in school and as a result, a significant number still leave at 16. Research by Biggart (2002) also suggests that, in contrast to males, these girls face a much more uncertain and precarious position in the labour market. Using secondary data from the Scottish School Leavers Survey, Biggert found that it was these girls who were also most likely to see motherhood as the only viable option for their futures. In some respects this finding supports that of the Joseph Rowntree Foundation (2006). In a study of planned teenage pregnancy, bad experiences at school was one of a number of reasons given by young people who viewed motherhood as preferable to low-paid and unsatisfactory jobs. As teenage birth rates are amongst the highest in Europe, the fact that young people consider motherhood as preferable to further education is a very real concern. Research by Osler and Vincent (2003) found that the working-class girls in their study were generally considered to have low expectations and were often judged to also have low levels of self-esteem and confidence. Of those who did aspire to academic success, limited knowledge about post-16 educational and training opportunities seriously limited the options they considered open to them. This means, as Arnot also suggests, that when working-class girls do stay on, they are still typically identifying with gendered courses, courses that reflect both their background and 'the realistic expectation of their future' (Arnot et al., 1999: 121).

Reay (1998b), drawing on Bourdieu, points to the notion of a 'gendered habitus' and suggests that whilst girls recognize a need for educational credentials, their aspirations will reflect opportunities perceived as available to them in the labour market, alongside the gendered experience that shapes habitus. Whilst drawing on different theoretical perspectives, this point is somewhat similar to that of Beck (1992). Beck suggests that, whilst the process of modernization and individualization has given women a 'freedom from', it has not provided 'freedom to', that is, although there has been liberation for women from the traditional 'female status fate' (1992: 111) paradoxically their choices are still constrained by their gender. This is because as long as children remain an essential part of women lives, women will always have obstacles to overcome. For Beck, ties to children affect ability to compete in a competitive labour market and to achieve economic autonomy. In terms of females' future aspirations, 'values of autonomy [and] independence . . . are valued much more strongly than in the past. A job or career has become part of a women's life project because it promises recognition [and] money of their own' (Beck and Beck-Gernsheim, 2001: 102). However, as the structure of the workplace does not reward women, in terms of income relative to men, and offers little support (in terms of good, affordable childcare) for combining these goals with motherhood their choices are restricted. Whilst young people believe, in principle, that childcare should be the joint responsibility of both parents, they are also aware that in practice, this role is most often carried out by women (Tinklin et al., 2005). Aspirations are therefore constrained and limited by this understanding. Implicit then, is the idea that gender remains, despite some ideological shifting, very salient within the aspirations and related future identities of young girls, defined as they are by a reflexive understanding of their gendered self.

Despite the fact that gender inequality remains, young women do aspire to higher education. In 2006, 54 per cent of accepted applicants in to higher education were females compared to 46 per cent who were males (source: ONS). Whilst it is true that in 2005–2006 only 29.3 per cent (Source: Higher Education Statistics Agency) of male and female students were from backgrounds considered as working class, the fact is that numbers are slowly rising. Some working-class girls clearly do aspire to higher education and some do make it. In understanding this, it could well be that working-class parents are pushing their children because they 'want to transform their children's educational fates [recognizing] higher education as necessary because of changes in the labour market' (Miriam et al., 2003: 29). Hubbard (2005) also suggests that observing under-educated mothers struggling financially serves as a powerful motivating factor in aspirations for higher education. The young women in her study cited the fact that mothers' lives were hard as the reason their mothers encouraged them to 'aim high' and avoid the same fate. Lucey et al. (2003) note that, in trying to understand why some working-class girls aspire more highly than others neither liberal discourse that focus on the pedagogy and practise of teachers and parents, or theories concerned with reproduction, adequately address the problem. They advocate that if serious about addressing educational inequality, it is fundamentally important to understand the psycho-social processes involved in the shaping of individual aspirations. An approach that tries to account for the psycho-dynamic factors involved in the choice making process, particularly of aspirations for higher education, would go some way in understanding and hopefully addressing the aspirations, of those girls who do not aspire highly and intend to leave school at 16.

Ethnicity

Modood states that for many academics and educationalists 'ethnic minorities continue to be more associated with educational underachievement than success' (2006: 247). Yet as statistics for 2001–2002 reveal, the likelihood of government targets of 50 per cent participation rates in higher education was significantly lower for whites than for all nearly all other ethnic groups. Indeed all but two ethnic minority groups have achieved, or almost achieved, this target (Modood, 2006: 248). Osler and Vincent (2003) note that many ethnic minority girls have aspirations for educational success and aim high. In addition, Ahmed (2001) draws attention to the fact that, despite popular negative stereotypes that view Asian women as 'passive victims' (Shain, 2000) without ambition, in reality the opposite is true. Not only do Asian women aspire to be upwardly mobile, they also aspire to higher education and good careers and are encouraged in these ambitions by the families (Basit, 1996, 1997; Siann, 1996).

In terms of educational attainment at key stage four, variation amongst different ethnic groups is evident and an abundance of research demonstrates that whilst there has been a decrease in inequality in terms of the educational attainment of all ethnic minority groups there remains a great deal of disparity. For example, the gap between African-Caribbean and Pakistani pupils and their white peers is bigger now than a decade ago (Gillborn and Mirza, 2000) whilst the achievement of Chinese and Indian pupils supersede that of all other ethnic groups (ONS, 2006). In addition, evidence also suggests that gaps in attainment become greater for African-Caribbean students at the end of their secondary schooling, when compared to the end of their primary education. More importantly, Gillborn and Mirza also state that black pupils from middle-class backgrounds remain the lowest attaining of middle-class groups 'in some cases barely matching the attainments of working class pupils in other ethnic groups (2000: 21). Research by Platt (2007) also found that Pakistani and Bangladeshi groups appear to suffer an 'ethnic penalty' (2007: 505) in terms of levels of educational attainment and subsequent potential for upward mobility. Persisting differentials in the educational attainment of some ethnic minority groups clearly demonstrates the complexity surrounding issues of ethnicity in educational attainment and as attainment is important to the realization of ambitions this is a significant concern.

In exploring factors that account for the lower levels of educational attainment amongst some ethnic minority groups, Gaine and George (1999) suggest it is difficult to disentangle how much of the inequality can be explained by class and how much by race. They note that whilst a significant proportion of ethnic minority groups are poor and live in poor areas these factors have similar results for white children. They suggest instead that it is a plethora of processes, specific to minority groups, colluding together which results in low attainment. For example, they point to lower levels of self esteem, low teacher expectations, gender differences as well as racism. Gillbourn and Mirza (2000) highlight the number of barriers to attainment that black pupils face, for example, in terms of being disciplined more harshly and in terms of ability assessment. Mac an Ghaill (1988) also suggests a curriculum that primarily focuses on the interests of dominant groups will not engage students and thus effectively excludes minority groups.

Despite the lower levels of educational attainment of ethnic minority groups, variation is evident between groups of different ethnic backgrounds. As already noted, children from Indian and Chinese backgrounds have levels of attainment that exceed the average for whites. In exploring this, research by Archer and Francis (2006) found that one of the ways that the educational success of Chinese students could be understood was as the result of 'family capital'. In their study parents and families were considered a resource that countered the more negative effects associated with a lack of cultural or economic capital. Participation in supplementary Chinese schooling, social competition between families to motivate academic achievement and a discourse of 'Chinese valuing of education' (2006: 42) combined together to promote both a desire for social mobility and educational success of the Chinese students and families in their study. Levels of academic attainment amongst ethnic minority groups are also differentiated by levels of language proficiency. Exploring ethnic minority under-achievement using data from keystage one, two and GCSE results, Demie (2001) found pupils in early stages of English fluency perform at very low levels. Children who were bilingual and fluent in English however, perform better than English-only speakers. As educational attainment links to aspirations and ability to achieve ambitions, persisting inequality in educational attainment is clearly significant.

In terms of higher education, more Pakistani and Bangladeshi males than females attend university; however, this is slowly changing. Statistics show that 44 per cent of all Pakistani students attending university in 2001–2002 were females (Modood, 2006). For black-females the picture is also very positive, with 75 per cent of black-African and 52 per cent of black-Caribbean students in higher education also being women (Modood, 2006). Clearly this represents a positive trend in terms of gender balance and gender representation. However, despite this positive trend research suggests a more complex picture with ethnic minority students applying and attending university still facing particular disadvantages that are important, for example, bias against ethnic minority students in pre-1992 universities, in terms of pre-entry attainment levels, geographical constraints, over-representation in certain subject choices, final degree result and so on. (Modood, 2006) as well as over-representation by certain groups in less prestigious universities resulting in a 'two tier system of higher education' (Archer and Hutchings, 2000: 568).

Whilst the proportion of ethnic minority applicants to higher education does exceed that of whites, they do not achieve the same level of success in the employment market as white graduates and are more likely to be unemployed relative to whites (Conner et al., 2004; Platt, 2007). Within ethnicity, differences in terms of rewards are also evident. Research by Battu and Sloane found that 'under-educated, non-native non-whites suffer a wage penalty which is twice as great as for under-educated whites, while the wage premium for over-educated non-native non-whites is lower than for whites and over-educated native non-whites receive no significant wage premium' (2004: 557).

Despite a variety of inequalities females from ethnic minority backgrounds are aspiring to higher education and some do make it. In understanding these aspirations and ambitions, research by Tyrer and Ahmed (2006) suggest that for Muslim females there are a multiplicity of factors shaping aspirations. From interviews with 105 Muslim women either at university or who graduated and were in employment, the view expressed was that generally higher education is seen as the route for enhancing the prospects for social mobility and status of students and families. In addition, and on a personal level, attending university had an important influence on other factors in their lives, such as marriage and work choices. Exploring the educational experiences of black and Asian students attending a sixth form college in his study, Mac an Ghaill (1988) also found that academic aspirations for some of his female participants were a response to the desire for social mobility as well as the means by which to achieve economic security and personal development. Educational qualifications were viewed by some of the female students in his study as an external measure of worth and were seen as a means by which to challenge racial and gendered stereotypes and assumptions. For the Asian- and black-female students in Mac an Ghaill's (1988) study, high aspirations present as a resistance strategy and may explain, as other research also shows, why black and Asian students aspire more highly than whites and believe education is important to their futures (Hutchings and Archer, 2001). Whilst Modood found that on average ethnic minority women earned more highly than white women where 'the highest average earnings were of Caribbean women'[4] (1999: 114), research also suggests that ethnic minorities still expect difficulties associated with race and gender in terms of employment opportunities open to them (Bhavnani, 2006). Higher education is clearly valued by some ethnic minority students as an entirely rational response to potential discrimination.

As well as individual motivations, research by Tyrer and Ahmend (2006) found that overwhelmingly, Muslim women cited encouragement of their ambitions by families as important to their aspirations and whilst research suggests that parental influences in career choices are less important for black-Caribbean girls than for Asian (Bhavnani, 2006) families appear significant. Conner et al. (2004) suggest that it is the influence of family alongside the positive value, in terms of economic rewards, associated with education, which drives ethnic minority students to aspire highly and in their research strong parental support alongside commitment to education was observed as important to alleviating some of the negative effects traditionally associated with class and aspirations (this view is also supported in Modood, 1999).

In 1999 two-thirds of Pakistani and Bangladeshi entrants to university came from households headed by manual or unemployed workers (Modood, 2004). Platt (2007) exploring the role of educational qualifications on social mobility for ethnic minority groups using data from the Office of National Statistics longitudinal study, found that class background indeed had a much smaller role to play in the subsequent class position of ethnic minorities than for whites. In an additional study of two different Pakistani communities, research by Dwyer et al. (2006) found that a strong commitment to education could not simply be explained by class background, as the educational commitment of the Pakistani girls in their study was as strong amongst more working-class families, where other family members had not been educationally successful, as the other young women with more middle-class parents. Conner et al. suggest then that family influences offer a powerful explanation as to 'why ethnic minority groups enter full-time degree courses, despite having lower than average class profiles' (2004: 2).

Research into the role of families in the educational attainment and aspirations of ethnic minority students is increasingly focusing on the role that social capital plays. Khattab (2003) for example, suggests that low socio-economic status (SES) and low minority status do not automatically lead to low educational aspirations. For the Palestinian students attending Israeli schools in his study, the effects of low SES and school setting on aspirations was significantly mediated by students social capital (conceptualized by the author to be family values and norms) as well a student's perception of the importance of education to future opportunities. This idea is supported in Dwyer et al. (2006) who also suggest that the community values, norms and networks of specific ethnic communities have a particularly positive influence on educational aspirations and outcomes. They suggest that the values specific to ethnic minority groups should thus be considered as 'social capital' because it is a resource that is utilized. In their study, the values specific to the communities explored had positive educational outcomes, particularly for Pakistani females. For example, whilst norms around gender constrain and limit the socialization of girls outside of the home, they are not then subject to the distractions of street peer culture cited by the males in the study. In terms of further and higher educational aspirations, whilst a very small proportion of the girls in their study had aspirations that reflected a delaying strategy to postpone marriage, other girls saw education more broadly. For the girls, education provided an opportunity to support themselves, and if necessary their parents, if their marriage should fail and was a means by which they could contribute positively to the Pakistani community in which they lived. Whilst drawing out the ways that ethnicity can be useful in exploring and explaining the educational success of some ethnic minority groups compared with others, the authors are also clear that the suggestion of conceptualizing ethnicity as social capital is tentative. They also acknowledge the complexity of ethnicity, in terms of the ways that different power relationships, class, gender, generation and structural constraints may influence community's values, norms and networks and how this may impact on the social capital available. As Boeck (2007) notes, whilst the social capital of ethnic minority groups is a positive resource to be utilized it can also hinder and limit opportunities. For example, strong social networks and a desire to remain close to family and neighbourhoods dictate choice of university for some. Boeck states that rather than choose an institution most relevant, some students opt to attend a university close to home that are also attended by other students of the similar backgrounds.

Drawing on data collected through interviews with 157 families and over 400 members in two towns in the north of England, Crozier and Davies (2006) conclude that social capital should be considered as ethnicized. They argue that whilst Pakistani and Bangladeshi parents are often criticized for either not being involved enough in their children's education or for having unreasonably high educational expectations, these communities contribute significantly, in terms of educational support and home-school relationships, but that these resources are rarely recognized by schools and so remain unharnessed. However, Crozier and Davies also state that despite the high value placed on education by British south-Asian families and communities , the actual social capital that members have to draw on has limited value in terms of accessing 'high status educational knowledge' (2006: 692). Therefore, for Crozier and Davies, the networks and social capital of the ethnic minorities in their study remain classed as well as ethnicized.

Despite the fact that ethnic minority students have high aspirations for themselves, research suggests that the experience of schooling is not necessarily conducive to fostering and nurturing these ambitions. Research by Bhavnani (2006) for example, found that 50 per cent of black-Caribbean students felt they had received inadequate careers advice in terms of options and were likely to experience racism and negative stereotypes in the classroom (Lindsay et al., 2006). Research by Shain (2003) also found that often Asian girls do not talk about their ambitions to teachers at school and also do not always receive adequate career advice. In some cases, negative stereotypes surrounding ideas of marriage are suggested as influencing a teacher's assumptions as to what an Asian student's aspirations are for themselves (Basit, 1996) leading to teachers having lower expectations of Asian girls (Singh Ghuman, 2001). Research by Singh Ghuman (2001) also suggests that while Asian female students are clearly doing well in terms of closing the educational attainment gap and in rates for staying on, the experience of school can be particularly difficult for some. He adds that this is because Asian students are likely to experience tension between home and school as well as racism. Shain (2003) suggests that Asian students in school both challenge and reinforce 'dominant definitions and cultural assumptions' (2003: 126) and many adopt different strategies as they strive to create/maintain their individual identities.

For some, educational success reinforces these identities whilst for others it does not.

Despite the complexity and differences in terms of educational attainment, research suggests that some ethnic minority students clearly do have aspirations for higher education and statistics reveal a greater proportion of ethnic minority students attending university than white students (Modood, 2006) and this is predicted to be a growing trend. In explaining this, the literature appears to suggest that whilst class and social disadvantage appears to impact on educational attainment, it does not appear to impact so directly on the aspirations that students from ethnic minority backgrounds have for themselves. Implicit in the literature is the idea that aspirations are more raced than classed yet the inequalities experienced by some ethnic minorities groups should not be considered as homogenous (Gaine and George, 1999; Wright et al., 1999). Whether differences in the aspirations of ethnic minority students can be understood as the result of students adopting strategies to counter potential future discrimination in the employment market or, as the result of other mechanisms and processes such as the family and social capital (particularly if social capital is conceptualized as Dwyer et al. (2006) and Crozier and Davies (2006) suggest as ethnicized) is not clear. Fostering and encouraging these aspirations, however, is important as is raising the attainment necessary to achieve ambitions.

Theory and Educational Policy

The role of class in determining both educational attainment and aspirations for further and higher education has been identified as key. Whilst educational differences can also be observed across gender and ethnicity, for many sociologists, the effects of these variables will still be influenced, in the first instance, by class. Class is therefore of primary significance and underpins all other explanatory and causal mechanisms. Whilst different perspectives debate exactly how the mechanisms of class determine outcomes, the broad consensus is that class matters.

The field of education then, is perhaps one of the very real ways that theoretical ideas can be observed directly translating into practice. It is the arena where one sees how theoretical contributions are adopted and then applied by policy makers, in this case, as they strive to raise rates of educational attainment and further and higher educational participation. The Children Act 2004 and its focus on education is one such political initiative that can be observed as encapsulating many class based concepts.

Every Child Matters: Change for Children in Schools (2003) emerged from the Children Act and has at its heart the ethos that education is the most effective way of raising young people from disadvantaged backgrounds out of poverty. Alongside promoting healthy eating and lifestyles and raising the educational attainment and aspirations of individuals, it also recognizes the need for families, local communities and schools to work collaboratively together. *Extended Schools: Access to Opportunities and Services for All* (DfES, 2005) is a programme that offers a range of services and activities which aim to encourage young people to achieve their full potential. In particular, children from disadvantaged backgrounds are targeted. A key component of the programme is the opening up of schools to make them more accessible. By offering a range of after schools activities, access to school facilities for community members and the provision of parenting support and parenting programmes, the implicit idea is that schools develop into a central feature of community life.

In many ways extended school can be seen as utilizing ideas associated with social capital. For Coleman (1988) community relationships, in this instance between community and schools, promotes a sense of belonging, shared expectations and trust which in turn translates into a greater educational engagement of both student and parent. Extended Schools therefore are '. . . not only about tackling underachievement but also about tackling the causes of underachievement' (DfES, 2005: 2). In addition, from September 2007, schools are required by law to promote community cohesion in a more formal manner (DfES, 2007). A targeted focus on community cohesion requires that schools build links with local organizations, for example, different religious groups, the police and so on, encourage students to engage in volunteer work, build links with local employers as also with others schools that reflect the diversity of society and so on. Building on the original principles of extended schools, the specific focus on community cohesion appears to address issues of social capital associated with Putnam's (2000) conceptualization of the term. For Putnam, social capital is acquired through social networks and relationships that emerge through civic engagement. Engagement and interaction amongst community is considered highly beneficial for society, particularly in terms of democracy.

As well as addressing social capital, the extended schools programmes also appear to address the relationship between educational achievement and cultural capital. For example, extended schools offer additional tuition for students who have fallen behind as well as providing extra-curricular activities. In addition, parent learning programmes provide tuition and advice to enable parents to support their children through their schooling, for example, by providing literacy, numeracy, information technology and practical parenting courses.

The extended schools programme then takes a multi-level approach in its attempts to raise the levels of educational achievement of socially disadvantaged young people. The benefits of this approach are anticipated as serving the needs of both the individual and community members. Services that support students learning whilst also encouraging and developing a strong sense of community, are clearly attempting to bridge an important gap amongst the socially disadvantaged, identified through research, in terms of their social and cultural capital. The relationship between class and educational outcomes appears to be acknowledged and the extended schools programme appears to be one attempt at addressing the issue. In terms of raising aspirations for post-16 education, the extended schools programme is clearly geared towards raising the levels of educational attainment essential to the choice making process. This is because if students do not achieve a certain standard educationally, then programmes that focus on widening participation in higher education are doomed to fail. Indeed, widening participation is a central concern of government and policy makers who, in 2003, set out their commitment to do just that.

Widening participation encompasses many goals, with the primary one being that young people, who have the potential and are from backgrounds not traditionally associated with going to university, should aspire to a higher education. Academy schemes for gifted and talented students, re-designing of careers advice with the provision of the Connexions Service and the introduction of the Educational Maintenance Allowance are just some of a number of ways the government are trying to engage with students through their Aimhigher programme. In addition, universities themselves are also taking a number of steps to encourage students to apply, for example, offering university taster days, master classes, student mentors and summer schools (DfES, 2004). In addition, more information is being provided that will enable students to make the applications to universities that match their interests and abilities. Whilst widening participation in higher education is geared towards providing for the estimated six million job vacancies that will require graduate employees between 2004 and 2014, widening participation is also concerned with providing benefits to the individual. For example, government research suggests that the average graduate can expect to earn over £100,000 more during their working life than a similar individual with A levels (DfES, 2006). Therefore, to provide a competitive global economy as well as raising the standards of living of the socially disadvantaged, the government is reaching out 'to groups who have not traditionally benefited from higher education' (DfES, 2006: 1).

Alongside the need to raise educational attainment fundamental to the widening of participation in higher education is the need to raise educational aspirations. In a report on widening participation (DfES, 2006) non-educational factors such as pupils' aspirations accounted for 25 per cent of the difference in the likelihood of different social groups staying on to do A levels. The report also states that this increases to 50 per cent when different aspirations are considered in terms of their effects on pupils' GCSE achievement. Aspirations clearly matter and schemes such as Aimhigher have been introduced to promote higher education in a positive and engaging way to young people in socially disadvantaged areas so as to encourage those who might not have normally done so, to aspire to higher education. By communicating more effectively information regarding costs and courses available, as well as opening up universities so that students can see for themselves what university life is like Aimhigher programmes aim to make young people feel positive about choosing to pursue a higher education.

Despite still being in its infancy the Aimhigher scheme has had some initial success. For example, a government report states that the proportion of students in Year 11 stating they intend to participate in higher education was 3.9 per cent higher in schools running the Aimhigher programme than in similar schools that were not (DfES, 2006). In addition, a survey of higher education institutions claimed that Aimhigher had resulted in increased applications to their universities (DfES, 2006). However, a report by Ireland and O'Donnell (2004) suggests that Aimhigher activities were more likely to be taken up by young people who were already interested in pursuing higher education, whilst Morris and Golden (2005) suggests there is no evidence as yet that participants in the scheme who did not want to pursue a university education then went on to change their minds. In many ways it is not surprising that schemes such as Aimhigher are able to claim some degree of success. This is because raising aspirations is significantly easier to do than dealing adequately with the complex array of factors that impact on the levels of educational attainment necessary to realize the aspiration.

Chapter Summary

Despite achieving some success, research suggests that government targets for university participation rates for 2010 are highly unlikely to be met. This is despite the introduction of broad and multi level schemes to address educational inequality, in terms of attainment and aspirations. Part of this failure may well be explained by the ambiguous nature of the concept of class itself; a concept on which much of government policy initiatives depend. As illustrated in this chapter, disagreement as to what class is, how the mechanisms of class operate and whether it exists at all dominates much of the sociology of education discourse. An inherent problem may be, however, that addressing educational inequalities by focusing on macro explanatory variables such as class ignores the importance of individual complexity, contextual differences as well as disregarding how the practice of class may be experienced differently, dependent on the individual. In terms of understanding educational aspirations, assuming the experiences of class are collective experiences merely because class outcomes appear to demonstrate collective patterns is unsatisfactory. As a result policy initiatives, however well-intentioned, are only ever likely to achieve moderate success and are why disparities in educational attainment and aspirations, within class, in terms of gender and ethnicity, remain.

Notes

[1] Bernstein discusses how children develop particular speech patterns through family socialization, patterns that are distinctive to class. Working-class children use restricted linguistic codes, whereas middle-class children use elaborated linguistic codes. An example of restricted and elaborate language would be: 'I ain't going'; 'I do not intend to go'. Pupils are expected to operate according to the elaborated codes.

[2] I am very grateful to John Goldthorpe for providing me with clarification on the points made here.

[3] The authors do not refer to this as Rational Choice but as Relative Risk Aversion theory.

[4] Although Modood does state that this findings may be 'inflated by the high levels of non-participation of Pakistani and Bangladeshi women whose potential earning were very low and the greater likelihood of higher qualified white women working part-time rather than full-time' (1999: 114).

Chapter 3

The Low Aspirers

However gifted an individual is at the outset, if his or her talents cannot be developed because of his or her social condition, because of the surrounding circumstances, these talents will be still born.

Simone de Beauvoir [1908–1986]

Characteristics

The low aspirers are those students who intend to leave schooling at the end of compulsory education and who largely (although not in all cases) consider school as 'useless' and 'pointless' to their futures. In many respects low aspirers personify traditional sociological theory that characterize the working and middle class as those who reproduce their class background through their educational choices. Just as in Willis' (1977) study of The Lads in *Learning to Labor*, the low aspirers reject the educational system and do not see the school curricula as relevant to their futures:

All we ever do is copy out of text books and it's irrelevant, we don't even use it. It's not just that they teach you stuff that if you were gonna do something, like in science would be useful, but, we get put into all three sciences and I'm not interested in doing any of them cause I don't wanna carry it on but, they don't make it broader so that you learn stuff that you could use later on, its no use to you and we're just learning things that we don't need.

Jessica, Focus Group, Year 10

OK they say we need to know them but we don't really, I mean, like half the things you learn in biology, I mean . . . you don't need to know all the bits inside a flower; you just wanna look at it!! [Laughs]

Pippa, Focus Group, Year 10

They aspire to leave school at the end of compulsory education and are eager to commence work as soon as possible. Yet, whilst further educational qualifications are often dismissed as 'not everything', surprisingly, they are not entirely considered as irrelevant either. This is illustrated by Mary-Anne and Lucy who believe that whilst future employment is possible without further education it is not guaranteed without effort and at least a little bit of luck:

CF: *so, you think it is possible to get a good job without more qualifications?*
All: *Yeah.*

Mary-Anne: *It depends what you want to do, like you can work and still do good in the end but it will just take longer and take more work 'cause you have to start at the bottom of the company or wherever you go to work. It takes longer to work up rather than if you've got the A levels 'coz then they will take you in at a higher job quicker.*

Lucy: *And I think it depends on who you are and if you are lucky or not. You might still find a good job that doesn't need more qualifications and then you're not stuck.*

Year 10 Focus Group

School Work and Academic Setting

The fact that future employment is risky without additional educational qualifications is acknowledged by the students, yet the desire to leave outweighs the possibility of continuing. This, in part, appears to be explained by the fact that the educational experience of these students has been marked by a general disaffection with school and poor relationships with teaching staff. These factors appear to be the one most important contributing influence on the choices that students make. For example, Lilly does not enjoy school and has found it a struggle to keep up with the demands of course work. She complains that the teachers are always 'in her face' and it makes her feel pressurized and anxious. To cope with the pressure she simply opts out and does not do her work. This often results in her getting into trouble, for example, by receiving detention.

It's always GCSE's, GCSE's, GCSE's and I'm like, shut up about it! . . . They are always coming in our faces, 'finish this and this and this!' and I'm like, just calm down, what more do you want from me? God! It stresses me out man and then I'm like, fuck it, I'm not doin' it . . . I just wanna get a job now . . . start earning money, like, I do earn money now . . . but it's not very much . . . I just wanna earn more, earn loads! I wanna get out of here.

Stress around course work was a general complaint from all the students that I spoke to but this pressure was felt more by the low-aspiring students who found it difficult to manage. Whilst the higher aspiring students adopted strategies for managing their workload, for example, a day off school feigning illness was a common solution for catching up with coursework and was approved of by parents, low-aspiring students coped by simply not doing it. It is beyond the scope of this study to explore whether such 'opting out' is a common or gendered response. However in a study of truancy, Attwood and Croll (2005) found that self reported truancy rates increased significantly amongst female students in Years 10 and 11, with more female than male students reporting truanting 'several times' or 'often' and this does suggest a link. Whilst students often expressed a desire to complete the work, particularly in subjects that they enjoyed, often the task of 'catch up' became too much of a mountain to climb. In large part students felt unprepared for the demands of school work and the level of expectation when they reached Year 10 and low grades were received, it became a downward spiral:

I don't think I will do that well, I've got too much to do still and I am mostly predicted E's.

Lucy, Focus Group, Year 10

In RE I am one mark from a C and it is so heart breaking cause I know I ain't gonna make it and I studied hard for it so, I don't think I can get a C in anything so what's the point in bothering?

Lorraine, Focus Group, Year 10

. . . and in child development I studied so hard and she's like, 'nah! You ain't done good' I just said 'shut up!'

Lilly, Focus Group, Year 11

I might try really hard on, say Art, take two hours doing something and all you get is 'its OK'. ITS' OK!!! It's' never good enough and it gets you down so then you think 'Oh why bother!!' And so I stopped bothering.

Georgina, Focus Group, Year 10

It is simply not true to say that help is not available for these students. A variety of homework clubs, after-school revision classes plus teacher support is available for those that want it. In addition, as the school strives to improve its examination attainment record the school opened during the Easter and half-term holidays prior to the examination period for students that wanted to come in and work. The difficulty in seeking support often appeared to centre round students' relationships with particular teachers. For the low-aspiring girls relationships with staff were poor (though not with all staff) and in some cases openly hostile. A common reason for non-completion of course work was 'I don't like her'. Paradoxically, students rationalized that not working for a particular teacher punished the staff rather than themselves:

> *I don't always do my work if I fall out with my teacher. I don't want them to think I care enough to be bothered to do it. I don't want them to think that they beat me.*
>
> Farah, Focus Group, Year 10

> *If I don't like the teacher, then I don't go to the lesson!*
>
> Lilly, Focus Group, Year 10

Unpopular teachers were those teachers who students felt did not respect them and this was a common theme amongst the low-aspiring students:

> *I like it when a teacher treats you equally. Some teachers treat you as a student, others treat you like they are just talking to you about something you don't really understand and know about. If they treat you equally you can get respect for them! Someone who treats me like a student then they don't respect you and I am just like . . . fuck you!*
>
> Lilly, Focus Group, Year 10

> *I stopped going to his class. He gave me a bad report and a part of me thinks, well, if you're gonna write that and disrespect me even though I did more work than everyone else yeah, then right, why should I fucking bother?*
>
> Katy, Focus Group, Year 10

Leanne is a good example of this stance.

Case Study 3.1 – Leanne

I met Leanne in Year 11 and she informed me that she had not done any of her course work since the beginning of Year 10. She recognized that she was unlikely to perform well in her exams and was not in the least concerned. Her only regret, she said, was not completing her coursework for CACHE (childcare course) as she had hoped to work with children. When I asked why she had not done it if it was important to her, she informed me that it was because she had not attended any of her lessons because she had 'issues' with her teacher:

She don't like me and I don't like her! So, I stopped going. We was always arguing cause she made things bad for me, kept sending letters home to my mum telling her how I hadn't done this and I hadn't done that! It caused problems!

Leanne, Focus Group, Year 11

I offered to help Leanne catch up with her coursework and liaised with the teacher on her behalf. To begin with, Leanne, a persistent truant, was unreliable and often failed to turn up to our appointments. However, as we began to make progress she became more enthusiastic and began to complete tasks at home (something that Leanne often remarked was the first time she had done so). Once the project was almost completed and we needed further advice, Leanne came with me to meet with the teacher. Mrs Knowles had seen the work completed thus far and was really impressed with the effort that Leanne was making. She informed Leanne that she was going to be sending another letter home to tell her mother how pleased she was with Leanne's progress. At this Leanne looked close to tears and hugged Mrs Knowles asking, 'Could you send one to my dad too?' After this Leanne required very little help from me, meeting with her teacher alone.[1] In her final exam, Leanne achieved a D and was really thrilled with it. It was the top mark for all her exams.

The point that Leanne's case illustrates is that relationships with teaching staff are fundamental to attitudes to schooling. The significance of teacher/student relationships is also confirmed in the findings of Attwood and Croll (2005) who found that poor relationships with teaching staff was a major explanation, given by students, for explaining unauthorized absenteeism and truancy. That is not to say that students wish to be friends with the staff, merely that they wished to be respected. All students, regardless of setting, stated that a good teacher was one who showed respect to a student.

Respect, in some ways links to a student's sense of status within school and in terms of how they feel staff and other students view them. The low-aspiring students were generally in the lower sets (although they had not necessarily started their secondary education there) and felt that because of this that they had less status in school. This view is illustrated in a focus group by Melinda (mixed race) in set four 'the girls in the top set look down on us 'cause they think we're stupid but we're not . . . they're just snobs who think they are better than everyone else'. This is confirmed in student interviews with OfSTED inspectors (2005a) where students complained that teachers expect less of those not grouped into set one. This in a sense places staff in a Catch 22 position, that is, if students find the work too challenging they do not do it, staff then learn to expect less from these students, students then feel they have less academic status and, therefore, feel they are less respected than other students.

Respect in education appears to be an important issue and might explain why, when students feel 'disrespected' they become 'disaffected, challenging, and problematic'.[2] As Pahl (2006) discusses, in modern meritocratic societies people must *win* respect on the basis of their abilities. When you are banded low, you are marked out as 'not very clever' (Pippa, black) by the teaching staff and pupils and it impacts on social relationships. Higher banded girls are often seen as 'snobs' or 'gifted', by the lower sets, while the lower sets are seen as 'thick' or 'stupid'. This finding is similar to Hargreaves (1967) and Ball's (1981) studies of boy schools that discussed how banding in schools serves as an indication to staff and other students as to ability and difference. Two teachers explained the difficulties of teaching set 4:

Teacher 1: *They are so difficult to teach . . . it's like they don't understand anything despite the fact that I explain it really well.*

Teacher 2: *They are seriously disadvantaged. It's not their fault . . . they were born that way. Of course there's no reinforcement at home because the parents can't help.*

Whilst Katy explains why she would not consider doing A levels:

I never thought of doing A levels 'cause I'm not clever enough . . . well not clever enough for those anyway. I'll be lucking if I get any C's . . . [Its' because] I'm in set 4; I'm one of the bottom ones.

Katy, Focus Group, Year 10

Once you are banded, you are marked and students feel this. In an institutional environment that places so much emphasis on achieving A–C and defines the individual in terms of examination success, it is no wonder that lower banded students, who can only hope to achieve the lower grades, feel a lack of motivation and interest and experience, as Osler and Vincent note, 'a second class version of success' (2003: 134). During my time in school six of the girls I saw were moved down sets for some of their subjects. This was the result of poor mock exam grades. Whilst academic setting may be an accurate indicator of ability for some, the girls who were moved cited problems at home, boyfriend preoccupations but, most commonly, lack of revision 'because its not the real thing' on their poor exam performance and not necessarily their ability to perform. Yet, they felt self-conscious of the down grade. It had bearing on their perceptions of themselves, how they felt others now perceived them and on how much future effort they felt they would now make.

Divisions are equally apparent amongst the Year 12 students, with a distinct physical separation noticeable in the sixth form area between the studious, high achievers who sit working quietly in the dining area and those who spend their study time socializing on the soft seats. Even in A/S level classes, where all are essentially equal, banding is felt. As Sandy (middle aspirer[3]) explains:

> *In media I feel like, God! I am going to fail! Basically, she has split us into 2 groups. There's the four of them who are going to get A's then there's the rest of us. She gives us handouts but spends much longer explaining things to them than us. We get the handouts and they get her time! When I asked her why she treats us differently she said that she wasn't but, well, it makes you feel thick, like your gonna fail so what's the point of making the effort?*

Students Who Withdraw

Banding shapes self identity, friendships (more on this later) and impacts on self-confidence and self-esteem. For some lower banded students this banding appears to result in their withdrawal and self-exclusion from education whilst others attempt to challenge the system. As Lauren so eloquently puts it:

> *I hate school . . . I just don't want to be here. I'm rubbish at everything; well that's what they tell me so I might as well not come.*

Rather than confronting the system, Lauren's response was to remove herself from it through the process of self-exclusion. Lauren's truanting was so bad that the Educational Welfare Office was involved and had threatened her family with a fine. Despite her mothers' exasperation and the fact that a fine could be ill afforded, her absenteeism continued (indeed nearing the end of Year 11 she only ever came in regularly to see me). Her time not in school was spent in bed:

I get up and get dressed and then leave the house so that my mum thinks I'm going to school. When they've gone [her parents] I go back and go to bed. I don't watch telly; listen to music, or nothing. I just think . . . I got so many problems and I just think about 'em. Just before school is gonna finish I get up and leave the house and then go to my mates, that way my parents don't suspect nothing.

Case Study 3.2 – Lauren

Lauren is 16 and lives on a council housing estate not far from the school with her mother and step-father. She does not see her biological father and has no wish to. She has two older sisters; one whom she does not see (with two children in local authority care) and another with whom she is close, also with two children who do not see their father. Lauren also has a brother currently in jail who is estranged from the family. Lauren describes her home life as gloomy. Her mother is on medication for depression whilst her step-father is often drunk. Both parents work as part-time cleaners in the same factory but do not get on very well, 'I think they're gonna split'. Because of conflict at home Lauren spends a great deal of her time staying with her sister who does not work. Lauren describes her childhood as unhappy stating that she was never cuddled as a child and particularly hates the constant family rows. The only person that she ever felt close to was her maternal grandmother but, sadly she died the previous year and Lauren still misses her dreadfully. Lauren has had several long term relationships already, primarily with men older than herself and who are out of work.

Lauren is a pretty yet scruffy girl who always sits on her hands or picks at her fingers when we meet and avoids giving me eye contact. Her hair is long and she uses it like a curtain to hide her face. When we met on one occasion in May 2005 Lauren informs me that she is six weeks late for her period. She is quite excited and informs me confidently that 'if I am pregnant then I'm keeping it'.[4] Lauren is rarely in school, has not done any of her course work and did not intend to take her exams. In part, she explains her dislike of school as the result of the fact that she is 'thick', does not get on with any of

---

her teachers, has few friends and is constantly the source of gossip and rumours, that is, that she is 'a slag and a slapper'.

Lauren considers that she is useless with no talent or skills and she has no plans for when she leaves school. Her experiences thus far have taught her that she is a failure and she accepts the label. Consequently, she had developed a cynicism and hopelessness towards life that belie her 16 years. She feels she has been marked as a failure and she has accepted the label. She has no aspirations, no hopes and no dreams. At 16 she is already a heavy drinker, is using drugs and had begun to self-harm.[5] Lauren could be considered in terms of Merton's model of individual behavioural responses to cultural goals as 'retreatist', in that she rejects the culturally prescribed goals of academic effort and attainment as she does not feel that she has the means to achieve them. She therefore retreats and 'escapes from the requirements of society' (1938: 678) or, in this instance, the requirement of the institution of education. Lauren believes that society has singled her out as 'a loser' so she in turn rejects school and the educational ideology that promotes the principles of meritocracy, that is, success through effort, by retreating and removing herself from it.

Students Who Challenge

Whilst some students withdraw from education others become more disruptive and attempt to challenge the system. The students who challenge are those most likely to be found in the isolation room and in detention. They are the students who exhibit more openly their hostility to the staff and school, for example, by walking out of lessons, listening to music or using their phones in class or by smoking on the school premises, and who articulate their frustration at a system the believe treats them unfairly. For example, Lilly recounted, in a group discussion, an unsubstantiated episode the previous week when a teacher was seriously assaulted[6]:

Lilly: *Mrs X, she just wants to get beaten again!*

[Laughter and shrieking!!]

Lilly: *And she deserved it and when she's walking and talking around, she will get it again! 'I've worked in a kids' prison! I got lots of experience!' Yeah, she acts like she's so big and bad! Please!!!!!!*

CF: *So, why do you dislike this teacher so much?*

Lilly: *She don't respect no one and she's ugly and really small and she's got black hair and she's got some buck teeth going on and those horrible dresses she wears! Oh bad!! She got beaten up by a student! [Laughs] She was running around crying and I was going 'what the fucks up?' and she was shaking and crying like a little baby . . . [Inaudible] we were all in the next room when she started shouting . . . she was asking for help but we were like, 'go away!' and I was like, what do you want me to do about it? She was crying but I was just standing there watching her getting beat! [Laughs] Boo hoo!!! And I was like, move, I am trying to see! It was so funny man!*

CF: *Is the teacher still in school?*

Lilly: *She had a broken limb apparently or something . . . [Laughs] She was away with stress 'cause she was very distressed . . .!! But people get beaten up 24/7 and I don't know why she's crying about it, she had to take like a month off 'cause she got beaten up but people get beaten up . . . children get beaten up. Its' happened to me and it happens to others and they go to school the next day . . . you see them so . . . don't know what she's crying about!*

Lilly and her friends were pleased that this particular teacher was attacked as they believed she showed students no respect. They stated that she is 'so up her own arse . . . [She] got what she deserved'. This episode illustrates, for them, an opportunity to fight back. They are proud of their ability to challenge the teachers and challenge the system. For example, they recount with satisfaction the story of a friend of theirs who is currently excluded from school for setting off the fire alarm four times over two days stating 'the teachers were going crazy, it's great!' They enjoy the disruption in school and the frustration of the staff who attempt to maintain discipline.

Lilly herself had a reputation amongst her peers as something of a bully:

Lilly is the type of girl you don't ask questions about, you just stay out of her way. You just don't ask cause if you do and she finds out about it then your dead! She's one girl that nobody messes with. You just do your best to stay out of her way. If she likes you you're fine but if she don't, then watch out.

Deborah, Focus Group, Year 10 (high aspirer)

Yet, when I dug a little deeper, I discovered a young lady with little self-esteem or confidence and a fragility that she carefully guarded with a hostile and aggressive exterior.

Case Study 3.3 – Lilly

Lilly is a black-African, who was brought to Britain from East Africa when she was four years old. She was reluctant to discuss her earlier years but what I did learn was that she had been in 'foster care' since around that time. She has not seen her mother or younger brother since arriving here but holds on to the dream that one day they will return for her: 'man, she owes me so many birthday and Christmas presents it's not real'. Lilly dislikes her foster family and does not feel close to anyone except her friends. She stays out until the early hours, even on school nights, 'just hanging'. There appears little supervision and she states her foster mother 'just lets me get on with it'. By the time she was 16; Lilly had been 'kicked out' of her foster family home and was no longer the responsibility of the local council. Essentially Lilly has been abandoned twice more in her young life, by her foster carer and by the local authorities. In her formal examinations Lilly achieved no A–C GCSE's despite predicted and targets scores of at least four.

Lilly tells me about her time at junior school, a time she considers as a very unhappy period in her life:

Well I was bullied at junior school. They picked on me 'cause I was black and 'cause I was fat and 'cause I had no mum. I used to just take it and go home and cry. I really hated going to school, I was always scared then, one day this girl hit me and she got me backed up in a corner and I was like, oh man what am I gonna do and then, like, I dun know what made me do it but, I just hit her back. I hit her hard, punched her right in the face and she was bleeding [laughs] and I thought, God I'm in for it now but she backed away. I got respect then and no one bullied me again. I realized then that I had to stick up for myself.

Lilly was probably the most difficult of all my participants to get to know but, in many ways, she was the most intriguing. Quintessentially, she was considered 'cool' and tough amongst her peers, whilst some staff deemed her a bully with a bad attitude. The Lilly that I saw, when she allowed me a glimpse, presented as a gentle, vulnerable and inse-cure girl who appeared to lack self-esteem. For example, there were many occasions in the library when she would ask me to choose her a Disney picture to colour[7] on the computer, yet this activity seemed so at odds with her reputation. In addition, when I asked her and her friends whether they were going to the Year 11 prom she replied 'no 'cause it will be crap'. However, when we are alone later, she admits that this is because she is overweight and believes that she will not be able to find a suitable prom outfit that will fit 'someone like me'. Her defence mechanism therefore appears to be to challenge and to confront those she finds threatening or who she simply does not trust (adults, in particular). It is the means by which she protects herself and enables her to 'stick up for herself'. In some respects Lilly's behaviour is an individualized response to her personal biography yet, her behaviour is also the product of learnt group behaviour, that is, where students who rebel against the system are rewarded with the respect of their peers, whether through fear or admiration.

Brief summary

Hallam and Ireson (2006) discuss how structured ability groupings lead to 'low expectations, limited opportunities, and the stigmatization of those perceived to be of low abilities, with consequent negative attitudes to school' (2006: 583). The examples of Lauren and Lilly, whist extreme, are used to illustrate this view. Whilst confrontation or withdrawal within school might appear as simple 'disengagement' from the academically least able, individuals are complex and have a number of factors shaping, influencing and impacting on their attitudes to education and their future aspirations. Within an institution that they feel has marked them as failures, in terms of the broad rhetoric of academic success, their reaction is simply an individualized reaction; a 'fight or flight' response to the 'feather and tarring' of educational setting that in some respects reinforces and amplifies the views that they already have of themselves. For those who challenge, their behaviour is simply the means of 'fighting for recognition and esteem in a society where some people count more than others' (Lutterell, 1997: xv) whilst those who withdraw are simply giving up and opting out of an institution that they feel has given up on them.

Work Experience and Career Guidance

The low-aspiring students who plan to leave school at the end of compulsory education aspire to work that could be considered as replicating class in terms of low pay and low status, for example, shop work and nursery nurse assistants. The most frequent reason given for leaving school was 'so I can get a job, earn some money and then move out!' Most of these low-aspiring students have complicated home relationships and a desire for independence over-rides any lingering doubts they may harbour with regards to going on to college or staying on into the sixth form. The allure of the instant gratification of having a wage now, outweighs the possibility of deferring work for the potential of earning slightly more after further education. As Samantha states:

> *Getting a job is just as good as going to college. My mate works at Comet and she gets £900 per month! That's a lot. And when your friends got money it makes it hard . . . like if they're going out a lot and that. We wanna get our own flat and I wanna learn to drive and get a car. I wanna have some fun with my mates.*

When I asked Samantha whether she could imagine herself employed in shop work for the rest of her life she replied that she did not know but, having enjoyed her school work experience placement in a store in the town centre, she imagined that it would not be too bad. Interestingly, Samantha had briefly considered going to college but as her best friend was leaving, she had also decided to.

For the low aspirers, work experience[8] placements do emerge as significant in terms of the impact they have on determining future career aspirations. Osgood, Francis and Archer (2006) found that students with no clearly defined career goals 'construct work experience placements as directly related to choices of future career' (2006: 318) They also note that work experience placements tend to be both gendered and classed and in this study nursery and junior school placements alongside work in retail outlets and basic clerical work were overwhelming the norm. This view is supported by a recent study carried out by Girl Guiding UK that found that career advice was highly gendered. Interestingly, low-aspiring students who had, for example, not previously desired to work with children found that this was now their career goal after undertaking a nursery school work experience placement. This was the case for six of the students in my study. Even students who had shop based placements which they described as boring, repetitive and unfulfilling stated that they would consider a shop based career despite the lack of status they believed was implicit in such work. For example Lilly describes her experience of working in an up-market older ladies clothes store:

> Lilly: *I had found one (work experience placement) myself and then the school gave me one and so I decided to do the one that the school had given me but it turned out*

to be stuck up people who think that they are hot but need a good slap! They were sooo rude . . . They tried to get me to mop the floors and I was like . . . me? Yeah! Sure! Like I am gonna mop the floors!! They were giving us work while they just stood around and talked to customers. I wasn't allowed to talk to them and when anyone tried to ask me some think I just walked away 'cause I didn't wanna try and answer them. Most of them that come in there are like really stuck up. There's this cube thing that goes around the hanger that tells you the size. I had to change all of them around the shop. Then you have to hang them in the right size, from ten onwards to 20, then they have to be colour co-ordinated. It takes so long and then you just have to keep going round the shop cleaning up, cleaning up! You're not allowed to sit down and you have to be on your feet for like, three hours straight. Then you get a little break and it's another two hours.

CF: *So could you see yourself doing this kind of work in the future then?*

Lilly: *I don't mind the work in the shop, yeah it's boring but it's just the people there that really got on my nerves . . .*

Felicity: *Like when Grace went there and they told her to go away!*

Lilly: *Yeah, my friend only came and asked me what time I was getting out [for lunch] and she [the supervisor] just went up to her and told her to get out . . . and I was thinking what ya doin'!! I just walk about, I done everything I could at the shop. And they got so annoyed 'cause I was so loud! When I laughed I was really loud! So it was a good experience in one way but not in another . . . and another thing! They were so rude! They never give me anything when I left.*

Felicity: *I had a card from all the children and I had chocolates* [smiles].

Lilly: *I didn't even get a thank you!*

Felicity: *I got a thank you every day!*

Lilly: *All I got was a bye! I was hoping to get a job out of it in the end but, I am not old enough yet. I wouldn't mind working there though, not really.*

Clearly, Lilly had found the work unfulfilling and implied that she had felt under-valued and experienced a sense of having less status than both the staff and the customers who shopped there. Yet, surprisingly, she expressed a desire to repeat the experience by possibly making a future career out of shop work.[9] Why is it that work experience placements hold such sway over these low-aspiring students? In the first instance I would suggest that the school is seen as indirectly advising students as to their suitability to certain types of work through the allocation of work experience placement. As one student said 'I wanted to do something with sport but I ended up in a junior school'. Whilst students do complete a form that assesses their interests and their preference for work placements, ultimately allocation seems some what arbitrary and subject to what is actually available. Stringent health and safety concerns, as well as the need for insurance[10] which covers students' in the work place hinders individuals from finding their own placements, for example, either in a family member's work place or in a particular field of interest. Where family support and guidance is lacking then school, and in particularly career guidance explicit in the work experience placement, can become the only source of direction that some students receive. Thus the education system, however unintentionally, emits a clear message as to suitability for work in their allocation of placements for those students who lack the confidence, the vision or the guidance to choose for themselves. As Osgood et al. (2006) note, these placements are classed and gendered and at a time when 'adolescents . . . are seeking to construct "acceptable" and normative constructions of . . . identity' (2006: 318) they appear to exert a powerful influencing force.

Despite all students receiving career guidance, primarily through the Connexions service, the overwhelming consensus of all the students in my research was that it was irrelevant and pointless at best. The overwhelming critique was that guidance and advice, however well intentioned, was remote and disconnected from the real world of work. What students felt they needed, but did not get, was assistance in exploring the choices that were available to them, in terms of their individual interests, abilities and skills:

CF: *Did you find career advice helpful?*

Aisha: *No . . . not really.*

Catherine: *No, 'cause they just give us a book to look at. We can read case studies and you can go out on trips to career fairs and stuff, although they didn't do that for us . . . so no, uhmmm, that made it hard and when they did do it [bring people in], it was accountants and . . .*

Aisha: *. . . it's just too general, it's not specific to you . . .*

Catherine: *if they brought in people from different occupations to come and speak to us and, uhm, it might appeal to someone who then might want to work in that kind of area. That would be better 'cause then you could talk to them, maybe go and see what they do and then see if its right for you.*

Aisha: *Yes, careers advice needs to focus more on the actual careers, like, what do you want to be?*

Focus Group, Year 12

Rachel: *I never went to talk to like a careers advisor for careers advice 'cause when I went there and told them what I wanted to do they were like, No! Why do you wanna do that? And they just kept asking me really shitty questions.*

Susan: *I remember I only went once I went to this meeting and I was talking and that and they just kept coming up with really random things and I was like, I am never gonna do that!* [Laughter]

Rachel: *Yeah, I suppose it's alright if you already know what you wanna do but, like, if you don't . . .*

Sarah: *They call it giving you careers advice but, they're so boring! They just sit there asking you a load of questions and you get nowhere in the end of it . . . especially if you know what you're gonna do.*

Focus Group, Year 12

Conclusion

I am not suggesting that careers advice can and should do more than what it does already. It would no doubt be virtually impossible to tailor a service that fits the needs of each individual student. What I am hoping to do here is to illustrate the futility of the current service in light of the needs of those low-aspiring students. High aspiring students with some anticipated future direction find career guidance unhelpful; if this is so, then it is easy to understand why low-aspiring students describe the careers service as 'pointless'. Yet, in some respects, it is arguably these students who are most in need of direction and support in terms of the choices that they make. What became very clear to me through my role as mentor in school was that some students do not have anyone to offer advice, encouragement or find out the information that will assist them in making informed choices concerning their future plans. In some respect my role as mentor very much replaced the parental figure, for example, I ordered college prospectuses, went through the entry requirements, assisted with filling in application forms with students and, on one occasion, attended a college interview with a student. Many students were often surprised to learn that there were a whole host of courses that had very basic entry requirements and, consequently, three students did go on to apply to college for courses which had no formal entry pre-requisites (in this instance two students went on to do child care courses and another to do a basic catering certificate).

Career Choices

As previously mentioned most of the low-aspiring students express a desire for low-level and low-skilled future employment; for example, work in retail outlets and nursery assistants. However, not all low-aspiring students lacked future goals. Indeed some students did have ambitions and dreams although it is fair to say they tended to be unlikely in terms of future educational plans. For example, Georgina stated that she was going to be a paediatrician after she had finished compulsory education whilst Samantha stated that if she grew bored with shop work she would leave and become a physiotherapist. Neither student had any knowledge of the additional training nor educational qualifications required for these occupations and did not consider these ambitions to be unrealistic for students educated to GCSE level. I admit to feeling somewhat perplexed as to how these students, both of whom were predicted to do poorly in their exams, should foster such ambitions. In addition, three of the lowest educationally achieving girls in this study had the sole ambition of being a famous pop star; the lead singer of their own band. However research suggests that this is not such an unusual ambition. Research by Croll (2006), using data from the British Household Panel Survey (BHPS) to explore the occupational choices of 14–16 year olds, found that a surprising 10 per cent of respondents expressed a desire to be professional entertainers and sports people. This is true too of Schneider and Stevenson's (1999) study of American students which also found that many students had occupational aspirations that did not match their educational plans. It would be easy to dismiss these ambitions as unlikely pipe dreams as only a small number of people ever achieve real fame but, as Pahl (2006) notes, as so many of today's respected media celebrities often 'boast about their lack of formal skills, education or even intelligence' (2006: 175) it is easy to understand why these ambitions are so attractive to the low aspirers. These ambitions do pose an interesting question in terms of attempting to understand and explain the disparity between occupational expectation, obtainability and predicted educational outcomes. Whilst a lack of adequate career guidance appears to be a likely explanation, when considering these ambitions in terms of the individual, they can also be viewed as the ambitions and dreams of those most lacking in self-confidence and self-esteem and are the ambitions and dreams of those students predicted to do the most poorly educationally. In some respects, ambitions of high status occupations or of fame could be considered as ambitions for respect and status of those students who, consciously or unconsciously, believe they cannot achieve it through the traditional meritocratic route of educational achievement.

Both Samantha and Mary Anne have parents whose occupations can be classified as working class, for example, Samantha's father is a lorry driver whilst Mary Anne's labours on building sites. Whilst both students professed ignorance to the concept of class Mary Anne's comments concerning an aunt she dislikes suggests she is aware of social difference and differences in status:

> *She thinks she's better than the rest of us just 'cause she got a good job and lives in a nice house. She won't let me see my cousins cause she says I'm a bad influence. She don't like the way I talk and that, says I am too common, but we all talk the same in our family, she's the one who talks funny. I don't care anyway. We're better than her.*

Status, or a sense of a lack of status, appears implicitly in many of the comments of the low-aspiring students and is thus considered as an important link in understanding both attitudes to education and the occupational choices of these students. This is because status appears to be so strongly associated with a student's sense of self in terms of their abilities, self-worth and self-esteem.

Whilst some low-aspiring girls make an independent decision to leave school at the end of compulsory education, some girls are actively encouraged by their families to leave and to seek work, in particular, work that will be secure. The view expressed in a focus group by Claire (white) in Year 10, a view that is quite common amongst those who intend to go straight into employment:

> *My dad says what's the point in going to college to learn gardening when you can just get a job and learn it that way? At least you're earning at the same time!*

Some students, however, discuss how they would have liked the option of continuing their education but are simply not able to:

> *I would've liked to have gone to college, maybe done a child care course or train to be a midwife but I can't. My mum would love me to do it too but she can't afford it. She say's that if she helps me then it wouldn't be fair on all the others, there's five of us see. If she does it for me then she would have to do it for all of us and she's right . . . It is hard for her 'cause she's on her own.*
>
> Jennifer, Focus Group, Year 10

Jennifer was not aware that as her mother was in receipt of welfare benefits she would probably be eligible for the Educational Maintenance Allowance (EMA).[11] However, after collecting the information and application form for Jennifer and her mother to read, she decided against applying. Jennifer was a bright student in set 2 who achieved seven A–C grades at GCSE. However, she did leave school after her exams had finished and took up a full-time post in a shoe shop in the town centre. Jennifer is a good example of a student whose initial occupational outcome did not correlate with her academic abilities.

Brief summary

In understanding the aspirations of those students who aspire low, it is clear to see that they are, in the Bourdieuian sense, replicating and reproducing their place in the social order, that is, their external position in terms of their family's place in the occupational hierarchy, as well as their position internal to the school. When considering the role of education in this reproduction, it becomes difficult to disentangle the role of structure and individual biography in understanding how these low aspirations are shaped. What is clear to me, however, is that alongside the influence of class, the individual's sense of self is also important. I would suggest that because of this more can and should be done to assist these low-aspiring students to foster belief in themselves and to understand that there are a range of choices available to them. This can be done by getting to know and understand the complexities of the individual as well as understanding the constraints imposed by class, for example, through a wider, rather than selective, use of one-to-one mentoring, mentoring that incorporates and indeed targets 'disaffected' students as well as those with C/D borderline predictions for GCSE.[12]

Family and Friends

Family and friendships are fundamental to understanding those girls' with low aspirations. This is because they appear to link significantly with their sense of self and their ability to trust. Therefore, family relationships and friendships have an important impact on a students self identity.

For the low aspirers, relationships with parents ranged from good to poor though in most cases were often complex. Many students report little in the way of parental sanctions or support. For example, Samantha recounts a surprisingly common event just before the Christmas holiday 2005 when she received a fixed-term exclusion for being drunk in school:

> Samantha: *I sneaked out of schools with my mates at break time and we went over to the park and got drunk. It was just for a laugh. But then, when we got back into*

school we got into so much trouble and then the school called my mum to come and fetch me. I got suspended till after the holidays.

CF: *And did you get punished by your mum?*

Samantha: *No, she said I'd been punished enough, what with being excluded and feeling so sick.*

In another, separate incident, Diane's mother discusses how she had felt about an occasion when her daughter was clearly intoxicated, she said:

Well naturally, I couldn't believe it; I was horrified to be honest. I don't know why she did it . . . she was so upset, she kept crying and saying she was sorry. I couldn't bring myself to punish her, I just couldn't. Well, to be honest I think she'd been punished enough, she felt soo sick and I don't honestly think she would do it again, I really don't.

Many of the low-aspiring students' can go to older boyfriends' homes for the weekend and can stay out very late with little parental interference or dissent. As Nicola states, 'when I get bored I go just out with my mates, go to town and have a laugh . . . we do stuff that's a bit naughty, that's wrong and my dad he don't know'. The perception of this approach by students ranged from a sign of parental trust to a lack of care. For the large part, many of the low-aspiring students appear to have complex home relationships, for example, having step-parents and step- and half- siblings, students living arrangements split between the households of both parents and so on. When asked how they get on with their parents, the general responses of 'not very well' or 'we argue a lot' would no doubt be typical of the parental relationships of many teenage students. What was interesting to note in some cases, however, were those relationships between student and mother that appeared to be almost 'friendship' in type. For example, students discuss how their mothers get on particularly well with their friends, give relationship advice, share a drink or a cigarette occasionally and how they go clothes shopping together. For some, mothers are, as Samantha states, a student's best friend. These 'friendships' might explain why in both the previous examples of excessive drinking neither mother felt able to reprimand their daughter and why, in some cases, parents appear to rebuke the school while implicitly condoning the behaviour of their daughters. For example, in January 2005 a very heated argument broke out in the corridor between two students which quickly escalated into a physical fight. The dispute was concerning a boy who had been sleeping with both students and was very physical and aggressive. The instigator of the fight was temporarily excluded from school. A few days later, whilst in reception, this same student was brought back into school by her mother.[13] The mother was shouting and swearing and demanding that someone needed to sign her daughter back into school immediately as she had 'work to get to'. When it was explained that as she had missed her scheduled appointment with the head teacher at 9.00 a.m. and as it was now 11.00 a.m. she would have to wait she replied, much to her daughter's amusement, 'I don't give a fuck we're late! We're only late 'cause we was up late celebrating her [the student's] birthday'. Finally the mother lost her temper, refused to sign herself into the visitor's book and left without meeting with the head. This example, whilst extreme (i.e. it was the only incident of this type I witnessed) does give pause for thought. This was one of a number of instances where parents appear to challenge the authority and legitimacy of the school. For example, one student informed me how her father had came into school to complain about the grade that her Design and Technology teacher had given her for her course work, believing that the low grade was the result of the students belief that the teacher did not like her whilst another told me how her mother had challenged the setting for foundation level GCSE child care rather than the higher tier[14] her daughter had wanted to do. In both cases neither parent's intervention changed the outcome.

At the other end of the spectrum, some students' experience almost hyper-parental surveillance and have parents who are very authoritarian. For example, in a focus group Sedra, tells me how she is not allowed to stay up in her room for too long in case she is texting boys on her phone, whilst another student is not allowed to go to the local shop alone as she 'cannot be trusted'. Sumera also states 'I can't go out 'cause girls are not allowed out on their own and once you hit puberty it's even more important [that you don't] 'cause you might start talking to boys'. This perception of a lack of trust at home can sometimes lead to students being defiant in school. For example in a focus group discussion Shagufta discuss how she often engages in low-level disruption, for example, answering back or disappearing in school between lessons. She states 'When you have no power at home, then school becomes the only place you can have some.' Shagufta is keen to point out, however, that she is careful and knows when to stop 'I try to make sure I don't go too far 'cause I don't want them ringing my parents'.

For parents, getting the balance between boundaries and freedom right is obviously difficult and Nicola offers an illuminating insight into the important messages that are implied by different parental responses. Nicola, by her own admission, is difficult[15] and because her mother found it increasingly hard to manage her was sent to live with her father. Whilst

Nicola is fairly happy with the move she has found it difficult learning to cope with her new and largely unfamiliar step-family. Nicola stated that she has pretty much given up on school and has not completed any course work in more than a year. When her father learnt of this after receiving a call from the school, he immediately imposed a rule that prohibited Nicola from going out in the evenings unless she had spent at least an hour on her school work. As mentioned earlier, Nicola's father had little knowledge of her whereabouts or what she was doing whilst out, yet Nicola appeared to welcome the rule and believed it was a sign that proved 'he loves me'.[16]

For the large part all students state that parents have little involvement in their education, preferring to let students 'get on with it'. In terms of future choices, they are encouraged to 'do what I want to'. However, as we will see in the following chapters which discuss the middle and high aspiring students, this is not necessarily the reserve of the low-aspiring parents but is a consistent theme for all students. The only real difference between parents of the low aspirers and other students was their noted lack of attendance at parent information evenings. However, as the following focus group discussion reveals, this is not an inevitable sign of a lack of parental interest but an illustration of the desire of students that they do not attend:

CF: *So, it was parents evening last night, did any of your parents come?*

Lilly: *Nope.*

Felicity: *No. They have never been and I am not about to let them start now! Anyway they couldn't come 'cause I don't tell them about it!*

All: [laugh]

Kirsty: *I went, but not my mum, I never told her either!*

Kelly: *I never.*

Lilly: *All they do is go on at your parents.*

Felicity: *Then they just send the report home any way.*

CF: *Do they post them?*

All: *Yeah.*

CF: *So why don't you think that parents evening is a good thing?*

Lilly: *You know what they are gonna say basically . . . she isn't doin' this . . . she's always late . . . she has only done one piece of course work . . . of yes wonderful! They only have one good thing to say about you and about 20 others that are bad so, really, there's no point in going. You know at the end of the day your mum's gonna be mad at you when you go home.*

Focus Group Discussion, Year 10

Finally, friendships appear to be very important for the low-aspiring student and seeing friends was most frequently cited as the best thing about school. Whilst most students claim to make independent decisions concerning their futures, the choices of friends were often explicitly referred to and do appear significant. For example Samantha, as we have seen, plans to leave school at the end of compulsory education and find work in a retail outlet. However, she did temporarily consider further education:

> *I did want to go and do P.E. at college but only if my friend was gonna do it. But actually I find the theory side of it quite hard and I don't really know if I could really be that bothered to do it. Anyway, it wouldn't be no good without my mates.*

As Ball (1981) found in his study of a mixed sex comprehensive, friendships tend to be amongst students from the same sets and in this case more importantly reflect friendships amongst those who share the same aspirations (who might not necessarily be in the same set or even the same school). For the low-aspiring students relationships with friends were cited as being more important than those with family and all of their closest friends were also planning to leave school after their GCSEs. However as we will see when we consider the importance of friendships in aspirations amongst the high aspirers, this influence had the strongest significance on the low aspirers. In part this may be explained by the fact that 'having good mates' appears to be a considerable aspect of a low-aspiring students self-identity and associated sense of self-worth but may be also be intrinsically linked to gendered identities, as I will discuss in the following section.

Brief summary

In all cases, whilst family relationships are very important to a student, educational aspirations cannot be understood solely in terms of the role that parents play, that is, in terms of directly shaping aspirations through their guidance and advice. Whilst families are important in reinforcing the value, authority and legitimacy of the institution of education itself, they also appear important in shaping students self-identity in terms of self-esteem and self-worth through the degrees of independence they offer their child. Getting the balance right appears significant. Too much autonomy appears to leave students directionless and self-reliant in terms of their decision making processes and, for some students, appears to indicate a lack of concern and care. Too little autonomy however, appears to make students feel stifled. In either case, student/parent relationships appear to be associated with trust. In addition, friendship and the choices of friends are important because friends appear to be such a central component of self-identity. This is because students, who achieve very little self-esteem through their experiences at school, find it instead through their relationships with like-minded friends.

Gender

The career aspirations of low-aspiring students can be considered not only as replicating class but also as replicating gender. For the large part career aspirations typically reflect a gendered stereotyping in that child care and retail work (which are overly represented by female workers) were the norm. This is also true in the gendered curricula choices of students, who were overwhelmingly represented in courses such as child care (CACHE), food technology and textiles. In addition, whilst it is apparent that students acknowledge that modernity has afforded them greater freedom of choice in their life course than previous generations, that is, they no longer have to follow the traditional trajectory of marriage and children, and do freely discuss their ambiguity to ideas of marriage, most still foresee a steady relationship and children as an important part of their futures. These ambitions appear so intrinsically woven into student's identity as women that, as O'Connor states, 'gender is [clearly] a repressed but crucially important framework in the construction of self' (2006: 107). Whilst gender was only ever referred to explicitly when I raised the issue, what is implicit in my data is that low-aspiring students do define themselves in terms of their gender and, more importantly, in terms of their relationships with men.

During the course of my time in school two of the low-aspiring students became engaged to their older boyfriends whilst another sported a 'commitment' ring. None of these men were in employment and all had finished their schooling at the end of compulsory education. What was apparent in discussions with students regarding these relationships was the obvious satisfaction they felt in being part of a couple. For example, Heather told me with great delight that her friends were very jealous when she had shown them her ring and that having one made her feel 'grown up and special'. Heather, a largely shy, plain and overweight young lady discusses in a focus group how she now no longer meets up with her friends outside of school:

> There's just no time anymore and Darren don't like it, he likes it when we're together.

Lauren was another who very much appeared to define herself in terms of the males in her life and many of our conversations would end in a discussion of her current relationship problems. Despite boyfriends being a big part of Lauren's life, what was interesting was her unwavering belief that men could not to be trusted and that relationships based on meaningful affection were unlikely:

> *Men! they tell me they love me but they only want me for sex . . . men never love you . . . sex is all they want. Its' hard for teenagers like me round here 'cause you have to accept that you won't ever have someone to care for you.*

In the time I spent with Lauren there was only one occasion in which she appeared animated, excited and had a sense of purpose. This was the time that she thought she might be pregnant (as mentioned earlier) by her previous boyfriend. What was notable was that Lauren happily acknowledged that, if true, this potential event would be something that she would have to go through alone and she willingly accepted this:

> *David said that if I am [pregnant] he doesn't want me but he will give me £50 a week and see it three times a week. He promised he would never go for custody of it. I told him if I am then I have to keep it . . . I could never get rid of it.*

For Lauren, potential motherhood appeared to offer a sense of direction and purpose to her life that she was unable to find through the educational route. It also appeared that being a parent would enable her to acquire an identity that she considered had status and value. This idea is similar to findings in a study conducted by the Joseph Rowntree Foundation (2006) that also found that young people with unsettled home lives and bad experiences at school viewed parenthood as 'an opportunity, within their control, to change their life and to gain independence and a new identity' (2006: 1).

Brief summary

For the low aspirers, gender and gendered roles appear to be an important construct in the creation of future aspirations. That most of these students lack confidence, appear to have low self-esteem and do not do well academically is interesting. Conventional gendered roles, both in the occupational career choices and as future wives/girlfriends and mothers, appear to offer a familiar, traditional role that has value and some status to the students who choose them. In this sense for the low aspirers gender presents as a very powerful construct in terms of a students sense of self and who she will become in the future. However, as we will see, this is not simply the reserve of the low aspirers. Indeed, as the data for the mid and high aspirers reveal, gender is highly significant for all the students included in this study.

Chapter Summary

The low aspirers are distinguished by their low levels of self-esteem and self-confidence. Thus their rejection of post-compulsory education as a viable route for future career paths is understood as a response to their negative perceptions of education, shaped in part by their experiences of schooling and through their reflexive understanding of their potential to achieve. That these students feel alienated within school goes some way to explaining their lack of attachment to the institution of education broadly, as well as providing an understanding of why students reject the principles of meritocracy that is inferred from their comments. That some of these students consequently challenge or withdraw, via truanting and the like is presented as a rational response by students to a system they feel rejected by. In addition to a student's understanding of her place within the education, a lack of support and encouragement outside of school often leaves low-aspiring students directionless and dependent on the guidance and advice of school. Unfortunately, and however unintentionally, the careers guidance and work experience placements often appears to encourage the highly gendered low status, low-pay career ambitions of the low aspirers. It also explains why for some, motherhood and relationships were so predominant in future life course plans.

Notes

[1] See methods section for a more in depth discussion on the impact of my role as participant observer.
[2] These are the terms used by staff to describe the low-aspiring students in my study.
[3] Whilst Sandy is a middle aspirer, her comments are included here as they clearly illustrate my point.
[4] On this occasion the pregnancy scare was a false alarm. However, I was informed in July 2006 that Lauren was now expecting her first child.

[5] It should be noted that once I became aware of Lauren's behaviour I notified the appropriate teaching staff, who then took the necessary action. This was done with Lauren's awareness although not necessarily with her agreement. What was interesting in this particular case was that once her parents had been informed, Lauren's anger at the ensuing 'grief' she received from her parents was directed at the school and teacher involved and not at me, the person who had informed on her in the first instance.

[6] Although I did not verify this story it was re-told by several students and I did no longer see the teacher around the school or in the staff room.

[7] From the Disney website.

[8] Work experience tends to take place in the summer term of Year 10.

[9] Surprisingly Lilly did come back to the sixth form because her best friend had. However, Lilly was rarely in school and was experiencing great difficulties at home. Essentially, her foster parents had washed their hands off her and she was now sleeping on the floor of a friend's. As she was now 16 she was beyond the concern of the local authorities. Concerned teachers were powerless to help Lilly and get her into school and expressed their frustration at a system that was clearly letting Lilly down. When I went into school to see Lilly (as she had asked to see me) I was told by her best friend that she had been forced to leave school and move to a large town in the South West to stay with a relative she barely knew. When I last spoke to her (end of 2007) she was unhappy and still not in work, education or training.

[10] This insurance appears to cover the school in case of being sued by parents in the event of a work experience placement accident.

[11] EMA is a maintenance allowance paid directly to students whose families have an income of less that £30,000 per annum. £30 per week is paid to students whose families earn less than £22,000; £20 per week for incomes under £24,000 and £10 per week for those earning less than £30,000. On top of this bonuses for attendance and performance are also possible.

[12] In my first year in school I primarily mentored students who could be best described as disengaged from education. However in the second year the school, having been placed on special measures and under pressure to improve GCSE A–C attainment rates, appeared to shift their priority for mentoring to those students who were D/C boarder line in terms of predicted GCSE results.

[13] It is common practice that parents and student, on the return of the student to school from a fixed period of exclusion, meets with a senior member of staff to discuss the incident and agree future behaviour.

[14] In the England and Wales students sit GCSE examinations. The GCSE adopts a two tiered approach where students can be entered for GCSE at the foundation or higher levels. Foundation level means that students will hope to achieve a grade between G and C. There is no option of a grade higher than C. The higher level GCSE grades are D–A whilst in maths there is an additional tier, the intermediate tier, which assesses grades E–B. There are no tiers for examinations in history, religious education, music or art and design (Source: QCA website, accessed 13 September 2006.)

[15] Nicola would not elaborate on what she meant by 'difficult'.

[16] Unfortunately for Nicola, later in 2005 she was forced to leave her father's home due to conflict with her step-mother and she returned to her mother's home. Again, after just a short space of time, she had to leave her mother's home and found herself temporarily homeless. After staying at her boyfriend's for a while, she was given council accommodation and now, I am told, lives with him there. Nicola achieved three and a half Cs and two Ds at GCSE.

Chapter 4

The Middle Aspirers

Custom, then, is the great guide of human life.

David Hume [1711–1776]

Characteristics

Students categorized as middle aspirers are those who intended to continue with further education at the end of their compulsory schooling but did not intend to continue into higher education. Education refers to vocational training at college, for example, hairdressing, catering and child care courses and so on. and includes GCE A level[1] examinations at either college or a sixth form. Students categorized as middle aspirers, in contrast to most of the low aspirers, are generally fairly positive about school and value education, deeming it necessary for future job security. The middle aspirers are found across the range of academic setting but tend to cluster more predominantly in sets two and three.

Mid-aspiring students are distinct from the low-aspiring students in that they have clear career goals and essentially see education as valuable, worthwhile and believe continuing with it is crucial for their future. This is because students believe that finding work will be harder without some additional education. For mid-aspiring students, leaving education at the end of compulsory schooling is considered as too risky because they believe GCSE qualifications are now no longer enough in terms of the market place:

Karen: *Some people can get by with just GCSEs but there is that pressure you know . . . that GCSE's aren't enough.*

CF: *So do you feel pressurized to stay on?*

Karen: *I would love to leave but it's not really a choice.*

Naomi: *Yeah. But then, there is the choice but it's more of a . . .*

Melanie: *You have to do it, you should do it.*

Belinda: *Yeah, you could get a job but . . . not a very good one.*

Karen: *I think the same.*

Focus Group, Year 10

Rene: *I would be like, if I didn't stay on . . . I'd be like . . . I'd have no qualifications because GCSEs, everybody has them. So, it wouldn't be like . . . well . . . it would be an achievement but . . . it's not a big achievement.*

Seema: *It's like worthless now.*

Rene: *And you don't understand that when you are doing them.*

Focus Group, Year 12

All students stated that they had been sure for some time that they wanted to pursue further education in some form, yet complained that the decision making process, that is, deciding what to study and where, had felt rushed. Students stated that they felt there had been little time available to think things through properly and weigh up all the available options and believed that post-16 options were something that they should have begun thinking about much earlier in their school life. Whilst all the mid-aspiring students were sure that they wanted to continue with further education, what they did state was that they would have preferred to have been able to consider *what* they were going to study much earlier:

When you start your GCSE's you gotta start thinking about what A levels you wanna do and even if you wanna do them. You tend to think 'yeah I'll do them' and choose subjects that you think you're gonna do good in but that you're not actually sure about 'cause you haven't had enough time to think about it and then you might start dropping lessons.

Seema, Focus Group, Year 12

For some students, the pressure they experienced in having to make what they considered quick choices, resulted in some choosing to stay on at school in light of no attractive alternatives:

Ruby: *I didn't know what else to do really.*

Lisa: *No, like me. It was all a rush in the end.*

Focus Group, Year 12

. . . my parents were quite supportive of me but, at the end of the day they realized it was my choice, what ever I want to do had to come from me. I felt that there was

a lot of pressure on me to make a quick decision and I felt rushed . . . I think we should have started thinking about it a lot earlier.

Sarah, Focus Group, Year 12

Whilst not planning to pursue higher education, mid-aspiring students consider that future job security and choice in the market place is fundamentally linked with further education:

CF: *What's the main advantage for you in getting more qualifications?*
Zaharie: *You will get a better job at the end of it, a career.*

Rene: *If you continue in education, I personally feel that you feel better about yourself . . . that you did something, that you achieved something for yourself. You waste your education if you just leave school and get a job, start work . . . something like that. If you got an education you can get a better job and you can get paid better anyway. So, you kind of secure your life after that because with education you always have some where to work and you will always have something to do.*

Seema: *If you leave it's your own choice yeah and it's like, if you wanna go and work then that's your choice yeah but then some people wanna go further in their life and by doing that they have to carry on in education.*

Focus Group, Year 12

The mid-aspiring students believe that they are free to make their own choice regarding their educational future yet they contradict these claims with their very explicit observation that these choices are in fact constrained by the market place, that is, in terms of what employers expect. This view is supported in the work of Gallie (1996) who found that in the employment market, whilst there has been a noticeable rise in the number of qualifications required for jobs for both sexes since 1986, the shift was particularly significant for females. He also noted that of those aged 20–25 it is more likely that females will be employed in work requiring qualifications, including A levels. Therefore, it is not necessarily unrealistic that students consider that taking a chance and not continuing their education is highly risky due to market place competition. Students also note that further education is something they need to pursue now as they felt it would be harder to rectify later on:

CF: *What do you think would happen then, to students who didn't carry on?*
Rene: *At some point they're gonna realize that they'd missed out and by the time they realize that exams are actually important, specially if there's a job they want to do, by then it will be too late to go back.*

Karen: *It's never really too late, it's just harder to do the work at college when you are older . . .*

Naomi: *. . . and if you are not young anymore and all your friends are years ahead of you, its hard, really hard on you.*

Focus Group, Year 10

I just . . . I would like to get A levels because of a back up, you know, you could just like leave now but then if you actually realized what you actually want to do, your actual path then . . . you actually need to get these qualifications, it will set you back so much if you have to go all the way back, retracing. At least now, even if I get them and even if I don't, at least I'll have them as a back up cause I don't know what's gonna happen in 20 years time. It's kind like preparation basically.

Sandy, Focus Group, Year 12

In addition, middle aspirers appear to suggest that a distinction is made and a certain element of status attached to those people who have these additional qualifications:

CF: *So why do you think further education matters?*

Lisa: *I think it just does.*

Ruby: *Yeah. Some people say, like, loads of people who have left here thinks like, that experience means more but I don't think it does. I think when people like, met you, education means more than what you done . . .*

Lisa: *. . . 'specially when it's written down on a piece of paper . . . all your qualifications and everything, it's more important.*

CF: *So qualifications matter?*

Ruby: *I think today it's really important, yes.*

Lisa: *They defiantly do.*

Focus Group, Year 12

Just as the participants in Warmington's (2003) research found that students appear to believe: 'you need a qualification for everything these days' (2003: 101) and appear to have evaluated and calculated the costs and benefits of continuing with education in some form. These students perceive the employment market place to be competitively driven and therefore believe they must strive to attain, in advance, the qualifications needed for their chosen career paths if they are to have anything like a fair chance. Beck states that 'competition . . . compels people to advertise . . . their own accomplishments' (1992: 94) and this view seems to be supported in the data from the middle aspirers who appear to view further education and the associated qualifications as a metaphorical badge of merit and suitability. Further education is overwhelmingly the preferred route for students as opposed to gaining the skills through the 'hands-on' experience of being in the workplace, for example, through apprenticeships in hairdressing and catering. Students appear to view additional qualifications along the lines of low-risk investment in the stock market, believing that these additional qualifications will pay small dividends in terms of their ability to negotiate choice to some degree and, more importantly, compete for a place in the work place. Further education for the mid-aspiring students is therefore understood as offering a safety net that minimizes risk, ensuring future employability and future security.

School Work and Academic Setting

The mid-aspiring students are drawn from sets two to four although they are predominantly found in sets two and three. For the large part, middle aspirers are happy with their academic setting, believing that they are appropriately allocated in terms of their abilities. However, just as with the low-aspiring students, they too complain about school work and the demands of heavy course work schedules. Mid-aspiring students are generally happy in school and state they have reasonable relationships with most of the staff and in general state that they respect and like the teaching staff. However, whilst the middle aspirers have only modest expectations in terms of examination success, for example, most are working towards target grades of Cs and Ds at GCSE, they are differentiated from the low aspirers because of their desire to do well and because of the measures they adopt in their attempts to reach their educational targets. For example, mid-aspiring students were often willing to speak to teachers regarding their school work, attend after school revision classes and come into school and revise in the school holidays, prior to their GCSE exams. Middle aspirers were also the group who expressed, most often, anxiety in terms of their ability to do well by achieving the goals that teachers assessed them as capable of. Kelly, for example, was one of several students who informed me that she had started doing a small amount of revision in the evenings before going out, after getting several Ds in her mock exams. Anxiety connected to the pressure felt around the exam period often manifested itself through the occasional skipping of school with questionable ill health as well as some occasional sanctions for late handing-in of school work.

As well as expressing anxiety over their academic abilities, middle aspirers also expressed the least confidence in knowing how to prepare for their exams in the practical sense and this created additional worry for students. To illustrate, it was most frequently the mid-aspiring students who came to me and asked for practical help, for example, in drawing up examination revision schedules and for tips on revising. Whilst striving to achieve their academic targets, students appeared reluctant to approach teachers for any help that they perceived to exceed the teachers remit. For example, students stated that simple revision skills and help with revision timetables and the like are not covered explicitly in school. However, some students believed these were valuable skills that they needed and would be keen to learn.

The mid-aspiring students generally lacked confidence in their own academic abilities and unquestionably trusted and accepted the academic assessments and targets of others. No student expressed a confidence in aiming much higher than assessed. Giddens suggests that trust in others 'links self-identity in a fateful way to the appraisals of others' (1991: 38) and, for the middle aspirers, this would appear to be true.

Sixth Form Students

The mid-aspiring students completing A levels in the sixth form were also similar to those doing GCSEs in that they too lacked confidence in their academic abilities (as opposed to those planning to go into higher education) and whilst happy to ask for help on matters they were unsure of, expressed a self-consciousness about doing so. Whilst the high-aspiring students express the belief that their educational performance is the result of collaborative efforts of both staff and student, mid-aspiring students appear to suggest the main onus is on themselves.

I don't know . . . I'm struggling with the work at the moment and I know it's down to me really. I've got to do it 'cause there's no one else who can do it for me.

Ruby, Focus Group, Year 12

I am actually doing media studies but, I find it goes on because I don't like doing the press section of it because my weakness is being able to read and just . . . well I can read . . . I find it easier to learn when I can actually see the things, like pictures . . . looking tends to be group work and it helps me. I find writing so hard, putting down what you think in the right words . . . reading you have to, read beyond. I find that really difficult and I find that it's hard to ask for help because I feel like I should be able to do it because everyone else can.

Sandy, Focus Group, Year 12

Despite finding it difficult sometimes to approach teaching staff for academic help, teachers were generally well respected and were often cited by students as being important in their decision to stay on into the sixth form:[2]

I wanna be a teacher like Mrs Smith, it's 'cause of my English teacher I'm here; she's a really good teacher. I don't wanna leave until she does [laughs]. *And she's really good to talk to, she doesn't make you feel like there's a staff and student divide.*

Sarinda, Focus Group, Year 12

Despite sometimes expressing some rather negative opinions of the school after it was placed on Special Measures following its OfSTED inspection,[3] students still felt that staying on at their own school was preferable to going anywhere else:

Sandy: [in this school] *time is wasted . . . and sometimes those little things just bring it down for everyone else and its just like, for example, like, you know . . . 'cause the school is in a general . . . you know, everyone tries to be encouraged where as in 'Queens' and 'Churchfield' if you mess around then your out and that's why its higher when you come to think of other things. Everyone knows they're there to learn, that they're expected to learn whereas here, they just want people to stay on and it doesn't matter if you're not good enough . . .*

Charlotte: *. . . they just sell the subject and they let the lower down people do it . . . those that aren't really willing to do it.*

Sandy: *. . . and it drags it down for us, even for teachers who might lose their motivation when they are getting all of this all the time so . . . sometimes it might be beneficial* [to go to college instead] *but, at the same time . . .*

Charlotte: *. . . mind you, I say this and I just end up staying here and doing my A2s. It's just a thought I've been thinking about recently* [leaving and going to college instead]. *Most likely I will stay on here, I'd prefer to.*[4]

Sandy: *me too!* [laughs]

Staying in a familiar school does appear a significant consideration for mid-aspiring students. Research on truancy by Attwood and Croll (2006) found that changing secondary school during the years of compulsory schooling is clearly difficult and disruptive and was cited by several persistent truants in their study as the cause of their truancy. Students overwhelmingly expressed the view that it was better to stay on in a 'poor' school as going elsewhere is considered very daunting:

I knew that I did want to carry on with something but I wasn't sure what I wanted to do exactly. And I was like 'ah no . . . what am I gonna do?' but, I knew what I was interested in but I wasn't sure what subjects matched with that. So, 'cause they encouraged me and even though I was looking at different places to go but then I was like 'ah . . . I'll just stay here' 'cause I know the environment, I know the teachers.

Seema, Focus Group, Year 12

I didn't know what else to do really . . . and I didn't feel ready to start work yet.

Ruby, Focus Group, Year 12

I just didn't want to go straight into work.

Lisa, Focus Group, Year 12

Basically for me was that I didn't kinda want to start somewhere fresh where I had to like learn everyone again, learn who they are . . . meet new people and stuff. I thought it would be easier, less of a transition and I think I was scared about the jump from GCSE to A level it would be like really hard and I didn't wanna have to heap extra work on to it, having to get to know the teachers and the pupils. I just thought it was better to stay where I was, where I knew everyone.

Charlotte, Focus Group, Year 12

It's just like cause you know the people you feel more confident asking for help. Whereas if you didn't know the teachers you would just be wary and that's a problem you just don't need to be dealing with if you are going into A levels. 'Cause you need to concentrate on what you are doing.

Sandy, Focus Group, Year 12

Lara: *It's just easier for me to get here.*
Rosie: *That's what I was gonna say! . . . you know what your doin', you don't have to start somewhere new.*
Lara: *You know everyone.*

Focus Group, Year 12

A desire to remain local is similarly true for those going on to college for vocational training. They too expressed a desire to attend college locally rather than go to either of the other colleges that were but a relatively short travelling distance away. The reasons most often given for choosing to study locally was that the college was easy to get to and, most importantly, friends would be going there too.

Brief summary

For the middle aspirers the view that education is important and legitimate can clearly be seen as relevant in understanding student aspirations. Despite sometimes expressing rather negative views of their school,[5] those who opted to remain articulated well the reassurance, security and comfort afforded by remaining within an institution that was recognizable to them in terms of the staff, students, routine and expectations. As many of these students express a lack of confidence in relation to their academic abilities and for making new friends in unknown environments, it is understandable then that what is familiar should be the preferred choice. For the middle aspirers then, institutional attachment appears significant. Giddens (1991) suggests that some institutions within post-modernity are important unifying agents and for the middle aspirers school does appear to fulfil this role. This is because it creates a sense of security and belonging as well as promoting a confidence derived from feelings of familiarity and belonging. As Berger notes 'stable identities . . . can only emerge in reciprocity with stable social contexts (and this means contexts that are structured by stable institutions)' (1973: 86).

For those mid-aspiring students pursuing vocational training at college, attachment is also important but for these students it is attachment to locality, rather than institution, which appears implicitly to matter. All of the students planning vocational training intended to study at the local college. No student seriously considered the option of going elsewhere. This finding is similar to Hutchings and Archer (2001) who, although looking at higher and not further education, found that attachment to locality was fundamentally important to the respondents in their study in determining their choice of higher educational institution. Attachment to locality was strong primarily because of the desire/need to stay close to family and friends and was often cited as a valid reason for not pursuing higher education, particularly where the only viable institution was to far away.

Work Experience, Career Guidance and Occupational Choices

Those students planning vocational training have clearly defined career paths, for example, aspiring to be hairdressers, chefs, or to work with children. However, when asked to elaborate on why they had opted for these particular vocations, as opposed to others, they were ambiguous and unsure:

> Katy: *It was just something I always wanted to do. I don't know why really, I just know it's something that I really want to do.*
>
> Clara: *I dunno. I guess I've always been good with kids 'cause I know quite a lot and I just thought I would like a job like that. I don't remember when I actually thought it.*
>
> Focus Group, Year 10

Despite being unclear as to the reasoning for opting for a particular vocation, students believe that these occupations will be enjoyable and have advantages in that they are steady and reliable and offer the potential to acquire an element of job security. As Clara states in a focus group discussion 'people are always gonna be having kids that will need looking after!' Middle aspirers differ from the low aspirers in that they have basic knowledge of the requirements of the college courses they wish to attend, are willing to ask parents for advice and generally find the Connexions service helpful in terms of guidance and information. School work placements were also a positive experience in that they appeared to help some students either clarify or cement ambitions. For example, Fatima had had a vague idea of wanting to work with children and after enjoying her placement in a nursery was now sure that this was the career she wanted to pursue. In a focus group Katherine discusses how she too also wanted to work with children and had considered training to be a mid-wife. After enjoying her work experience in a nursery, she also decided to opt for child-care training instead. Her change of heart was attributed primarily to the belief that a child-care career was more attainable in terms of time, that is, one to two years as opposed to four. Interestingly, both students stated that the staff and the work had made them feel valued during the time they were there.

The school also runs a scheme similar to work experience that places students in college during school time. Despite the fact that only two students in this study are actually being involved in the scheme, it is still worth mentioning, particularly as the LA has recently provided the school with additional funding to pay for a member of staff to go into college to liaise with tutors as the number of students being included rises. Generally, the scheme involves students attending college for one or two days a week and is usually offered to pupils most at risk of permanent exclusion. Being included in the scheme effectively decreases the amount of time a student is required in school and assists in holding on to the student until the end of her compulsory schooling.[6] In addition, the scheme is also used for students who are specifically selected by staff to participate in subject-related courses.[7] For example, food technology staff select a few students to participate in a catering course, and students would then attend for one day a week.

Case Study 4.1 – Abby

Abby was a persistent truant who, in her last year of compulsory schooling, spent more time out of school than in. Abby was given a two day a week placement in a local hairdressing salon where she began training as an apprentice. This meant that Abby was only required in school three days a week.[8] Abby discussed with me her dislike of school and how truanting was her response to the point-lessness she saw in the school. Abby was however thoroughly enjoying her placement in the hairdressing salon and felt that what she was doing there was both meaningful (because she hoped to pursue a career in hairdressing) and was also something she felt she was good at. Importantly, because Abby was aware that her continuation on the scheme was dependent on good attendance on the additional days she was required in school, she now attended regularly. Despite admitting that she was still 'counting down the days until it's [school] finished and I can get out of here', Abby was grateful to the school for giving her the opportunity to finish her education in this way. Whether Abby could have made it on her own without the school intervening is impossible to know. However, what the scheme did was catch a potentially permanent drop out and place her on an alternative road which would enable her to acquire skills and training and thus secure her employability.

Case Study 4.2 – Helen

Helen had always known that she had wanted to be a chef. Whilst realistic in her ambitions, her dream was to own a restaurant. Despite initially being reluctant to participate on the college placement scheme ''cause I wouldn't know anybody', Helen ended up thoroughly enjoying the experience. The course, she stated, had given her confidence in her skills and abilities to try something new and in making new friends and she was now determined to pursue a catering course at college. Asked why she was chosen, she stated that she believed it was because she consistently achieved good grades for her food technology course, 'it's the one thing I am really good at'. However, whilst the experience of going to college was clearly viewed as positive, it was not without its own problems. The flip side to the college placement scheme is that it brought with it additional stresses for the students involved. For example, Helen informed me that students who were released from school for one day a week to attend college were expected to catch up with the school work they had missed, for example, writing up lesson notes and finding out about course work assignments. The onus is squarely with the student and no free space is allocated to their timetable, for example, with a study time period. Given that mid-aspiring students, for the large part, express high degrees of anxiety as they struggle to keep up with heavy work loads, this seems an unnecessary burden. A consequence is that it can lead to students falling behind in other work. For example, Helen (behind in her course work for several subjects) stated that she was not concerned if she could not catch up anymore 'because I won't need most of it for catering anyway'.

However, if Helen's view was true for all students who participated in the day release scheme (and I am not suggesting that it is), then the benefits, that is, in terms of confidence and experience, could prove to be counterproductive. This is because if they fall behind in their other subjects further educational choices then become restricted, particularly as some choices, for example A levels, will be dependent on a reasonable A–C pass rate at GCSE.

Finally, the career choices of those students who opt for A level study in the school sixth form, whilst less clear, centre primarily within the realm of administrative roles, for example, work in banks, as receptionists and office workers. Just as with those students aspiring to vocational training and associated careers, these students are also seeking work in an area they perceive to be available and safe, that is, aspiring to occupations they trust will always need employees and, additionally, employment which has a certain element of social status and respectability attached. For these students, A levels are perceived as providing a more enhanced opportunity for employment, as opposed to vocational training, in work that is perceived as having less risk attached because the occupations appear to offer longer-term security in terms of the availability of such posts. These students could be considered as having aligned ambitions (Schneider and Stevenson, 1999) that is, as having ambitions and aspirations that reflect knowledge of the labour market. This is because research conducted on behalf of the local council in 2003 found that administrative posts did account for 50 per cent of all employment in the town (Mercia, 2005). However, these occupations locally are now in steady decline and predictions suggest that by 2010 will fall by up to two-thirds.

Conclusion

The occupational aspirations of the middle aspirers could be considered as structurally determined in the Bourdieuian sense in that students aspire to careers which they perceive as being available and realistically achievable when evaluated relative to their abilities. Given the changing nature of the occupational structure in the UK today, the occupational aspirations of the mid-aspiring students could thus be considered as conditional to and restricted by the social context, with only marginal aspirations for social mobility expressed by some students. The aspirations of the mid-aspiring students therefore suggest strong support for the theoretical concept of habitus (see Chapter Two), particularly when understood in relationship to the role that the experiences of school have in shaping them. Whilst Bourdieu is often critiqued for not making clear the distinction between aspirations and expectations (Swartz, 1997), his idea that future aspirations are 'objectively conditional' has credence:

> [aspirations are] an acquired system of generative schemes objectively adjusted to the particular conditions in which it is constituted . . . all the thoughts, all the perceptions and all the actions consistent with the conditions, and no others. (Bourdieu, 1977: 95)

However, whilst the concept of habitus works well for explaining the aspirations of these mid-aspiring students, it does not so readily account for why it is only *some* students' aspirations that can be understood in this way. As a concept, it appears to leave gaps in the theoretical understanding as to why some students, that is, those with high aspirations, have ambitions for occupations that appear to fall outside a class framed objective criteria.

The work of Beck might offer some illumination. Beck (1992) discusses how traditional ties to class have been replaced, or at least superseded, by ties to institutions. For Beck, it is institutions and not class culture that is now significant in shaping individual biographies and it is institutions that are now the most influential determinants of a person's self and social identity. Implicitly Beck is suggesting that an individual's identity is tightly bound up in the labour market. This is because social inclusion or exclusion is dependent on that market and where you are within it, that is, your identity is bound by what you do for a living. For Beck then, the institution of education is a corner stone of modernity because an individual's ability to negotiate that market will depend largely on their educational credentials. Education can thus determine whether an individual enters society or merely 'drift into the margins' (1992: 133), and without it one will 'face social and material oblivion' (1992: 133).

Beck offers a theoretical perspective that is useful in that it allows us to move beyond an over-reliance on concepts such as class dispositions and class values to explain aspirations (this is not to say they are not useful merely; they tend to be over-used as an explanatory 'catch all'). Yet Beck's theory of institutionalization can also be criticized in the same vein as Bourdieu, in that it also fails to account for how it is, if attainment and economic resources are held constant, there are differences in aspirations, that is, why it is that some students acknowledge a relationship between education and employment whilst others are unconcerned. However, by including the family in the conceptualization of 'institution'[9] then the relationship between institutions and aspirations would be much clearer. As I will show in the following section (and Chapter Five), it may be that it is not necessarily that institutions shape aspirations independently, more that, it is degrees of attachment to those institutions that is important.

Family and Friends

The relationships of the mid-aspiring students with both their family and friends present as being significant and illuminating, both in terms of understanding a student's sense of self-identity but also because they provide an explanatory window for understanding their aspirations. As we will see, the parental relationships of the mid-aspiring students' are an implicitly important factor in promoting a students sense of emotional security because they appear to support a sense of belonging. These same factors are also suggestive in the importance that students attach to their friends.

Whilst families may be fragmented and complex, for example, with step- and half-siblings, mid-aspiring students appear to maintain a strong bond with at least one of their parents which, in most cases, tends to be with the mother and have some contact with extended kin.

The relationship of the middle aspirers and their parents can be inferred as structured in that they appear authoritarian yet loving. Parents provide students with clear boundaries and expectations, for example, by setting curfews, and their authority appears to be resignedly accepted and rarely challenged. As one student in Year 10 told me 'I might not always like the rules but at least it means she cares.' However, parents do permit some degree of independence, for example, in terms of dating. An implicit theme in the relationships of the middle aspirers to their families is that of dependency. In this instance dependency refers to emotional reliance/security as opposed to physical and/or economic needs. Unlike the low aspirers and, as we will see, the high aspirers, mid-aspiring students express no urgency in seeking independence away from the family home, at least in their immediate future plans. Whilst they may complain, for example, if they share a bedroom with a sibling, their grievances appear superficial and would probably be representative of many teenagers. Dependency is inferred, for example, in the importance that they attach to their future abilities to maintain daily contact with their families when they are adults and is expressed also through the significant weight that students attach to the guidance, advice and reassurance that parents offer them. For example, Rene stated that staying on in the sixth form to do A levels had been her own choice yet it was immensely important to her that her parents agreed:

> *Basically, I moved here (UK) five years ago and my parents' English is not that good so, most of the decisions I made so far were down to me and . . . um . . . and I'm happy for that cause it made me a bit more independent and I know exactly what I am gonna do with my life and where I want to go with it. But, at the same time I have had loads of support from my parents. I ask them 'do you think this is the right thing for me to do?' And they are always telling me this is the right way to go and your doing the right thing and that matters a lot to me.*
>
> Rene, Focus Group, Year 12

Most of the mid-aspiring students stated that, to their knowledge, their parents had not participated in further education. Despite this though, they still demonstrate concern and interest in their daughters' education. Although these parents rarely gave practical help, for example, with homework, their interest was expressed through things such as attending target-setting days and showing interest in school examination attainment. These parents could therefore be considered as providing their daughters with an emotional investment through the support and interest they offer. The following example of Fatima provides a good illustration of one type of emotional support that some of the mid-aspiring students receive.

Example One – Fatima

Fatima was banded for most of her subjects into set four and was predicted four borderline C grades for her GCSEs. Fatima though was not optimistic. However, when she came to see me after receiving her mock exam results she was both buoyant and cheerful, having managed to achieve three Cs. Her mother, a first generation immigrant from Gambia with no formal education, was delighted with her daughter's success.

> *My mum's so proud, she's been telling everyone in the family . . . she's just so proud of me and it makes me happy . . .* [laughs] *and because I really did try my best she's gonna buy me a nice dress for my Prom now, as a reward.*
> Fatima, Focus Group, Year 11

Despite going on to achieve only two Cs of a predicted four in her GCSEs, Fatima's decision to stay on into sixth form to do A levels was attributed as solely due to the encouragement of her mother. Indeed during the course of this research Fatima's aspirations moved from low to mid and then high aspirations. This will be discussed further later in the book.

In many instances, mid-aspiring students discuss how proud they believe their parents are of them and how, as a consequence, they feel they 'owe it' to their parents to do the best they can. This implicit sense of obligation is noted particularly amongst students who are first generation migrants to the UK but is also expressed by students who live with just one parent. This may be due to the fact that these students believe that their parent(s) have made sacrifices to support them, for example, by leaving families behind through migration or because of financial hardship.

Case Study 4.3 – Sandy

Sandy arrived in the UK with her mother and older sibling when she was eight and was reunited with her father who had travelled ahead of them the previous year. Sandy remembers this period in her life vividly and often referred to the cultural 'shock' she experienced at that time. Shortly after arriving, Sandy's parents separated. The consequence of the ensuing divorce was that the family were unable to settle in one home for any real length of time and Sandy became estranged from her father.

Sandy discusses with passion the love and obligation she feels for her mother and provides insight into the sacrifices she believes her mother has made for her:

. . . she brought me here because she wants me to have a good education. In Kenya women with an education can do well. Although schooling is available for everyone it becomes harder for women to continue after a certain time. Mostly you have to get married. My mum wanted more for me and my sister; [she] wants me to succeed and I can't let her down. She works so hard to support us and she had to leave all her family behind just to bring us here and have this opportunity!

Sandy explains how her mother has always been the bread winner and that financially things are difficult:

My mum works six days a week to support the family. She is a cleaner. She leaves home at seven and doesn't get back until eight in the evening and she gets so tired. That's why I try my best to work hard, because I feel guilty . . . When I have finished my education I want to return to Kenya and get a job, I can look after my mum then and she won't have to worry anymore.

Sandy's educational aspirations can be understood explicitly in terms of her sense of obligation but they can also be inferred as resulting from her understanding of her own biography as her experiences and that of her mother compel her to achieve the best that she can educationally. Such strong familial bonds could possibly be understood as the result of having no extended family in the UK, Sandy however, attributes it as the result of their shared history. Shared history and perceptions of parental sacrifice promote strong feelings of belonging and unity which, as a family, they consciously reinforce:

> *We are Seventh Day Adventists but since we moved we don't live close to a church anymore. We don't have money for a car and 'cause we can't go we spend Saturdays in worship at home. We pray and sing and my mum's, well she's like the minister and we're her congregation. We have a day of service at home because it's very important to us and it makes us feel close.*

Siblings

In addition to support from parents, encouragement of siblings is can also be just as important in terms of choices.

Shazia describes herself as very shy and stated that she found it difficult to talk to teachers to ask for help and translating constantly for her parents was difficult when she came to consider her options. In the end it was her elder brother, who has attended university, who offered her the advice and guidance that she felt she needed:

> *My parents were educated but here their education means nothing. Without him* [brother] *I would not have stayed on. I would've just stayed home and then maybe got married. My parents didn't continue in education but my brother got a degree. He's always encouraged me and always helped me out and when it came to sixth form I keep thinking 'I'm gonna fail so I'm not going to carry on' and I kept thinking 'no, I'm not gonna do this' but he was always encouraging me saying I had to try harder, think positive and you will pass and get the grades and that's exactly what happened . . . he's a good role model. I tried harder because of him even though he is finding it really hard to get a job. My parents did think about it a little but my brother was more encouraging 'cause he had experience.*

Shazia was repeating Year 12 after failing all her A2 exams. Prior to sitting these exams for a second time, in Year 13, she left school. She remains in sporadic contact with me but would not elaborate further than 'family difficulties' and 'ill health' as to why she dropped put.

Friendships

Granovetter (1973) suggests that the strength of a relationship between two individuals can be determined by '[a] combination of the amount of time, the emotional intensity, the intimacy (mutual confiding), and the reciprocal services that characterise the tie' (1973: 1361). Whilst no systematic analysis of the strength of friendships was undertaken in this study, based on this definition it is implicitly clear that the friendships (or the relationships between two individuals) of mid-aspiring students appear to be very strong and indeed are very important.

Friendships amongst the middle aspirers matter and seeing friends, as with the low aspirers, was cited as one of the best things about coming to school:

CF: *What do you like best about school?*

Katy: *It's fun!*

CF: *Do you mean the lessons?*

Naomi: *You get to see all your friends.*

Katy: *It's sociable.*

Karen: *It's got a good side and a bad side. The good side is that you get to see your friends and learn new things and the bad side is the teachers.*

All: *Yeah!* [laugh]

Melanie: *It's good 'cause you're gonna see everyone, all our friends.*

[All voice their agreement.]

Focus Group, Year 10

Students enjoy coming into school to see their friends and the view that school is primarily a social setting was expressed by many. Relationships amongst students in school continue, for the large part, outside of school and disputes among friends can be a huge source of anxiety and distress. As with the low aspirers, most of the friendships of the middle aspirers do tend to be amongst girls who are in the same academic stream or tutor group or, are friendships with those who live close to their own home (see Hargreaves, 1967: Ball, 1981). There are some students, however, who do have one or two friendships with students in different streams.

Most of the mid-aspiring students discussed the importance of friends and often made further educational subject choices that could be considered as mirroring the choices of their closest friends. For example, several of the students planned to stay on into sixth form because their friends were doing so. Others, who were unsure of what to do, opted for college because their friends were going whilst a few, who wanted to go to college but did not know what to study, selected courses that their friends had chosen. What was interesting was that students planning to go on to college made no secret of the fact that they were going because their friends were. Students who had already stayed on in the sixth form appeared concerned that it should be seen by me as an autonomous decision. For example:

> *. . . my friends are all doing completely different subjects to me 'cause I'm interested in different things to them but, its like, I didn't stay 'cause of them 'cause . . . it's just the subjects were there. I did like it. I liked it when we were together but I didn't choose it 'cause they were here, its just . . . 'cause I thought this is the best place for me but then it is nice to have them, I am glad they're here yeah, it's nice that they are.*

Seema, Focus Group, Year 12

For middle aspirers (and as we have seen, the low aspirers) friends and friendships appears to be significant in understanding the educational aspirations of the mid-aspiring student. Partly this is because having 'good' friends situates students within a social network that offers support and appears to gives students confidence to make choices that they may possibly not have made without friends to lead them, for example, by going to college. The view of friends as confidants, someone who was trusted was constantly reiterated. The following comment, for example, illustrates this recurring theme and was a view that was expressed by many students:

> *. . . you can talk to your friends about stuff you can't tell your mum and, you know you can trust your friends.*

Naomi, Focus Group, Year 10

As discussed in this chapter, students talked explicitly about the importance of familiarity when deciding their post-16 options. It could also be inferred that the same is also true for friendships as a common remark from students was, for example, 'I just thought it was better to stay where I was, where I know everyone'. Making new friends, whilst welcome, did not appear a priority for mid-aspiring students who, for the large part appeared happy and comfortable with the networks that they had. However, as we will see in the Chapter Five on high-aspiring students, the opposite is true and that 'meeting new people' was a factor in selecting where to study post-16.

Brief summary

In many ways, strong family relationships can be seen as underpinning the further educational aspirations of the mid-aspiring students because students feel encouraged and supported and, in some cases, obligated to continue with some form of further education. However, whilst these relationships appear to promote aspirations for further education it could also be inferred that indirectly and however unintentionally they appear to discourage aspirations for higher education or, aspirations that could potentially remove the student from close proximity to the family. Mid-aspiring students frequently discuss strong feelings of attachment to their families and are explicit in their desire to remain close, in the physical sense, as they get older.

Whilst family relationships appear to promote confidence in students in terms of the self *within* the family, they appear to discourage confidence *without* the family. For example, when I first met Sandy she aspired to higher education and indeed had completed the UCAS application process. However, at the end of Year 13 despite doing well in her A levels and being offered a place at Brighton University, she opted to find work instead:

> *I decided it's not for me, it's too far away. There's not many of my family here in the West, they're all back home and I wouldn't wanna be too far from them. It would make a big difference to my relationships . . . I might just take a year out but for now I just want to get a job.*[10]

Sandy, Focus Group, Year 12

Mid-aspiring students could be considered as those who, like the low aspirers, look to others (the collective) for their sense of self. In contrast to the low aspirers however, middle aspirers appear reliant on family and friends to feel secure, valued and confident. Middle aspirers expressed high levels of trust in their family and friends as well as a great deal of emotional attachment. This implicitly suggests that higher educational aspirations are restricted in these students, despite being academically able, because potentially it would mean 'going it alone'.

Anomalies – The Undecided

A significant proportion of those students opting for further education are those who simply do not know what else to do. These students, unsure of what work they want to undertake, are the students who remain in the sixth form for want of something better to do. What marks these students out as different to the mid-aspiring students is that they lack the commitment or enthusiasm for further study and, consequently, are frequently absent, switch subjects, drop out or do not attend classes and do not complete assignments. It is these students who are the most likely to leave during or, at the end of Year 12. In many respect, these students could be considered as simply biding their time until they decide what they want to do with the rest of their lives. Ruby, for example, was one such student. Ruby had originally made the decision to leave at the end of Year 11 but when it came to it decided that she 'couldn't be bothered to start working yet'. She opted instead to return to school and study for A/S levels. However, by her own admission, Ruby did not want to be at school and despite switching and then later dropping some of her options, Ruby confessed that she had pretty much given up on going to classes. Ruby had a long term boyfriend and was engaged to be married and what she really wanted to do, she said, was to quit school and plan her wedding. When her friend left to have a baby at the beginning of the school Easter holidays, Ruby made the decision that she was going to quit too.

Other students could be considered as staying on at school simply because they feel they should despite preferring to leave. Lisa is one such student who decided to remain on at school because most of her friends had opted to. However, Lisa was never sure that she had made the right decision and, consistently struggling to keep with subjects that she found hard to understand, she opted to leave school during Year 12 and work full-time in the pharmacy where she already had a Saturday job. This, she felt, was a better option as the training that she would be given (she was promised a place on a pharmacy assistant course) would be more relevant and useful to her than the A/S subjects she was finding so difficult. Staying on, although only for a short while, had given Lisa the opportunity to feel confident that she had made the right decision for herself. What is interesting is that the decisions of both Ruby and Lisa were autonomous choices made without parental direction or advice. Both students were advised by their mothers that they were free to do that which they wanted to.

Pakistani Students

Whilst I am interested in issues of race and ethnicity, no analysis was undertaken which explored these variables as separate discrete entities. This was because my interest lay more in interpreting a student's own sense of identity, rather than pre-supposing one. Whilst it is undoubtedly true that racial and ethnic categories are a fundamental aspect of self-identification and do, as suggested here, impact on social relationships within school, what I wanted to do was to understand possible interaction more inductively. It soon became apparent that it was primarily the Pakistani students who appeared to face particular issues in terms of their education. Whilst of course, I do not claim that these are necessarily exclusive and specific to this community of students, the issues faced did appear to have a significant bearing on the educational experience and further educational choices of the students included in my study. For this reason I have chosen to discuss Pakistani students separately.

Nearly all the Pakistani students I met were either already in the sixth form or moved on into it after completing their GCSEs. For the large part, the decision to remain in their current school rather than going elsewhere, for example, to college, was explained as the result of parental preference[11] for single sex schooling.[12] Many of the Pakistani students in my study who had opted to stay on did so because they aspired to achieve additional qualifications. For the high- and mid-aspiring student, the experience of school was described positively and most stated that they generally had good relationships with most of the staff. However, this was not the case for all of the students I came to know nor was it true for many of their friends who were not included in the research. For some students, school was perceived negatively with some students believing that they were treated differently by staff in the school. For example, Momena was one who believed that teachers singled out the Asian students for differential treatment.

> . . . *staff here are racist. They single Asian girls out for reprimands but ignore the white girls even when they do the same and it makes me so angry!*
>
> Momena, Focus Group, Year 11

Noticeable around school was also clear distinction among apparent friendship groups, that is, groups of Asian students clustered together and the other, more mixed groups. The following view expressed by Sophia (White) was a view I heard a number of times:

> . . . *there is a very high number of Asian students in school and this creates divisions. They stay in their groups and they don't want to mix, they're not interested in getting to know us and we end up feeling the same, it creates a divide between us.*

Some teachers also stated, informally, ideas associated with racial stereotypes, for example, concerning differences between black-African and other students:

Teacher A: *African girls have a better work ethic.*
Teacher B: *Yes, it's because they are brought up stricter and are told to work hard.*
Teacher A: *It's so obvious when I mark their work.*

Alongside this view is the opinion that the decision to remain in education for some of the Pakistani girls was not so much about gaining additional qualifications but was more to do with delaying marriage:

Many Asian girls will deliberately fail the exams so that they can repeat the year. They need to know that they can have the things that they want, but there is no one in their culture to push them. If they get a good education then they can marry well but, it's not about careers . . . Asian girls stay on at school to prolong the time until they must get married. They stay on but they don't work. This skews the statistics for exam results . . . and lowers the statistics for achievement of the school.

Teacher

When I tentatively asked a couple of the Asian students[13] who I had come to know quite well about this issue, they agreed it was true, particularly for many of their friends:

. . . some Asian families will allow you to do A levels but nothing more after that. They don't see the point of more than that when there is marriage to think of! But in our faith education is highly thought of . . . [If I hadn't] *stayed on . . . I would've stayed home and then maybe got married . . .* [but] *education is so important. People can take your money and your things but once you are educated they can never take that from you. You have it forever. The more education you have the more you can get on in life. Loads of ladies have no education. They get into the wrong groups, do drugs and that and have no future. But education can really help you; I mean there's even EMA.14 EMA helps you get on, I mean money to help you get on!!!!*

Shazia, Focus Group, Year 12

Raheela: . . . *it will be my brothers next* [wedding]. *In one way I can't wait, you get new clothes and everything, it's great . . . so, I am kinda excited about when it happens but, I am not excited as well . . .*

CF: *Why not?*

Raheela: *Well . . . yeah its 'cause, once he gets married there's only me left and so the attention will turn to me, the focus will be for me to get married yeah, and like, I don't wanna get married, not ever.*

CF: *What happens if you say to your parents 'hey mum and dad I really don't want to get married, I want to stay home with you,' can you?*

[laughter]

Raheela and Momena: *Absolutely NO WAY!!*

Raheela: *It's just not an option, there's no way!*
Momena: *It just wouldn't happen!*

> *I wanted to stay on because I wanted the education because its hard being a girl yeah so, its like, in our family the girls that wanna go on, they do and the girls that don't, they just get married off and then they go or, after a while they do but . . . my mum was like 'I want you to study' and I wanna study myself. So, I don't just wanna get married or stay at home . . . I wanna do something with my life so, I stayed here.*

Seema, Focus Group, Year 12

Marriage is a fundamental aspect of both the Pakistani student's culture and her Islamic faith however, as many of the Pakistani students note, education and further education are highly prized too. Just as Basit (1996) points out, contrary to some stereotypes, this is something that many parents actively encourage their daughters to pursue. Interestingly, just as in the study by Tyrer and Ahmad (2006), for the Pakistani girls in this study, it is the fathers who are most frequently cited as the main source of encouragement and support to students' ambitions and aspirations. Whether this is because it is fathers, rather than mothers, who are more likely to be engaged in the work place and therefore recognize more readily the link between education and social mobility I do not know. In addition, whether the background of origin of the parents, that is, rural versus urban (where rural backgrounds could be considered as being more traditional and urban more liberal), has a bearing I can also only speculate upon.[15] Either way, support of fathers is very important to the girls and is important for their ambitions for themselves.

Many of the girls I met aspired to higher education and had specific career plans and goals. That education and further education is important to these students is clear. However, valuing education is not without its problems and, as Wafa explains, it can promote some conflict and issues for some students.

> *. . . my dad thinks I should concentrate on my education but my mum gets frustrated, she thinks that I should concentrate on the things that she wants to teach me instead, you know, the things that will be important when I am a wife and a mother, like how to cook and clean and that.*

Trying to get the balance right between home and school, that is, keeping up with school work and assignments (and Wafa was a very conscientious student) also posed difficulties. From a practical point of view this meant that Wafa felt overloaded at times whilst, on a deeper level, it brought a conflict between herself and her parents that troubled her.

> *. . . every evening I have 1 hour of study of the Koran, followed by one hour of Urdu. By the time I have done my housework we don't generally sit down to eat until 9.00 p.m. After that I am too tired to do schoolwork . . . and there are differences between us. I mean my parent's interpretation of Islam is different to mine. They were taught their understanding by their parents but I live in a different culture. It's the same for my friends. They say 'the Koran says this' but I see that it says something different. It's frustrating because we live in different times.*
>
> Wafa, Focus Group, Year 11

Others students discuss different difficulties that can provoke conflict. This conflict primarily appears to reflect a struggle for self-identity and some autonomy.

Case Study 4.4 – Amina

Amina's father is Pakistani but left her and her English mother when she was a small baby. She now has a Pakistani step-father who often leaves the family and then returns, as well as older brothers she has never met. Amina is a practising Muslim and wears the *Hijab* but does not like many of the rules imposed on her. For example, she discusses how girls are not allowed to go out on their own and once they hit puberty they are not allowed to talk to boys. She defies this rule and has had many Muslim boyfriends. Her mother gets very angry with her and they fight frequently. Alongside this, Amina is aware that she would have problems if her step-brothers ever found out who she was:

> *. . . if they knew me and they saw me out talking to a boy, even it was a family friend, they would stop their taxi and they would beat him there and then and then take me home for my mother to do the same. I don't think it fair; we should have equality but fathers they don't want their Muslim daughters to work. Nor do the mothers but, even if they did want you to, they would have no say over it. Most mothers, all they want you to do is cook and clean. All my friends, none of them go out, they are terrified of what would happen if they did but not me. One of my boyfriends told me that there's only one thing*

---

in life to be afraid of and that's Allah and it's true . . . I am very close to my mum and she wants me to be happy but we often fight, have proper physical fights. My mum tells me that it's normal because I'm a teenager but I get so frustrated and I have a very bad temper. I get in a lot of trouble, [even] teachers . . . try to humiliate me and then I just get mad.

Amina's conflict both with her mother and her teachers at school appears to arise out of a need for some autonomy in her life as well as a desire for her own identity rather than one she feels is imposed.

Whilst the example of Amina is an extreme one, similar issues around autonomy and self-expression can be seen, although to a lesser degree:

. . . It's like my head scarf. My mum kept saying that she wanted me to wear it but my dad said I would do so when I was ready. He knew I would rebel if I was pushed. It's the same with praying. My mum thinks I am ready but I'm not yet. You know inside when you are. I do wear my headscarf now because now I am ready, it's part of who I am and is important to my identity but, it's not for everyone and that's fine. It's like me and Nasrat. She's my best friend but she doesn't wear one 'cause she doesn't want to. People say 'you're both Muslim but you wear a scarf and Nasrat doesn't, why doesn't she?' and I say she doesn't want to and that's the way it is, it's not a problem, it's just not part of who she is. I am lucky. Some girls don't get to make that choice for themselves; their parents will just make them wear it, it really does depend on the parents.

Wafa, Focus Group, Year 11

When you have no power at home, then school becomes the only place you can have some. If you are bullied at home then you go out and bully. If you are controlled then you want to control.

Shagufta, Focus Group, Year 12

The role of family expectations in understanding the Pakistani student's sense of self and consequently her aspirations for herself does appear significant. Raheela, for example, was one student who really appeared to struggle against what she considered was a lack of trust on the part of her mother 'I'm not even allowed to the shops on my own.' Possibly as a result, Raheela was constantly getting into trouble at school and was frequently slipping out of lessons to wander the school. Raheela desperately wanted to get part-time Saturday work but was prohibited by her family. However, when I last saw her (and quite by accident) much to my surprise she was working in Argos. Not only this, but she happily informed me that she had also been allowed to go to college. Her family, she informed me, had a change of heart and she was now enjoying studying more than she had ever done previously.

That some students appear to experience a clash between family's cultural expectations and their own desire to achieve some autonomy over their destinies is evident. However, this is not to say that this is true for all students nor is it true that Pakistani students, in their quest to find an identity, reject their cultural history. As Shain (2003) notes, whilst social structures and practices have an impact on Asian students experiences, they do not necessarily determine those experiences, that is, there is space for 'the active negotiation of identities' (2003: 42). As the example of Raheela shows, the identities of Pakistani students are not fixed but remain fluid and for some students, cultural heritage is extremely important and underpins their aspirations for themselves and their families.

When I have finished my education I will go back to Pakistan and open my own business designing my own clothes for Asian women. I don't think any one's done that in Pakistan yet so there's a gap and I could get rich!

Wafa

What is particularly intriguing about this ambition is that Wafa's family try to discourage her. They believe that she would not be happy living in Pakistan and Wafa admits that she has not enjoyed her visits to Pakistan to date. Despite this however, being Pakistani is very important to Wafa and is a fundamental part of how she sees herself and how she defines her future. For other students, the struggle is not so much about being opposed to the cultural background of their families, as about accommodating it within a western context.

Research by Dale et al. (2002) found that *izzat* (family honour) created issues for higher education for Pakistani and Bangladeshi girls. For the most traditional of families, going to university would be extremely difficult because of the potential harm to family honour. Ideas surrounding *izzat* were mentioned on many occasions and it is likely that without the availability of single sex schooling, as in this case, it might well have been an issue for some of the students pursuing further education within the school.

So far I have painted a rather gloomy picture that talks of conflict and of personal struggle for identity. But, this is not true for many students. What I have presented is simply some of the issues facing 'some' of the students.

Clearly many Pakistani students do have aspirations for further education and a good career and many students actively strategize to enhance future applications that they may make, for example, for work. Both Wafa and Nasrat are good examples of this: both are House Captains and recognize that this will enhance applications both to university and for employment. Indeed, both stated it was the primary reason for taking on the roles. Nasrat, in particular, is very ambitious and desperate to secure the position of Head Girl whilst in Year 12, tried to ensure she got it by enlisting my help in writing her letter of application.[16] Whilst I helped her as much as I reasonably could, Nasrat was clear that if I wrote it, she would get it:

> . . . *If you help me I am bound to get it. The letter has to be really good and well, you're doing a PhD, so you could write me a really good one!*
>
> Nasrat, Focus Group, Year 12

Whilst Nasrat was unsuccessful in this particular quest, she has achieved many other successes. For example, I frequently spot her photograph on the 'board of achievement' in the main school corridor,[17] a place which recognizes students for their successes. Nasrat is given acknowledgment for both her efforts and her successes in her A/S and then later A2 subjects. Given that she was, by her own admission, a 'difficult student' in Year 11, this is a great triumph for her and one that she and her family are rightly proud of.

Nasrat does not appear to experience the issues that some of the other students face. Being the only daughter amid several brothers, she does not wear a *Hijab*, wears more make-up than other Pakistani girls and says that her family's name for her is 'princess'. Nasrat is confident and well liked and is achieving really well in the sixth form. She fully intends to go on to university and I, like the teaching staff I have spoken to informally, would be very surprised if she does not. Whilst Nasrat clearly has high aspirations and would not, therefore, have been introduced until Chapter Five, I felt it was important to mention her here. This is because she offers a balance to the other narratives I have presented and illustrates the diversity that surrounds attitudes to education, even amongst those students who share similar ethnic and religious backgrounds.

To conclude, for the Pakistani students included, attitudes to education and associated aspirations appear to be significantly shaped by the degree of autonomy that the family will permit. Where there is little autonomy, just as with the other students, further education appears to offer a temporary reprieve from making decisions, for example, what work to do or postponing marriage. In contrast, a student permitted some independence with regard to important decisions in her life, for example, as with Wafa deciding when to she was ready to wear the *Hijab*, appears to encourage higher aspirations. This is because, as we will see in Chapter Five, autonomy appears to signify 'trust' within families which appears to be directly related to self-confidence. Pakistani girls have the same issues, concerns and worries as any other student and are, as Shain (2000) notes, active in the creation of their own identities. Whilst these identities draw on the culture of their parents traditions, they draw too on the 'local and regional cultures that they currently inhabit' (Shain, 2000: 171). For the Pakistani students, there are multiple factors that impact on and help shape her sense of self-identity as well as her career and educational aspirations. To understand her experiences and the impact of them simply in terms of broad 'cultural' rhetoric is to deny the variability amongst students and the important impact that the role of differences amongst individual families has to play. The recurring issues of trust and attachment suggest that these matter.

Gender

Just as with the low-aspiring students gender also appears significant in understanding the mid-aspiring students, particularly when considering ideas around future identities. For the large part, middle aspirers predominantly aim for future careers that could be considered as gendered, for example, child care and secretarial work, whilst partnerships and families feature significantly in their plans for their future life course. Du Bois-Reymond (1998) discusses how adolescents aim for clearly defined professions and steady employment and that girls in particular, intend to enter fixed relationships earlier so as to start their own families. Middle aspirers could be considered as following the gender-specific 'normal biographies' of the type Du Bois-Reymond found (1998). This is because, in addition to following typical gendered career trajectories and opting for conventional GCSE options, for example, textiles, food technology and the like, gendered stereotypes also appear to feature significantly in how students believe their future role as a parent will have to be negotiated. This idea can clearly be seen when students discuss the need to be able to juggle between career and family rather than sharing the responsibility, as the following extract illustrates.

> . . . *it* [will be] *hard because you have to work at a job and at home so obviously it's extra work because you gotta try and balance it out and think, 'I gotta go to work*

and then I gotta go home to my children.' You've got to sort your plan out first . . . if you wanna do it.

Seema, Focus Group, Year 12

I mean if it gets too hard you could just leave work for a few years and go back again but that would be hard but, I guess, it would depend on the situation and the support you get. If your partner doesn't support you and your parents can't help it's gonna be hard for you but you can still do it.

Rose, Focus Group, Year 12

Whilst gender was only ever referred to explicitly when I raised the question, what is implicit in my data is the idea that gender remains an important construct within a students understanding of the future world of work, whether this is directly acknowledged by the student or simply inferred. As O'Connor states 'gender is a repressed but crucially important framework in the construction of self' (2006: 107) and this does appear to be true for the middle aspirers.

I think men without qualifications can do more jobs than women because they are stronger, they can do manual work and women can't. I do think it's more equal than in the past though . . . but women do need qualifications because it's easier for men.

Bryony, Focus Group, Year 12

For women there are restrictions but they will always be there, that won't ever change. You're not stopped from doing anything but there's a . . . oh what's the word? . . . people expect you to do one thing and don't expect you to do another or there's certain things that less women are expected in – you know, one profession and another but I don't think that would stop me from doing it but it might make other people more wary.

Caroline, Focus Group, Year 12

Rene: *Men are still seen as the dominant. Although I haven't had any personal experience to say 'oh yeah this happens' but, I know it still happens, in work places, university. Some people will say 'you are only a lady, you can't achieve much, what you gonna do? You're just gonna have a family' and things like that.*

Sarah: *I agree to an extent. I've got a part time job and it's not serious, serious but the men still dominant there. They are expected to do the manual labour, like lift the heavy boxes . . . in a way I guess that's not really fair to them.*

Focus Group, Year 12

In addition to a gendered understanding of the world of work and of parenthood, gender is also apparent in student's appearance, for example, in the wearing of jewellery, make-up and hair styles. Whilst there are limitations imposed on students as to what they can and cannot wear due to uniform regulations, some students do appear to get as close to the boundaries as possible, for example, by wearing shorter skirts, leaving their shirts un-tucked and dying their hair and so forth. Of course, it is as easy to interpret this as a demonstration of students striving for individuality with in a context of similarity, as a display of femininity. However, as conversations concerning boys, boyfriends and relationships feature so frequently, it is suggestive that being seen as feminine and attractive is an important facet of middle aspirers' identities as women.

These ideas become more pronounced once students move into the sixth form where, as a reflection of their new status, students are permitted to dress as they please. Whilst in the sixth form I witnessed lots of incidents of personal grooming, for example, the re-application of make-up and adjustment of hair. What was interesting, however, was that there were also some occasions when students were observed grooming each other, for example, playing with the hair or plucking the eyebrows of another. In addition, new hairstyles could also promote a great deal of excitement and discussion amongst friendship groups. Whilst these activities can be observed as tying in with the visual stereotypes that surround concepts of femininity, they also appear to be highly social and, in some respects, appear to reinforce and re-confirm friendship ties. In what could essentially be considered as an intimate act due to the close proximity required between persons, the somewhat ritualistic preoccupation with physical appearance appears to reinforce both the emotional attachment to close friends that have been discussed as important to a student's sense of self and also illustrating student's identity as women. This is because concern with appearance, make-up and the like appear to reflect cultural standardizations of femininity. As Connell (1987) notes, sexualizing oneself in the manner mass media like women's magazines dictate, serves as a very visual marker of gender because it emphasizes femininity and this certainly appeared to be true for some (though not all) of the mid-aspiring students.

Chapter Summary

The middle aspirers are distinct from the low aspirers in that further education in some form is both valued and deemed necessary. Thus further educational choices and aspirations for this group of students can be understood as an essential strategy that maximizes the probability of finding employment that is both long term and secure, whilst minimizing the risk surrounding competition, to a certain degree.

Whilst future employment security is very important to this group of students, in some respects it also appears to reflect a greater concern with security more broadly which is illustrated through the apparent comfort and reassurance that is given to students by what is known and trusted. The further educational aspirations and choices of the middle aspirers can be understood as appearing to reflect the degree of attachment applied to that which is familiar. In this case, attachment to family, friends and locality appears to be important. In addition, 'trust' also appears significant. For example, middle aspirers will readily accept the educational evaluations, that is, grades and academic setting made of them and unquestionably trust the judgement of others, for example, friends (and their choice of course/career), teachers and so on.

For the middle aspirers, self-confidence and autonomy in choice making processes appears to be intrinsically linked to interactions with, attachment to, and trust in 'others'. What accounts for this and why do they differ so distinctly from the low aspirers? In many respects, the middle aspirers fit well with theoretical explanations that would account for their choices in class based reproductive terms. However, it is also relevant to consider their aspirations and choices in relationship to the individual context in which they are located and also to understand how their subjective experiences and understandings of the self within this context have shaped their ambitions and aspirations for themselves. As I have illustrated, the social context is experienced differently dependant on the individual and it is this that accounts for why variations in aspirations and ambitions can be observed *within* and *between* families that appear to have many common social characteristics. I conclude, therefore, that whilst class theory may account for the aspirations of the middle aspirers, it cannot explain why middle aspirers appear to display much greater levels of attachment and trust than those with low aspirers.

Notes

[1] A (Advanced) level study is the typical examination route taken for entry into University. An Advanced level qualification is comprised of study at two levels: A/S and A2. Study at A/S level (Advanced Subsidiary) requires students to take

three components of a particular subject. Whilst the A/S level can be taken as a standalone qualification it is more usually followed by the A/2 examination (a deeper exploration of the same subject). The grade range is A–E, with grades A–C being the target grades required by Universities and employers.

[2] Although some students cynically remarked that this may have been because the school was trying to expand its relatively small sixth form.

[3] Interestingly students attributed the schools failure in the OfSTED inspection as being the result of bad teaching staff and did not feel that the pupils that attended were responsible.

[4] Charlotte did leave the sixth form at the end of A/S examinations, transferring to the local college (with another friend) to do her A2 exams.

[5] I should make clear that this was within a climate of general despondency within school following the OfSTED inspection. I am not sure whether students would have been as negative had the school not been placed on Special Measures.

[6] Attendance and truancy figures are important to the school and are included in OfSTED inspections. It is implicit that this scheme is for the benefit of both school and student, as students attending college doing something they enjoy significantly improves the schools attendance figures.

[7] I am not sure what criteria staff use for selection and placement on this scheme.

[8] Abby was the only student that I was aware of that had this work placement training as opposed to being in college. Despite the fact that this was a work and not a college placement, I believe the principles are the same.

[9] *Institution* – 'an established order comprising rule bound and standardised behaviour patterns . . . numbers of people whose behaviour is guided by norms and values' (Jary and Jary, 2000: 307).

[10] I have remained in touch with Sandy and, to date, she has not changed her mind. Indeed, when we last spoke she told me that she had taken up a full-time post in a pharmacy and was considering taking up her employer's offer of training.

[11] Students referred to the decision to remain at their current school as their parents' choice. This is not to say that this was not an acceptable decision for students.

[12] However, two students did go elsewhere: one to college and one to a mixed sixth form in another school.

[13] A discussion around the role of researcher is found in Appendix 2 – Research Methodology.

[14] EMA – Educational Maintenance Allowance.

[15] I am very grateful to a discussion with Reetinder Boparai for the ideas expressed here.

[16] Issues such as this are addressed in Appendix 2 – Research Methodology.

[17] Although when I discussed this with her she expressed her displeasure at the photograph of her used and was having another done.

Chapter 5

The High Aspirers

For what is the best choice for each individual is the highest it is possible for him to achieve.

Aristotle [384 BC–322 BC]

Characteristics

Students categorized as high aspirers are those who intend to pursue a higher education at university. High aspiring students are mostly positive about school and value education highly because of an explicit belief that a clear correlation exists between future security (like the middle aspirers), choice and the potential for independence. They are distinct from the middle aspirers in that although both groups of students intend a further education, high aspirers, whilst choosing to study further still, have no clear intended future career path to drive their choices and ambitions. For example, some students intend to attend university and study for an English or media degree but are not sure what job they would like at the end of it. Others hope to study law but have no specific aspect of law that they would like to work in. Whilst this is unremarkable in that many undergraduates are not sure what job await them after graduation, what distinguishes the high aspirers from the middle aspirers is that middle aspirers do appear to have a more clearly defined career path when making further educational choices, for example, to work in a nursery or as a hairdresser. They will attend university is the only certainty for the high aspirers.

Just as with the middle aspirers, these students value education and view higher education as both desirable and necessary because it is crucial for securing future employment.

Susana: . . . *to get the better jobs you need to have a high education.*

Sarah: . . . *Well, going to university means you will get a better job at the end of it, you get a career.*

Focus Group, Year 12

Choices regarding further education are viewed by some students as important, strategic decisions. For example, some students believe that choosing to study in a different place to their current one would be regarded favourably by admission officers at higher educational institutions. On this basis, high aspirers are further divided into those high aspirers who continue their further education in the sixth form of their current school and those who opt, on the basis of rationalized advantage, to study elsewhere. Interestingly, the decision of these students to pursue higher education, whilst a clear and assured one, is vague in its origins.

CF: *Why did you decide to come back to school and not leave and get a job after your GCSEs?*

Susana: *At the end of this I wanna go to university and get a better job.*

CF: *When you were doing your GCSEs did you actually have to sit down and think shall I leave or shall I stay? Shall I go to university or not?*

Susana: *No, I knew. I just knew . . .*

Jane: *I didn't know if I wanted to go to this school or college or to another school or something . . .*

Susana: *We didn't know where, we just knew we were gonna do A levels and then go to university.*

CF: *So, it was something that you talked about with your family?*

Jane: *No, it was just expected.*

Susana: *Yes . . . it's like an expectation.*

Jane: *Nobody really said anything to me . . .*

Jane: *It just came to me . . .*

Susana: *It's still your own decision though . . .*

All: *Yeah.*

Susana: *. . . like, even though my mum hasn't been to university I know that, like, she expects me to go.*

CF: *Were you encouraged by your teachers to stay on?*

Susana: *I think the teachers would have been like WHAT! if we didn't!*

All: *[Laugh] Yeah!*

CF: *What about career wise? Do any of you know yet what you might like to do?*

Susana: *I know I'm gonna go to uni but, no, I have no idea career wise.*

Focus Group, Year 12

. . . the kind of job I'm looking for, I wanna be like a professional, I don't wanna . . . I wanna have a qualification and go to university and get a degree and get that

extra bit to give me a better job and be able to live comfortably. I don't wanna . . .
and that's basically why . . . 'cause I just thought yes you can do the vocational
way, do the training and go and get the degree that way but, that's longer and
I think I'm more educational . . . to be honest I don't know why I wanna go, I
just know that I do.

Lotte, Focus Group, Year 12

CF: *How important were teachers to you, in your decision making?*
Carolyn: *I don't think it was that much affected by the teachers really . . . I made*
the decision to stay on by myself . . .
I: *They helped me. I think I talked to every single science teacher that there was . . .*
'cause I just didn't know what science to do . . . I just knew I wanted to do science . . .
I didn't have a clue so I talked to the teachers.

Focus Group, Year 12

Whilst many people are attributed as contributing to the student's decision making process, as we will see, students ultimately view it as an autonomous one, that is, one they can choose to reject. What is clear from the data,
however, is that whilst for some, higher education is viewed as the somewhat
natural progression of the intellectually-able, for others it is a determined
strategy that they see as linking strongly with self-improvement, social promotion and future independence.

School Work and Academic Setting

Some high-aspiring students are drawn from set one and whilst students
with higher educational aspirations were also found in others sets. Some
students expressing higher educational aspirations also tended to be the
students who most frequently changed their mind; dropped out when the
time came (despite completing UCAS applications and receiving offers
from universities) or were students who could be considered as having
misaligned ambitions, that is, ambitions without attainment. For ease of
writing, I will focus primarily on high-aspiring students whose ambitions
remained focused and unwavering. Anomalies will be discussed later.

As in the study by Hallam and Ireson (2006), students drawn from set
one expressed a strong preference for setting. In addition, these students
presented as the most confident and self-assured in their academic abilities and placement and this was evident in attitudes towards teaching
staff and their evaluations of students. For example, if grades are awarded
that reflect the student's expectation then the teacher is fair. If marks are

perceived as unfair then, in some cases, it is the teacher who is wrong and is disregarded. This is seen most clearly in predictions made regarding possible GCSE grades. For example, if a student is assessed as likely to achieve C at GCSE this will not diminish her aspirations to aim to achieve higher, for an A. The following quote illustrates the views of high aspirers on teaching staff.

> . . . *If a teacher starts on your case then that gets you down but, I don't tend to let teachers get me down 'cause there's no point. They're there to teach you, they're not there to get you down and if they are having a go at you then they've not really got any right to so, I just brush it off to be honest to be with you. If it's out of order then I don't listen.*

Emily, Focus Group, Year 11

In contrast to the middle aspirers, high aspirers appear to look to teacher's educational evaluations of them as reinforcing, rather than shaping, their academic identity. However, this is not to say that a student's character is inferred as solely self-determined. Indeed, students explicitly acknowledge that teachers are able to challenge their identity institutionally through the fluidity of academic setting. By far the greatest concern, expressed by a few, was that they could keep up enough to remain where they were and this appeared to be reflected in the attitudes applied to school work.

> Emily: *When I started Year 10 I got behind on a piece of course work and then it built up and then I sat myself down and said 'no! I'm gonna sort this out, I'm gonna sort this out now,' so, I sort of said 'if I do this, this and this tonight, this tomorrow' so I worked about three quarters of hour a day and caught back up. I was so scared of moving down . . . they try and warn you, they let you know it's not gonna be a breeze in Year 10 and what ever but, it never actually prepares you for the immense stress of it all. My first bit of course work for Year 10 was English, it was on Jane Austen and I spent 18 hours on it!! 18 hours!! I actually had to take a day off school to do it . . .*
>
> CF: *Do you do that a lot? Take time off for school work?*
>
> Emily: *Yes, when I have too. My mum lets me; it's the only way you can keep up.*
>
> CF: *And did you get a good grade for it?*
>
> Emily: *I got an A for my first draft which I was quite pleased but, 18 hours!! And that was the first piece of course work and at the end of it I was just like, I just couldn't believe it . . .*

An underlying theme suggested in students' comments was the implicit need to justify or validate their place in set one. The school operated a number of reward schemes for the top 15 of the set, for example, a day trip out to a local grammar school, and, as a consequence, the desire not to be the only one amongst friendship groups not to go created anxiety and competitive undertones. Whilst students included appeared to share close relationships with one another, they also appeared to engage in friendly but thinly disguised rivalry. Whilst the middle aspirers appeared to enjoy and find comfort in being 'the same' as their friends, for the high aspirers, except for being in the same set, the opposite appears to be true. Whilst being close on an emotional level was important (see section on friendships), grades appeared to be viewed as an institutional measure of individual success and competition amongst friends was subtle but clear, as in Reay and William's (1999) study of younger students. The importance of grades then, in determining a student's identity was apparent on several levels: they reinforced a student's sense of her right to a place in the academic elite; they illustrate a student's educational identity at an institutional level to staff, other students and friends and, finally, they reconfirm a student's sense of her own ability. In these terms, course work and examination preparation was taken very seriously with some students applying great amounts of time and effort to their studies. The following statement by Stephanie was one I heard, in a variety of forms, many times:

> *I stayed up until 4:30 am last night, re-doing some of my English coursework . . .*
> *well, I had actually done it but I wasn't happy with it so, I decided to re-do it.*
>   Stephanie, Focus Group, Year 11

Just as with all other students, high aspirers also complained about the heavy demands of school work. Most, however, resignedly accepted the need to be challenged. Whilst the high aspirers appeared to feel the greatest degrees of pressure in terms of examinations and course work deadlines, most appeared to adopt pro-active means of dealing with it. As seen in the comment of Emily, taking time off from school was a common response of the high-aspiring students and was one that was sanctioned by parents. Justification for taking time off was that a student could focus and apply a reasonable amount of uninterrupted time to the task in hand thus maximizing her potential to do a good piece of work and, consequently, achieve a good grade.

Students in set one believe that they are treated differently to other students, in terms of the level of expectation (this idea was also confirmed in the comments of other students allocated in different streams, see Chapter Four), with the comment of Annabel in a Year 10 focus group a common one:

> . . . *the pressure that they put on you and the course work that they give you and stuff is a lot higher than if you were in another set. There is a level of expectation in set one that isn't there for the rest of the school but I don't agree with it being there. I can pinpoint about two to three teachers who treat you differently. Like our English teacher. She treats us like we are college students. She'll talk to us like we are level to her and that's why I really enjoy her class, it's the manner in which she speaks to us, it's really good . . . and Mr H he treats us like college students also, just in a really relaxed manner that every one should do.*

This view is also expressed by the high-aspiring sixth form students who attribute this apparent deference as the result of their age and not their intellectual abilities.

Sahara: *It really changes when you get into Year 12.*
All: *Yes* [general discussion of Years 7 and 8 and how difficult it is]
Georgia: *You get more respect the older you are.*
Sahara: *It's probably easier for teachers to get on with the older people though . . .*
Lima: *We're on the same level, a mature level!*

Probably the most striking feature of the high aspirers, a feature that differentiates them from the middle and low aspirers, is their willingness to be actively involved in the life of the school. This is seen in students' keenness in volunteering to be student mentors, Millennium volunteers[1] within school, heads of school houses and head girl for sixth form students,[2] to members of the student council for the Year 10 and 11 girls. The high aspirers who opt to remain in the sixth form could be considered as conventional in that one might expect involvement of this sort. However, this is not so for the high aspirers who intend to study elsewhere. Indeed, as the following case study illustrates, several students could be considered as quite the opposite in that they were willing to adopt pro-active measures to get their voices heard if more conformist methods fail, even if it means that potentially they could get into trouble.

Case Study 5.1 – The Trouser Protest

The school uniform policy of 'Southwell' prohibited the wearing of trousers. However, several of the high-aspiring students who intended to study elsewhere believed the ruling archaic, discriminatory[3] and not in line with the practice of other schools. However, despite using the correct forum to air their views, that is, the student staff council,[4] the request for a re-think, according to students, was continually rejected. Two of the students then decided to take matters into their own hands and so organized a protest whereby they encouraged students to come, for three days, into school wearing trousers. The protest was largely unsuccessful in terms of numbers participating but, successful in that the head was now willing to see them (previous requests for an appointment had failed). The head informed the students she was willing to listen and suggested that they conduct a small survey of all tutor groups to see what the consensus of students was to the issue. The response was as expected. Students and many staff were overwhelmingly in favour of the wearing of trousers. However, the move to change the uniform rule was rejected by the head. Her justification was that she believed students had gone about making a case in the wrong way. She then prohibited the issue to be discussed at any future Student Staff Committee Meetings and any other protests would be punished. However, students refused to let the matter drop and sought out the OfSTED inspectors when they came into school, for help. They were successful. OfSTED inspectors criticized the school for disregarding a genuine issue with popular support, raised in an appropriate forum, that is, student/staff committee and urged the school to reconsider its position. The school did and, to the immense satisfaction of the students involved, pupils were at last permitted to wear trousers. However, despite being successful, the students involved stated that they would have persisted with the cause had they needed to, 'I was going to make a report and send it to the government if I had to' said one. Students also claimed a similar victory in a long standing battle for substantial improvements to school toilets.

What distinguishes the high-aspiring student from other students within school then is their willingness to participate and be involved in school at an institutional level. Whilst many students across the school participate in a variety of ways in school life such as, charity and fund raiser days, talent shows and school plays as well as sporting events, these are somewhat different in that they tend to be collective and social activities. High aspirers, in contrast to other students, participate on a level that appears to present them as active agents of the school rather than members within the school. Theoretical explanations which account for high aspirer's contribution and involvement in school would possibly attribute it to increased levels of social capital and certainly there is much utility in the concept in terms of the ideas surrounding civic engagement and social trust. In addition, a wealth of research linking social capital to educational attainment (Coleman, 1988; Croll, 2004) illustrates well why government and policy makers are so excited by the theory. Research by Gewirtz et al. (2005), for example, illustrate one of a number of government initiatives to raise educational attainment that can be understood as based on ideas associated with social capital, for example, the creation of Educational Action Zones. These were introduced to socially disadvantaged areas as a means to enhance and improve both parental and community relationships and involvement in schools.

Social capital as a concept is problematic, however, in that there are no clear conceptualization as to what it really is. For example Bourdieu (1986) states that economic capital lies at the heart of social capital. For Bourdieu, social capital is about networks and group membership but networks and associations that are marked by cultural and economic homogeneity amongst members. For Bourdieu, social capital is therefore stratified and classed and serves to reproduce and reinforce class distinctions in the same way that other capitals do. The utility of an agents' social capital is thus limited by his class.

For Coleman, however, social capital is somewhat different in that whilst family and community relationships provide social capital as for Bourdieu, the relationships are not stratified in the way he conceives them to be. Coleman (1987) conceptualizes social capital, with respect to education, as the relationships between adults and community to children; relationships 'that are of value to the child growing up' (1987: 36). The value that these relationships have relates to the promoting of norms and values and in generating social networks. Research by Coleman found that students who attended faith schools[5] achieved far greater educational success, regardless of class, than students who did not. For Coleman however, social capital is in decline because as parents spend less and less time in the home as they work, much of the responsibilities for generating social capital fall now to institutions such as schools. Evidence for this could be considered in the rising number of after-school activities such as homework clubs, careers and counselling services. Individualization, greater autonomy of young people alongside fragmenting communities is creating what Coleman refers to as a 'fundamental vacuum' (1987: 38) which has consequences for both individuals and society as a whole.

Putman (2000) also sees social capital in the USA as being in decline and agrees that this has negative consequence for society. For Putman, however, social capital is conceptualized as individual civic engagement and community involvement, as opposed to an emphasis on families, institutions or economics. For Putman, social capital is socially advantageous in that capital acquired via, for example, membership of voluntary organizations, looking after neighbours' children, or through union membership, promotes democracy and fosters relationships of trust and reciprocity and, as with Coleman, has positive consequences for educational performance.

Whilst conceptualizations of social capital differ, underlying is the premise that social capital creates trust, that is, that social capital increases with increased community engagement. Regular involvement generates greater degrees of trust between individuals and communities and this has positive benefits, in this case in terms of educational outcomes. However, what my data appears to illustrate is that whilst social capital as a theoretical tool can account well for several of the students included, it cannot account for all of them. This suggests that the direction of causality in terms of social capital and outcome is possibly incorrect. My data begins to suggest that the direction is in fact reversed so that, in the first instance, it is trust that matters. Trust is defined as the 'firm belief in the reliability, truth, ability, or strength of someone or something'.[6] Trust (and its degree), be it in terms of relationships with family, institutions such as schools or communities, facilitates willingness for civic engagement and this engagement in turn enhances social capital, that is, it facilitates its further acquisition. However, trust is what underpins this acquisition and is therefore the foundation stone on which individual people build. Conceptualizing social capital in this way makes it extremely useful for explaining why differences in educational aspirations and ambitions or community involvement differ, even when other social characteristics such as class are held constant. It is also useful in that it enables students to be understood as active agents in their own right, generating their own social capital, rather than viewed as dependents of family social capital. I hope to illustrate this point further in the rest of the chapter.

High-aspiring students express a general satisfaction with their school and with the experiences that they have had there. Positive experiences inevitably mean that some students are happy to continue on in to the sixth form but this is not so for others. Whilst moving on is tinged with sadness and nostalgia, strong ambitions and aspirations to study elsewhere drives and motivates these students to study elsewhere.

I have been really happy and although I wanna stay here and do my A levels I can't. I want to go somewhere new and meet new people. It's important to do that if you wanna go to university. I don't think it looks good if you stay in the same place. You need to try other places, meet other people and I think if you do that it will be good for when you want to go to university because it shows that you can apply yourself.

Deborah, Focus Group, Year 11

[I won't stay here] *I want to go somewhere where I will meet different types of people.*

Emily, Focus Group, Year 11

Both Deborah and Emily express explicitly their desire to study elsewhere and the advantages they and others feel this will have both in terms of experience and in meeting new people. Unlike the mid-aspiring students, remaining in the familiar was not desirable as it offered nothing new. Alternative places of study were viewed as offering greater curricula choice, providing opportunities for making new friends and useful for university applications. Rationalizing their further educational choices in this way demonstrates the planning applied to future pathways and the means that students adopt to maximize their chances of achieving their goals. In addition, these are strategies devised autonomously, without the influence of parents or teaching staff. In many ways, high-aspiring students who plan to study elsewhere could be considered as middle class in their planning. This is because planning and strategizing within education is typified as a being the forte of the middle class due to their higher levels of cultural capital (Devine, 2004). As Ball (2003) also notes '. . . the middle class have enough capitals in the right currency, to ensure a high probability of success for their children. The tactical deployment of these capitals . . . enables them to gain access to and monopolize advantageous educational sites and trajectories' (2003: 168).

The desires and motivations of some students to attend further educational establishments (that all require a certain amount of travelling to reach) could be partly explained by their view of education *per se*, that is, that educational success is a measure of individual effort:

School is fair, what you achieve is the result of your own effort.

Stephanie, Focus Group, Year 11

School is fair; teachers treat us all the same. Even if you're in set five you get extra help so you should still be able to achieve if you try . . . sure you have a label but . . .

Emily, Focus Group, Year 11

However, whilst Emily and Stephanie view educational success as fair and meritocratic this does not mean they believe inequality and/or discrimination do not exist. Indeed both believe that there is evidence of it within school.

. . . what is unfair is when a school that is achieving really well gets rewarded with money whilst schools that are struggling don't, where's the fairness in that? I mean why punish the ones that are struggling, help them and, when they do get money, spend it on what matters like good teachers. Don't spend it on painting the school . . . yeah it's nice to look at for a day but it's not the same as good teachers. And computers . . . stop buying computers. I mean, how many computers does a school need? We need good teachers and that's all we need.

Stephanie, Focus Group, Year 11

. . . I think there is some discrimination in this school, but discrimination about the way people dress, their dress sense. People get judged and labelled by clothes, they stereo type you. Some is self-imposed too like; it's difficult with the Asian girls. They tend to stick together and they don't mix with people like me and, why not? 'Cause we have absolutely nothing in common and I understand that but it's still discrimination!

Emily, Focus Group, Year 11

. . . There are some people that have things easier. For example, girls that go to 'The Queen's' [independent girls' school] have more opportunity than girls that go to a common school like I do. But, that's about it. I only think that from the things they do in school. But, if you want to work hard enough you can all have the same opportunities and I am willing to do that. I can have the same opportunities as them because I will work hard enough.

Emily, Focus Group, Year 11

Both Emily's and Stephanie's comment concerning educational success suggest a very individualized notion of achievement, and this individualized view is further empathized with the idea that prejudice exists over clothing. This comment is interesting and sits easily with modern ideas concerning the body and self-identification, that is, where 'appearance, to put it bluntly . . . becomes a central element of the reflexive project of the self' (Giddens, 1991: 100). However, their comments do also suggest a more structural interpretation of discrimination, particularly in terms of schools and their broader differences, for example, differential access to resources and in terms of homogeneity of students.

Conclusion

It is clear that high-aspiring students view further and higher education as the normative route for their future life course. For these students, education and educational success can be understood as presenting a central aspect of student's self-identity, both in terms of the perception of self, that is, a student's intellectual ability, and as linking with their future identities as credentialized workers. Significantly, high-aspiring students, in contrast to other students, appear to demonstrate high degrees of institutional trust, that is, trust in the educational system and those that work in it, demonstrated through their willingness to be active agents within school and through their faith in meritocracy. Whilst high aspirers recognize and acknowledge inequality and discrimination within school, the belief that they are, as Reay (1998) found, autonomous creators of their own future is apparent and appears to suggest a very rationalized and individualized interpretation of self. For example, even though students explicitly acknowledge that they are stratified within school through setting, they believe that this is something they can control through hard work.

Anomalies of Aspiration

One of the outcomes of government initiatives to improve aspirations through schemes such as Aim Higher is that some students are indeed encouraged to foster aspirations and ambitions for higher education they may not have had without such intervention. However, whilst this undoubtedly is a positive outcome, it does present some issues. For example, what does become apparent is that some students appear to aspire to higher education not necessarily because they want it but more because they feel a pressure that dictates that they *should* want it. As a sixth form environment appears very much geared towards progression to university some students therefore feel pressurized to go through the motions despite appearing to lack confidence in their choice. Typically they follow the A level route, complete the UCAS application process and then change their minds, deciding instead to work and re-consider the matter in a year or two. Some of the reasons given are that they are not sure if university is what they really want; decide that they do not want to move away from their families, or that they prefer instead to start earning now. These students were those who dropped out during Years 12 and 13. Therefore, whilst some students articulate a higher educational aspiration they are not classified as high aspirers as they did not follow the aspiration through (for those students in Year 13).

In addition, some staff feel that raising aspirations leads to some students fostering somewhat unrealistic ambitions, in terms of goals versus educational attainment, which they believe ultimately leads to students feeling rejected, disappointed and let down. These students are thus considered as having misaligned ambitions. For example, some students aspirations could be considered as are somewhat unrealistic in terms of their previous attainment. Of course, this presupposes assumptions on my part. However to illustrate, several Year 13 students who expressed very high educational aspirations and ambitions made applications to study law at Oxford or Cambridge University. Both the degree and the institution were selected on the basis of the perceived status associated with them. Yet all of the students who did this had little or no idea as to entry requirements in terms of UCAS points[7] required or with respect to required A level subjects.[8] In addition, most students had preformed average to below average at GCSE and were predicted C or below for A level. As might be expected for higher educational institutions that are extremely competitive in terms of places versus applicants, their applications were rejected and students were left feeling disillusioned and demoralized. These students, all first generation black-Africans or second generation Pakistani, did not believe that high ranking universities were 'unthinkable choices' (Archer and Hutchings, 2000: 563) nor believe their rejection the result of their background. However, having got to know some of these students quite well I could not help wondering whether the process was somewhat contrived and considered the possibility that, on some sub-conscious level, their applications had been set up to fail by themselves. Of course, this is just conjecture. It is equally likely that these unsuccessful applications were the result of parental aspirations for daughters to attend prestigious universities or simply be the result of a limited knowledge of British universities. The end result was, however, that students did not go on to university at the end of Year 13 because the choice had been taken out of their hands. The institutions of preference had rejected them.[9]

Aim Higher initiatives do succeed in raising aspirations. However, some staff feel that the programme can also, in some cases, set students up for failure. As one member of staff stated,

Yes, we have to raise aspirations and we are trying to do that, but if some are not academically-able then they end up disappointed when they can't make it and that's not fair.

Teacher

Thus some students, having had aspiration fostered yet not able to attain at the level required, end up disappointed when they consequently fail to secure the grades they will need for university admission. Failure occurs, in some instances, not because students are lacking in enthusiasm or commitment, but simply because they are unable to achieve the required academic grades. Some other students, having been disengaged throughout their compulsory years and underachieved at GCSE, find that they lack the necessary skills to 'catch up' and work at the advanced level of sixth form study and thus growing disillusionment leads to the aspiration dying. That the outcome might have been different had these students been caught earlier one can only speculate.

The consequence of raising aspirations then is that some students do not make it. At some point the aspiration falters. Whether down to a lack of attainment, unrealistic expectation with respect to those abilities or because they are simply 'going through the motions', what is clear is that strategies to raise aspirations have both succeeded and then failed in the same breath in some instances. These anomalies in aspirations could perhaps be understood and explained well using class as a concept, particularly those ideas associated with cultural capital (see Chapter Two).

Work Experience, Career Guidance and Occupational Choices

As already discussed, many of the high aspirers have only vague future career plans that underpin their educational choices whilst others, although not sure as to what role they will take, do have an idea of the field in which they would like to work, for example, media or law. However, the common theme, that is, of wanting to pursue a higher education, is consistently seen by all as the means to open up future occupational choices that would not have been possible otherwise. Primarily, higher education is seen as the route to occupations that offer employment that will be enjoyable as well as offering higher salaries. This is very important for high aspirers because greater earning potential equates with increased financial security and thus allows for independence and self-sufficiency, both of which are highly prized:

> CF: *Why do you want to go to university?*
> 3: *I just want to get a good job and you need to go to university to get one.*
> 2: *And choice! If you get a degree you get more choice about what job you can do.*
> 1: *Yeah, that's why I wanna go.*
>
> Focus Group, Year 10

> *I would like a good job, that's important . . . you know . . . to be able to look after myself . . . that's really important to me.*
>
> Stephanie, Focus Group, Year 10

> *I have to study . . . so I can make it.*
>
> Rhiana, Focus Group, Year 12

> 3: *I think I'd be really bored if I just left and got a job now and it would be so hard to find a job that you like, enjoyed.*
> All: *Yeah.*
> 4: There are jobs out there but, not necessarily the ones that you would want.
> 3: *. . . paying the money that you would want.*
> 2: *I just feel too young anyway, you know, to start work now.*
>
> Focus Group, Year 12

In addition to seeing high educational qualifications as offering enhanced job prospects and future security, some students also expressed the view that jobs at this level have some element of status attached to them. For some, having an occupation that says something about their identity to others was important:

> *I don't wanna do a job that no one looks up at you. I want one that people say 'you do that? That's brainy . . . you must be really clever to do that.' I did wanna be an Air hostess once and then I thought, well . . . it's just cleaning up other peoples mess . . . it ain't clever.*
>
> Nasrat, Focus Group, Year 10

Whilst the idea of social status was only ever explicit in a few comments, it was implicit in many others, particularly in relationship to the status applied to ideas associated with independence, that is, in terms of being socially desirable. Students also appear to infer a desire for social mobility. Students frequently comment on how hard their families work for less than satisfactory wages and discuss frankly how this is something they were keen to avoid. As Beck notes, 'people . . . within the same "class" can . . . choose between different lifestyles . . . and identities . . . knowing one's "class" position . . . no longer determine one's personal outlook . . . or identity' (1992: 131) and this appears true for the students here. In a study of 30 highly successful, low-income African-American public high school students, Hubbard (2005) found that mothers who struggled financially were a strong motivating factor in the aspirations of some of the female students in her study and this is also true for some of the parents of students here.

Because my dad didn't [go to university] *and he's having a hard time now, work wise, I want to make sure it doesn't happen to me.*

Emily, Focus Group, Year 10

Overwhelmingly careers advice was considered by high-aspiring students as less than helpful either because it was considered too broad to be useful or because students, having made the decision to go to university, felt there was little more that the service could offer.

When I went the careers advisor like, she used to be a journalist for New Women *magazine or something like that and she was giving me all these tips on how to get into journalism. I was really interested in it and then she got out this massive book and said 'you're gonna have to run up to people and you're gonna have to do this and this and this' and she really put me off* [laughs] *and I said to her 'OK then, I won't do that!'*

Rosy, Focus Group, Year 12

Echoing the comments of the low aspirers, career guidance was generally viewed as: 'irrelevant', 'too general', 'not specific enough' and 'boring'.

In addition to finding careers advice less than useful, work experience was also viewed as having little relevance with respect to future careers plans, primarily because the bulk of work experience placements tended to be in retail outlets which were the types of work the high aspirers were keen to avoid in their futures. On a positive note however, all the high aspirers that I spoke to stated that they had enjoyed the experience because it had been both fun and useful, first because it provided a break from the usual routine and secondly, because it gave students an opportunity to include some working experience on an application form when they began to apply for Saturday work. That work experience is generally enjoyed is similar to the findings of Hillage et al. (2001). However, their study also found that it was student respondents engaged in retail and leisure work experience placements that were most likely to find the work neither challenging nor interesting.

Conclusion

High aspirers could be considered as decidedly rational in planning their futures. Although somewhat vague, aspirations appear to clearly link to a desire for future security, choice and independence. As the employment market is considered highly competitive, higher education and the route it offers into different and desirable occupations thus becomes viewed by some as not a choice but a necessity if aspirations for social mobility are to be achieved. Hodkinson and Sparkes (1997) discuss how career decision making can be understood as the result of a series of turning points[10] in an individual's life, turning points that are pragmatic and rational and situated within an individual's culturally determined horizon. In their article Hodkinson and Sparkes address the relationship between structure and agency in individual choice and this is a useful approach for exploring differences in aspirations. However, the idea of turning points, whilst helpful, is somewhat vague in that, whilst turning points may indeed incline an individual to aspire to a particular career, it does not explain adequately why this career is more preferable to another, for example, graduate employment versus vocational. In addition, the idea that career decisions are made at different turning points within culturally defined horizons implicitly infers a structural determinism that does not allow for subjective decision making to be understood as the result of psycho-social process occurring over time.

Ball (1990) suggests that vocational training is a response to the needs of industry. However, the needs of industry appear not necessarily to relate to the aspirations of the high-aspiring students. Careers advice is found to be unsatisfactory by high-aspiring students and this viewpoint is echoed in the comments of both the low- and some mid-aspiring students also. Clearly then the careers service is in need of re-evaluation. This is because by Year 11, careers advice, whilst well-intentioned, appears to offer little of use. Research by Croll (2005) found that what Year 7 students stated they wanted to do post-16 was a good predictor of what they actually went on to do. If this is so then clearly career guidance and advice is coming too late for many students. Students appear to articulate a desire for a more nuanced approach and indeed such an approach would be beneficial. Many of the students, and particularly the high and low aspirers, go through their post-16 decision making process alone. A career service more individually tailored would therefore be extremely useful to many of these students in providing guidance and advice.

Family

High aspirers' relationships to their families and friends are very import-ant and trustworthy friends and a sense of belonging appears as equally important constructs within a student's self-identification. In addition, the relationships of high aspirers to their parents are also extremely relevant in understanding their educational aspirations because parents, whilst pro-viding emotional support and encouragement, also promote autonomy.

The parents of high aspirers are employed in predominantly skilled and semi-skilled occupations, for example, as cleaners, taxi drivers, carers, shop workers and so on. When occupation is not given, in the case of Year 12 students, whether they were in receipt of EMA was used as a measure of class. As with other students, the families of high aspirers are diverse and include divorced and single parents. In general however, students pre-dominantly live with both their parents and, unlike the middle aspirers, appear to have very little contact with extended kin. Whilst middle aspirers primarily enjoy a close relationship with at least one parent, most notably the mother, for high aspirers it can be either parent (as in the case for Pakistani Asian students or, as in one instance, a sibling who takes on the parental role).

Case Study 5.2 – Stephanie

Stephanie has aspirations for higher education and intends to leave school at 16 to study for her A levels at a college some distance from her home. After university she hopes to work in the field of media. Stephanie is a likeable girl and is popular amongst her friends. However, life has not been easy for her; she had been seeing a coun-sellor for the past year, provided by the school, to help cope with bereavement.

Stephanie is considerably younger than her siblings and conse-quently lived alone at home with her mother. When she was 11 years old her mother became ill and so her elder brother moved back home to help. Her brother, knowing that their mother was unlikely to get well, encouraged Stephanie to get to know the father she had never met. However, this was fraught with difficulties for Stephanie as she found it difficult to bond with a man and a family she had never known. When she was almost 14, Stephanie's mother died and reluctantly she was forced to uproot from her home to go and live with her father. She recalls this time:

> *I didn't really get a choice about living there or not 'cause, like, when my mum died my brother went really, really low and he didn't cope and, at that time, he wouldn't have been able to look after me. So, my dad just basically, he didn't ask me but, I had to go and live there. I'd only meet him when I was 12 I went and lived with them for a year and like . . . I'd never met my dad really and up until then I'd only seen him, like, once a month . . . and I had to travel for like an hour everyday to come to school. I fell out with my step mum. We went to France for a holiday and, you know how if you get put in a house with people that you don't know that well and, you get to know them, and you will either get to know them better or you completely fight with them the whole time. And we just fought the whole time. And then I ran out of my house, I ran away. I dunno, it's like, my dad he's quite old, not like the usual kinda age for a parent. And he didn't really understand and my step mum was meant to be retiring so . . . then like . . . they didn't understand and anything I wanted to do it wasn't . . . they didn't understand that teenagers make mistakes and so, anything that I've done, like . . . I dunno, anything stupid that any normal teenager would do and then regret it, even though they'd still do it. They didn't really get that and they were constantly pressuring me at school, questioning everything so . . . um, I just couldn't take it really . . . so . . . I walked out and my brother came and got me the following day and my dad was just like 'well, it's not really working is it?' and he just . . . so, I just moved in with my brother . . . I don't talk to my dad now.*

Stephanie clearly loves her brother and believes he has sacrificed a lot to care for her. They are very close. However, this does not mean that their relationship is without its issues or difficulties at times:

> *. . . sometimes he gets really strict and he's . . . I dunno, it most be really hard for him like . . . he doesn't know 'cause my dad's not around and he doesn't know where to draw the line. He doesn't know whether to be a brother or a parent so it can lead to rows sometimes . . .*

Despite undergoing a very difficult time emotionally, Stephanie's ambitions have never wavered, 'I've always known I wanted to go to university.' Whilst finding it very hard to cope with a double loss, that is, of her mother and her father, Stephanie has been able to retain a sense of belonging, in this case to her brother. Stephanie feels cared for but, more importantly, she feels her brother respects her and the decisions that she makes. The most important decision that she made, that is, that she could not remain with her father, was accepted by him. Having bereavement counselling was also of help. Being listened too was important to Stephanie and she believes it helped her gain confidence in her own ability to make decisions.

Several of the high aspirers refer to their parents' lack of further educational experience as a motivating factor in their aspirations. However, rather than hinder or limit aspirations, that parents had not 'made the most' of their education is used as a source of encouragement for their daughters:

CF: *Do your parents ever discuss their own time at school with you?*

Emily: *The only point that they will refer to is where they messed up. I mean, my dad left school at 16, he really . . . he got on really well at school until about the age of 14–15 and then he left school and he regrets that. He didn't go to college and he regrets it. My Mum . . . I actually don't know. It's really weird to say but I don't know. I've got a feeling that she left at 16 but, I couldn't say for sure which is weird . . . I guess I should know.*

Well, my mum didn't have a good time at school, she was glad to leave at the end of it but, well, like she regrets it now. She wishes she had gone on. She is always telling me to do my best . . . make the most of my education while I have the chance.
Deborah, Focus Group, Year 11

I'm always told university, university, university! That's what you're gonna do! And I agree with them. My parents say that you kinda know the people that haven't been to university . . . the people that haven't . . . my dad went back . . . he came over from the Caribbean and their schooling is different there and he was actually old enough to leave but when he got here he hadn't got the education so he had to go back and do school. He goes to college now, in the evenings and he is going to go to university when he's finished.
Lotte, Focus Group, Year 12

Encouragement for the high aspirers is seen as fundamental to their aspirations:

CF: *Does your family encourage your ambitions?*

Suzy: *Yeah definitely! They're a big part of it. You need their support and encouragement. You could do it independently, you know study, but it's good, like, to have that little bit of support and encouragement to make you actually just go that little bit further.*

Suminda: *My parents encouraged me . . . 'cause they didn't go on themselves. So, they want me to go to university and get a good job.*

Rachel: *. . . my parents can see how important it is to get a good job and you need education for that but, on the other hand our parents, they didn't have the opportunity to be well educated themselves but they want to offer that opportunity to their kids.*

Focus Group, Year 12

Despite lacking knowledge of further education, the parents of high aspirers appear to recognize the value of further and in particularly, higher education. As already noted, whilst opting to pursue a higher education is considered an autonomous choice, once made, parents encourage their daughters with enthusiasm and a desire to see their daughters achieve where they did not. Cultural capital theory is used to illustrate how different social classes are endowed with different levels of cultural resources which have an impact on their ability to provide meaningful involvement in terms of their children's education attainment (Lareau, 1987; Reay, 1998, 2005). However, whilst the parents of students were indeed not able to offer much more than simple praise and encouragement this does not appear to have been detrimental to the value students placed on education nor their aspirations and ambitions for higher education.

Susanna: *I talked to my parents and that's why I decided to do chemistry and biology basically* [at A level] *. . . 'cause of them. I had to fight to do history 'cause they didn't want me to do it.*

CF: *Have either of your parents studied those subjects?*

Susanna: *No they haven't actually but they thought they would be good subjects for me to do.*

Focus Group, Year 12

. . . I brought home my art course work and they were like 'wow! What have you being doing' I mean, they'll take an interest if I take an interest in wanting them to

know. Otherwise they just keep out of it because sometimes I just don't want them to know. But, sometimes if I say 'hey dad can you read this English essay for me and correct the spelling' then he'll read it and he'll be like 'yeah, well this is good' and he'll try and help me change it. So, they show an interest.

Emily, Focus Group, Year 11

CF: *. . . And does your mother help you with your school work?*

Deborah: *Well, not really, well . . . I mean she does . . . like, she is always interested in what I am doing and like, she will look at my work if I want her to.*

Parental interest in the case of the high aspirers appears to promote confidence and reassurance in their decision making processes. Whilst high aspirers frequently refer to the fact that how much involvement parents actually have in the academic side of their schooling is regulated by themselves, it appears that it is interest not active participation that is of primary importance.

In addition to this, inferred from students' comments is the idea that parental attitudes towards students have even greater significance than parental interest in education. High aspirers frequently allude to the idea that good parental-daughter bonds emerge through reciprocal relationships of trust. Student's decisions and decision making, both within and outside of school, are respected and trusted by the parent. This is not to say that students have *carte blanche* choice over all aspects of their lives, rather when families communicate they do so not on the basis of power relationships that are stratified disproportionately but instead present as relationships of equality. A result of this is that high aspirers appear as autonomous individuals within the family, that is, they are treated as adults. Li and Kerpelman (2007) in a study of parental influences on young women's career aspirations, discuss how daughters are often better prepared to make their own choices 'when they experience explicit permission to do so' (2007: 113) and this view appears to be supported in my data.

[Discussing her father] *. . . We sit there and we can usually end up talking until about four or five in the morning and it's just anything and everything and now 'cause we're not allowed to smoke in the house I go outside then five minutes later my dad will come out and we'll just sit there and have a chat and it's just really, really nice . . . he's not actually sat me down and told me 'oh! do this and this and this!' but he listens to me and we have conversations about stuff and I treasure that so much and it's something that I could not live without. My parents* *are quite decent. They're not out of order people at all . . . my mum's nice too. Like we can sit down and we can talk but I prefer to talk to my dad about something because he's so . . . he doesn't judge anything, he's so level headed. And even when I'm punished* [for example, when her parents discovered Emily was smoking] *I'm like, yeah, I deserve it, it's fair.*

Emily, Focus Group, Year 11

Families of the high aspirers appear important to understanding their aspirations because, whilst loved and supported by their parents, high-aspiring students do not appear dependent on them. For example, most of the high aspirers discuss how attending university will give them an opportunity to move away from home and become independent. Unlike the middle aspirers who express a preference for remaining close to their family, this is not so for the high aspirers.[11] Parental relationships that support some autonomy in important decisions and choices whilst providing guidance and encouragement also appear to promote independence and foster trusting relationships. Trust within the family is important as it appears to provide a sense of belonging that appears to promote self-confidence. Whilst parents of high aspirers do retain authority within the family, for example, with the issuing of sanctions and boundaries, generally these are viewed as fair.[12] In understanding the aspirations of the high aspirers then, one could infer that it is this promotion of autonomy and independence, coupled with trusting relationships within families that contributes to students investing trust outside of the family, for example, within school.

Friendships

Just as with the low and middle aspirers, friendships for the high aspirers are also very important and constitute a significant aspect of a student's self-identity. This is because having friends offers a network of support, creates a sense of belonging and appears, on a subjective level, to signify publicly the worth of the individual through her relationships.

Unlike the low and mid aspirers, the friendships of the high aspirers do not appear to matter significantly in terms of further educational choices. For example, whilst all the high aspirers appeared to share similar aspirations, this was not so in terms of subjects studied or institution attended. To illustrate, of the five high aspirers who went on to study elsewhere, only two attended the same college. Despite this though, they followed different courses and often travelled to college (which required a train journey) separately. Indeed, for some students, choosing to follow a course of action simply because your friends are doing so is considered as irresponsible.

> *. . . personally, since Year 10, the teachers would advise us not to do what our friends were doing cause at the end of the day we are friends and I respect my friends and they do me but, what I do with my life . . . I'm not gonna be with them for the rest of my life. I might choose a different career path to my friends. So, I considered the fact I had been here for four years . . . I chose what was right for me, not what my friends were doing. It is very important. Some people are making a mistake from GCSE choosing the subjects that their friends are doing. If it's not something that you enjoy, why choose it? Why waste your time doing it?*
>
> Rachel, Focus Group, Year 12

> *. . . like Daisy, she was my best friend and she went. She went to a different school but I stayed here and it didn't stop her from going and it didn't stop me staying.*
>
> Jane, Focus Group, Year 12

Indeed, during the course of this study two of the students, Sara and Lotte, who were part of a close group of friends, left to go to different institutions: one to college and one to a sixth form at another school. Both were considering the move during the course of Year 12 because they were not happy with the academic standards in terms of the challenge of the work and they left at the end of the academic year.

Whilst high-aspiring students acknowledge the importance of making one's own decision with regard to further study, similarity in aspirations, as already noted, does appear relevant. Friendships groups, although not exclusive, appear to be predominantly made up of students who share similar aspirations for higher education, that is, they intend to study at university. This homogeneity of aspirations is noted by some students and is explained as a natural consequence.

> Jane: . . . [friends] *have the same desires like what we had.*
> Susanna: *You're always going to want to gravitate to people that you feel at ease with.*
>
> Focus Group, Year 12

[Discussing her six closest friends] *. . . we are all similar when you cut us down but, we all branch off, if that makes sense to you? That makes the group even* *more interesting I think. We are all similar at the core but, then outside you've got all these different things that makes it varied and interesting . . . and we are all going to carry on our education, we are going to carry it on I think.*

Emily, Focus Group, Year 11

In addition to shared higher educational aspirations, many of the high aspirers also shared similar non-academic interests. For example; the high-aspiring students intending to study elsewhere had formed their own band. Each friend had a role in the band regardless of musical ability and these ranged from lead singer, to promoter, to official groupie. In addition, these students also shared a broader social network of friends that encompassed students from schools other than their own. For example, they enjoyed close and non-romantic friendships with a number of boys from a local boys grammar school. These friendships were considered as very important 'as it is good to know other people'. However, whilst high-aspiring students enjoy being part of a friendship group and value shared interests, what is noteworthy is that generally it is only one or two from the network who are considered as trustworthy confidantes. It is only those whom a student considers closest whose opinions are sought and are most valued and respected. The importance of trustworthy friendships is a theme also expressed by the low and middle aspirers and appears as very significant in terms of a students' sense of security and emotional well being. As noted in previous chapters, arguments and fallings out can be a great source of angst and distress and are much more significant in a students' life than rifts with parents. Close and trusting friendships provide students with a source with whom to discuss issues that students do not wish to talk over with parents. This appears particularly true when it comes to relationships with males, for example. Indeed for at least one student, it was her close friendship with two girlfriends that helped her come to terms with a significant aspect of her identity in a way that her parent could not.[13] For Stephanie, it was the opinions of her friends that gave her confidence to be herself, as the following example illustrates.

Case Study 5.2 – Continued

Stephanie discusses her sexuality and how being a lesbian was received by her closest friends. She discusses how she could never tell her father about this aspect of herself but it mattered little because of her friends' acceptance.

I can't tell my dad, he'll go mad, he just won't be able to deal with it. We used to have two gay vicars that lived next door to us and he just couldn't deal with it, he hated them and if it were his own daughter . . . he just won't like it.

She tells me how her sexuality was not an issue for her two closest friends as they suspected long before she told them.

I mean I liked guys and that and would say stuff like he's fit or he's fit but, I never had any feelings, nothing inside. I had guy friends but, I liked them for their personalities, nothing more. One day we saw this band and I was going on and on about the guitarist 'cause I really liked her and one of them were like . . . ur Stephanie you really like her don't you? I mean really like? Is there something you wanna tell us? And I was like, 'no, what do you mean?' And they just laughed and said 'come on Stephanie! You can tell us you know! You can tell us that you like her because we already know!' and so I did, and it was such a relief. It was such a relief that my friends just accepted me the way I am.

Stephanie discusses how whilst she experiences comments, looks of disgust or patronizing smiles as she holds her girlfriend's hand and does not like it, she says that because those closest to her accept her the way she is she can *deal with it.*

Conclusion

Trusting relationships, with both family and friends, are important in understanding a student's sense of self. Primarily, this is because close and trusting relationships situates students within an important, supportive network that appears to promote a sense of belonging. 'Belonging' is important because positive associations appear, on a subjective level, to provide a student with a sense of security that is beneficial in terms of self-esteem and confidence. Unlike the middle aspirers, these relationships do not appear to be characterized by an emotional dependency or reliance.

Friendships are important for all the students. However, whilst the friendships of high aspirers tend to be predominantly amongst like-minded friends, the further educational choices of high aspirers suggest that they are not influenced by the choices of their friends (e.g. students make their own choice regarding further educational institution based on subjects they want to study and not on where their friends intend to go). This is similar to the finding of Schneider and Stevenson (1999) who also found that whilst friendships were an important aspect of a young person's sense of self, they have limited influence on educational goals and career plans. For the high aspirers then, it is the relationships of students and their families that appear significant in understanding their aspirations. Families of high aspirers may be isolated (i.e. limited contact with extended kin) and lack the 'cultural capital' that research suggest is significant in determining the educational success of students', for example, knowledge of the educational system (Ball, 2003; Devine, 2004), educational abilities and skills with which to help their children. However, this appears to have little impact, in the first instance at least, on the creation of aspirations amongst high-aspiring students. What is clear is that despite lacking the cultural skills and knowledge of further education that enables parents to strategize in the way that research suggests middle class parents do parents of high aspirers do have ambitions and aspirations for their daughters and value education in terms of the opportunities they believe it potentially can offer. This appears to be important. In addition, the promotion of autonomy within the family appears to foster and encourage independence and determination, that can be infer as having positive consequences for a student's sense of self, ability to trust and thus her ambitions and aspirations for herself.

Gender

Gender for the high aspirers appears as significant a construct in the student's sense of self and future identities as for the low and middle aspirers. However, whilst for the low and mid aspirers conventional gendered roles, for example, as wives and mothers or as workers in gendered specific occupations, appears to offer security through social conformity, the opposite is true for the high aspirers. Both the low and middle aspirers appear to define their future identities with respect to the significant 'other' they hope to have in their projected future lives, that is, in terms of children or men. In some respects, they could be considered as finding security in future aspirations that conform to societal role allocations that are perceived as 'normal'. However, the opposite appears to be true for the high aspirers. This is because implicit in students' comments is the idea that self-reliance and financial independence are desirable pre-requisite before marriage and children. Therefore, whilst gender appears as an important aspect within the creation of high aspirers' future identities, it is significant in that they aim to re-negotiate typical gendered stereotypes, that is, that of dependent within marriage, rather than conform to them.

For high aspirers, education and particularly higher education is seen as the route to occupational choice and economic security. Economic security is synonymous with independence and self-sufficiency and these are important goals when high-aspiring students contemplate possible future relationships. It is fundamentally important that they are able to support themselves as non-dependents in any potential relationship.

I don't know about marriage. I'd rather get the best part of my life over and done with before I even thought about that. I'd rather go to college, go to Uni, travel for a bit and then . . . you know, settle down . . . I suppose when I've done everything. I think I'd prefer to live with someone than get married anyway. God . . . I just don't want to think about it just yet! [laughs] *Whatever comes my way, comes my way I guess but, I'd need to be in a good job first . . . you know, earning my own money.* [as for children] *Oh God! No!! . . . maybe . . . I don't know. That comes later, comes much later!!!*

Emily, Focus Group, Year 11

. . . 'where would I like to be in 20 years time?' Well, I'd like to have my own home that's for sure. Yeah, I suppose I wouldn't mind being with someone but I don't need to be. If I am on my own, it won't matter. What does matter is that I have a good job though, that is important to me. I want to be able to look after myself. I wouldn't wanna depend on anyone else if that makes sense. That's why I'd like my own home. My own home first and then maybe I would wanna be with someone but, like I said, it's not important.

Sophia, Focus Group, Year 10

The comments of Emily and Sophia suggest that economic self-reliance is an important pre-requisite before considering marriage and children. Beck and Beck-Gernsheim (2002) state that one of the resulting consequences of modernity and a 'rhetoric of equality' (2002: 102) is that women increasingly recognize the need to be able to provide for themselves and this idea is clearly expressed by these students. In addition, Giddens (1991) suggests contemporary feminism has been highly significant in the aspirations of women in that it has opened up possibilities that allow women to desire more than family life. Indeed, O'Conner found, in a study of 14–17-year-olds, that 'heterosexual ties and children were, for the most part, only tenuously integrated into . . . life plans' (2006: 120). However, marriage and families are not totally rejected and indeed for some are important, as the comments of Deborah, Year 11, illustrate:

> Deborah: . . . *well, I guess I would like marriage and kids but, it's important to have a career too. I want a career as well as being a mother; I see it as a 50/50 thing.*
> CF: *Why is marriage important to you?*
> Deborah: [laughs] *I don't really know . . . I'd want the whole white dress thing* [laughs] . . . *I just couldn't say why I wanted to get married and have kids, just that I do . . . I want a career though, that is important to me. I wanna be more than just a mother.*

All of the high aspirers do not see their gender as constraining and believe that equality of opportunity exists, alongside freedom to pursue any occupation of choice. Whilst some acknowledge that there remain jobs seen as traditionally male which may create apprehension in taking it up, the general consensus is that it should not.

The following comments refer to gender difference and its link with differing status.

> *As a woman, from my perspective, you have to work hard to prove to yourself that you achieved something in life. Part of me wants to work hard to prove to the men who say women can't do this . . . yeah look at me . . . look where I am now! I achieved something!*
>
> Rachael, Focus Group, Year 12
>
> . . . *if it was me and a male that go for a job I know I will get it if I have more qualifications than him. If I don't . . . well, then he'll get it!*
>
> Sara, Focus Group, Year 12

Just as Hey (1997) found, femininity is often on show and many girls appear to adopt the hypersexual behaviour that McRobbie (1978) also found. Just as with the middle aspirers, girls were frequently observed grooming themselves or one another. Indeed femininity, as expressed through the typical mode of make-up, hair and dress, was a striking feature of all the students, which was interesting given that it was a single sex school. Femininity therefore appears a significant defining feature of student's identity along with her heterosexuality. Heterosexuality, as expressed through associations and relationships with boys, appears to matter. Whilst relationships were rarely serious, being involved with a boy appears to implicitly infer desirability and adulthood both on a subjective level and as a signal amongst peers. Interestingly, none of the high-aspiring students who remained in the sixth form of their school were involved in relationships with the opposite sex because, as one student stated 'they are too distracting!'

Conclusion

What the comments of the high aspirers suggest is that while attempting to renegotiate traditional identities through individual choice, ultimately gender remains a powerful determinate of future aspirations. Whilst the students do not appear to see their gender as detrimental to aspirations and ambitions, the desire for independence and, more importantly, equality is evident from their comments concerning relationships and economic security. Overwhelmingly, high aspirers express the desire to be non-dependents and to have equality in any potential future relationship. Implicit is the idea that, for the high aspirers, education is the route to this emancipation. This is because educational success opens up far greater employment opportunities and thus presents prospects for achieving economic independence. As Kierkegaard states 'freedom is not a given characteristic of the human individual, but derives from the acquisition of an ontological understanding of external reality and personal identity' (cited in Giddens, 1992). For Giddens (1992) lifestyle choices are not open to everyone despite the idea that individual futures are reflectively defined. Autonomous choices are still influenced by 'the structuring features of stratification' (Giddens, 1992: 82), in this case, the structuring features of gender. As Swartz (1997) notes, the symbolism of gender, whilst contested in practice is still rigidly enforced. For the high aspirers then, it is gender that appears as highly significant in understanding their future aspirations, more so than ideas associated with class.

Chapter Summary

All of the high aspirers, by definition, intend to pursue a higher education. Whilst further education is seen as opening up future choices and opportunity, higher education is considered as offering a route to greater economic security and independence than further education alone. In contrast to both the low and middle aspirers, high aspirers are strategizers and clearly articulate the rationality they apply to their future choices, for example, calculating the various returns on the differing options available in terms of post-16 study. Unlike other students, high aspirers are explicit in the belief that the choices they make in relation to their futures are autonomous ones.

What marks the high aspirers as distinct from the low and middle aspirers is the very individualized notion of self. Whilst students acknowledge inequality and discrimination, they believe firmly in the principles of meritocracy. For the high aspirers, choice and ambitions are viewed as reflectively defined and made possible by personal application. In addition, high aspirers demonstrate greater levels of social capital than do other students, not social capital acquired via their families but capital achieved in the students' own right. Social capital is important as it appears to be inherently linked to the concept of trust. However, data suggests that the relationship is reversed and that trust precedes the acquisition of social capital rather than the reverse. Trust, particularly institutional trust, is important because data suggests it facilitates a students' willingness to accept the legitimacy of the educational system in terms of defining future identities but also because it fosters a willingness to become actively involved with the school.

Finally, high aspirers appear to differentiate from other students in terms of their relationships with their families. Whilst loving, supportive and trusting relationships within kin groups are significant for all students included here, it is the nature of the relationship in terms of autonomy that appears to matter in terms of aspirations for higher education. The families of the high aspirers appear to balance parental authority with individual autonomy and this appears to promote both a sense of security and independence. Interestingly, research generally suggests that the familial class background of students does not appear to have the significant influence on students' aspirations. For example, whilst none of the parents of high aspirers had experience of higher education (or indeed further education) this did not prevent them encouraging their daughters to pursue this ambition. Indeed, rather than hinder or limit, the educational disadvantage of the parents of high aspirers is used to motivate and encourage daughters. Therefore, whilst possibly low in cultural capital, the parents of high aspirers still endow daughters with a positive investment in terms of emotional support[14] which provides students with a secure foundation on which to project future identities that are alternatives to that of their families.

Whilst the social background of the families of high aspirers does not appear to hinder aspirations, to suggest that aspirations are not stratified is clearly incorrect. Whilst students do not recognize class, stratification and inequality appears important in ambitions none the less. Primarily, this is because high aspiring students recognize that they are stratified as students within school through academic setting and because they also suggest that the social backgrounds of their families is what inspires them to strive for more economically secure futures. Stratification for the high aspirers then does not appear to limit ambitions. Conversely it appears instead to motivate. What remains significant in the aspirations of all the students however, is gender. Whilst gender is something that high aspirers seek to renegotiate, it is an important underlying variable in the aspirations of the high aspirers. Ultimately, high-aspiring students consider themselves as individuals situated in a social context that is unequal. Inequality, however, is something students believe can be countered through individual hard work and application.

Notes

[1] Millennium Volunteers is a scheme aimed at young people aged 16–24. Students sign up and volunteer their time to help others and gain a certificate at the end. Source http://www.wearev.com/mv/index.php

[2] Head of school and of school houses require students to nominate themselves and then go through an interview process.

[3] Students felt the practice was discriminatory in that some students were allowed to wear trousers on the grounds of faith. Students involved in the protest felt that there should be no distinctions of this sort and were supported in the view by the girls that were permitted to wear them.

[4] The Student/staff council is made up of representatives from each year and tutor group. Interestingly, I was informed that student were predominantly members of set one.

[5] In the USA faith schools are private. However, in a report published in January 2007 The Sutton Trust reported that faith schools and single-sex schools are more than twice as likely to appear in the list of the top 200 performing schools for GCSE exam success. (Source: http://news.bbc.co.uk/1/hi/education/4640064.stm accessed 13 June 2007.)

[6] http://www.askoxford.com/concise_oed/trust?view=uk (accessed May 2007).

[7] UCAS apply a tariff for A level grades, with each grade worth differing points. For example: A = 120 points, B = 100 points and C = 80 points. Universities apply points tariff for admissions in to their degree programme. For example, Oxford University requires 360 UCAS points which equates to three A level grade As. In addition, performance at GCSE is also considered due to the high number of applicants versus places. All GCSE grades for subjects taken are expected to be A to A*.

[8] Despite the school processing the university applications and offering support and advice with the personal statements, from students' comments, choice of institution and degree were decisions made alone, with little or no support.

⁹ Statistics published on applications to Oxford University in 2003, show that of 107 black-African applicants 14 per cent (n = 15) were successful. Of 30 three Bangladeshi applicants 9 per cent (n = 3) were successful as were 18.6 per cent (n = 24) of the 129 Pakistani students who applied. Data was not available for the social classifications of applicants. (Source: The University of Oxford Admissions Statistics 2003 Entry, http://www.ox.ac.uk/gazette/2003–4/supps/entry.pdf accessed 13 June 2007.)

¹⁰ Hodkinson and Sparkes (1997) draw on Strauss to illustrate a number of different 'turning points'. Turning points are seen as facilitating a 'significant transformation of identity' (1997: 39). Turning points come under three categories: *Structural*, that is, determined by external structures of the institution involved, for example, at the end of compulsory schooling or retirement; *self-initiated*, that is, the person is instrumental in the transformation in relation to some event in their life; and, *forced* by external events or actions of others, for example redundancy. Hodkinson and Sparkes state that turning points alter the habitus of an individual.

¹¹ It is worth noting however, that most of these students believe that ultimately financial considerations means that it is probable that they will be forced to attend the local university and, consequently, remain in the family home.

¹² A good example of this is when Emily decided to tell her parents that she was smoking. Her parents were initially angry, disappointed and anxious for her health and did ground her (i.e. they would not permit out of the home) for several weeks. However, ultimately they accepted that as she was nearly 16 there was little they could do. After a long discussion, they forbade Emily to smoke in front of her younger siblings or in the family home and Emily accepted these rules. Emily, whilst not happy with her initial 'grounding', could rationalize her parent's response as resulting from concern for her. It was important to her that they had sat down and discussed the issue 'like adults'. It is also interesting to consider the fact that Emily decided to share the fact she was a smoker with her parents. Transparency does appear significant in parental/daughter relationships.

¹³ Although it is worth noting that Stephanie did not enjoy a good relationship with her father, who was absent for most of her life and who was, by her account, significantly older than the fathers of her friends.

¹⁴ A tentative discussion of the role of families will be provided in Chapter Six.

Chapter 6

Discussion: Exploring Within-Class Differences in Aspirations

Introduction

In addressing some of the different theoretical frameworks that are used to make sense of differences in aspirations I found myself faced with a theoretical conundrum; how to bridge, and at the same time make use of, very differing perspectives that are used to explain the role (or not) of class within education? Whilst initially adopting a very deductive approach, informed by the work of Bourdieu, I soon became uncomfortable with it. This is because whilst the work of Bourdieu offers a rich framework for exploring aspirations, I began to feel that ideas of class shaped values and dispositions, the result of habitus, were somewhat patronizing when applied to the working class. After all, is it not fair to assume that most young people recognize the 'value' of schooling to their futures, even if they choose to reject it? Do not most young people aspire to an enjoyable occupation providing a steady income, as well as a secure home? And, is it not possible that whilst class clearly imposes restrictions and constraints as to how to achieve these goals, are not other, more individual influencing factors just as important too? Through adopting a more inductive approach, what soon became clear is that aspirations and what shapes them are complex and multifaceted, and cannot be readily understood by adopting one theoretical framework alone. In particular, conceptual tools such as cultural capital and habitus associated with cultural reproduction theory are not always helpful as they do not easily allow for within group variation when applied broadly. In order to understand the aspirations of the students in this study I attempted to make sense of the mechanisms behind students' aspirations for themselves by considering ambitions with respect to the students' relationships with school, perceptions of family and friends as well as their experiences over time. In addition, attempting to explore a student's subjective interpretation of self enabled me to get some sense of the underlying mechanisms that motivated some students to continue in education and not others. In the rest of this chapter I shall discuss what the results of this study suggest are significant to understanding the differential aspirations of the students included in this study.

As illustrated in Chapter Two, class is a very powerful tool that is used to explain differences in both educational attainment and aspirations. Popular within the sociology of education is the idea that differences in educational attainment and aspirations can be understood as the result of cultural reproduction, the idea that class background is reproduced both subjectively (in terms of the individual values and attitudes of students) and objectively (via the institution of education itself, i.e. the nature and structure of learning and the awarding of academic credentials). Central to cultural reproduction theory are Bourdieu's concepts of cultural capital and habitus. Cultural capital refers to the cultural background of an individual in terms of the skills they possess, for example, linguistic abilities, their cultural knowledge and tastes. Families are important to cultural reproduction theory as it is the cultural capital of families that is endowed upon an individual. Within education, cultural capital is highly significant as it has a direct bearing on the academic attainment of an individual as well as the ability for parents to engage with their children's learning. In terms of class, the higher the social classification, the greater the cultural resources available. An individual's habitus is also important and results through a process of socialization; a process determined by the experience of class. Habitus provides a sub-conscious understanding about how society works and consequentially a framework for determining practice. Both of these powerful explanatory tools are significant in that economic resources, the primary axis on which class is operationalized, underpins their acquisition. Understanding the interconnection of class, cultural capital and habitus is thus considered important because they work in conjunction with one another to shape and determine values and dispositions towards education as well as educational outcomes, providing for some theorists a clear illustration of the socially reproductive nature of education.

Another capital considered important within education is that of social capital, that is, the social relationship that exist between individuals and between individuals and communities. Whilst different theorists conceptualize social capital differently, underlying the conceptualizations are the views that social relationships foster and promote community cohesion, civic engagement, shared norms and social trust. In terms of education, when individuals and communities develop relationships, for example, with schools and/or individuals with experience of higher education. The result is that trusting relationships emerge and this consequently encourages the reinforcement of school values. This has positive results for children's education. However, for theorists such as Bourdieu social capital is also classed and serves to promote social closure and reinforce class boundaries. Therefore, the benefits of social capital will be dependent on class. Whilst some theorists consider the role of social capital as an internal mechanism of families and others, as an external factor, its importance in influencing educational outcomes is increasingly the focus of educational policy.

Whilst cultural reproduction theory presents a powerful explanatory framework for understanding both educational outcomes and aspirations, supported with an abundance of research, other theorists prefer instead to focus on the secondary effects of class. For rational action theorists, it is the effects of economic resources that are important to understanding differential aspirations because even when academic performance is held constant, students from less advantaged backgrounds still make less ambitious choices. By focusing on the secondary effects, rational action theorists explain misalignment as the result of students from different class backgrounds evaluating and calculating the risks and costs of alternative options available to them differently. For rational action theorists, when considering differences in educational aspirations, it is the constraints placed on choices that are significant rather than cultural factors. This is not because cultural factors are not relevant but more, that cultural factors cannot explain the persistence of class differentials over time, despite educational expansion and reform or the slowly improving rates of educational attainment (Goldthorpe, 2007c).

Both cultural reproduction and rational action theory posit strong arguments for the usefulness of using class theory for framing an exploration of how educational aspirations are shaped and determined. However, counter arguments suggest that class is not as salient as research suggests and that, as a result of changes in the labour market, class as an explanatory tool is now defunct. Alternative theories of individualization suggests that aspirations can in fact be more readily understood as resulting from an individual's reflexive understanding of the labour market situation plus an evaluation of the course of action deemed necessary to ensure their own survival, in terms of preventing downward mobility and providing for future security. Increased labour market competition now compels individuals to credentialize themselves, whilst ties to family, cultures and traditions no longer matter (Beck, 2001). In terms of aspirations, theories of individualization suggest then that patterns of inequality should be considered as atomized rather than collective patterns and should be explored in terms of an individuals understanding of their own biography rather than the result of deterministic structures such as class.

Despite debate, class retains its currency and continues to be used to illustrate the relationship between social background and educational outcomes. This relationship is also supported with empirical evidence. Even when considering differences in relation to gender and ethnicity, class is still considered significant and underpinning their affects. However, in addressing within group variation, that is, explaining the working class who aspire high or the middle class who aspire low, class theory is not so clear. Indeed, critics of cultural reproduction theory, for example, dispute the claim that families are the sole source of the accumulation of cultural capital or that habitus is fixed (Halsey et al., 1980; Goldthorpe, 2007a), whilst critics of rational action argue that the theory does not account for how and why individuals chose to pursue different options. Finally, Lucey et al. (2003) state that no theory can adequately address differences in aspirations without considering the impact of psycho-social processes on the individual and it is this critique that I try to consider when framing my approach. In considering the role of class in the educational aspirations of the students included in this research, what is apparent is that its impact is not clear cut. For example, whilst economic constraints and considerations do pose significant issues and hurdles that affect students' choices, these do not determine similar outcomes for all students.

Aspirations and Theory

In terms of understanding aspirations in relation to theory it is clear that class does matter. Class matters because, as a plethora of research within education illustrates, there is a clear and important link between child poverty and educational attainment. Whilst I will argue in the rest of this chapter against an over-reliance on using broad concepts such as class (as it is currently conceptualized) to understand the aspirations of students in this study, one cannot ignore the important consequences that it appears to have on attainment. After all, a minimum level of attainment is necessary if many educational and occupational aspirations are to be realized. However, it is my contention that other factors are equally as important when considering aspirations (and attainment) and argue that practices within school, as well as trust and attachment are just as important as economic resources and/or class culture for the girls included here. These factors will be discussed in the rest of this chapter.

Attitudes and Practices

In the first instance future educational aspirations would appear to link with a student's attitude towards education, particularly in terms of how a student views the usefulness of education to their future life courses. Although complex and not a perfect correlation, most students who do not value education highly intend to leave education at the end of compulsory schooling, whilst students who consider education and educational qualifications as extremely relevant and useful to future lives aspire to further and higher education. To some degree then, attitudes towards education (which is different to attitudes towards a particular school) would appear to predict educational aspirations. However, attitudes are complex and whilst negative attitudes towards education initially present as oppositional, a straight forward rejection of schooling, on closer exploration this does not appear to be the case. For example, not all students who were negative about school intended to leave and not all students positive about school intended a higher education. In this study then, attitudes towards education appear multifaceted and are reflective, in some degree, of levels of self-esteem and self-confidence which has an impact on how the usefulness of education is evaluated in a student's future plans. This also appears to interconnect with a student's faith in meritocracy; that effort is worth it relative to rewards. Practices with in school then, appear important in reinforcing these attitudes.

Practices and relationships within school present as relevant to understanding how students understand themselves within an academic environment and appear significant to understanding a student's attitude towards her future, in terms of educational aspirations and their attainment. Building on Cooley's (1922) concept of the looking-glass self, practices and relationships within schools are perceived by the students included as a reflection of peoples' opinions of them. These perceptions then appear to become a principal aspect of students' own identities, with students becoming the kind of person they believe others see them to be. The practices and relationships within school, when considered in relationship to practices and relationships outside of the school, appear to impact on levels of self-confidence and self-esteem within education, which appears to shape attitudes towards education particularly in the sense of whether education is seen as being a viable route for providing future careers, as Bandura et al. note 'children ground their sense of occupational efficacy in their beliefs about their academic capabilities rather than their actual attainment level' (2001: 197). Thus, students take the route they believe they are most suitable for, which for some means rejecting education and others embracing it. The structural location of students within school is therefore important to understanding how students situate themselves within school, particularly with respect to the bench mark criteria for success of five A–Cs at GCSE. Setting and teacher evaluations assess students as those who will exceed the target, achieve it or simply fail to make it and this has important consequences for a student's understanding of self and her place within the educational system. This is a relevant consideration, particularly when considering low aspirers and the very low levels of self-esteem they appear to display. When life experiences have not been positive, the messages students receive within school, for example in terms of ability, particularly when reinforcing external messages, promotes a sense of fatalism, that is, 'I will not succeed so why bother?' Consequently, these students reject or challenge the education system and aspire to future identities they believe are attainable in low pay, low status jobs or as mothers. However, unlike The Lads in Willis's (1977) study, the oppositional position of the low aspirers is not a rejection of the cultural values surrounding education but is a response to an individualized defeatist sense of their own abilities that then impacts on attitudes to education. The same self-reflection process also appears to explain the aspirations of low and middle aspirers. Therefore, aspirations may appear to demonstrate an understanding of whom one is in class terms but they also offer a picture of how students in this study perceive themselves, in more psychological terms and how this in turn impacts on their attitudes towards education.

Families

Whilst no systematic analysis of families and parental roles in aspirations was undertaken and parents were not interviewed as part of this study, families still present as significant to understanding the attitudes and aspirations of students included in this study due to students' perception of the role their families play and the role these perceptions then have within school. Just as a student brings into school a level of self-confidence and self-esteem, so also she brings an understanding of her parents. Whilst clearly there is the possibility that a students perception of the role parents play in supporting her education may diverge significantly with the reality, it is arguably the perception that is relevant. Thus, whilst a discussion of families can only be tentative as I did not talk with families directly, the level of emotional support the students perceive that they receive from their families appears to be important. Families are still worth considering because they are a site from where students believe they learn to make decisions for themselves and get a sense of who they are. Perceptions of family were therefore explored in order to see how these perceptions operate as a process within school and the links with attitudes and aspirations. As Bandura et al. (2001) note, socio-economic status has only an indirect effect on children's ambitions and in developing aspirations, it is the belief parents have in their children that appears more important because 'aspiring parents act in ways that build . . . children's [own] academic, social and self-regulatory efficacy, raise their aspirations, and promote their scholastic achievements (Bandura et al., 2001: 198).

From student comments, families appear to encourage or discourage autonomy in varying degrees, which appears to have important consequences in terms of self-esteem and self-confidence and aspirations. For low-aspiring students, parental relationships presented as highly or weakly authoritarian, that is, relationships between mother and daughters that were described by students as over-controlling were highly authoritarian and those that presented as 'best friend' relationships were weakly authoritarian. For middle aspirers, relationships appeared to be ones of emotional dependency, that is, where daughters depended on and sought comfort from the advice of parents, and students appeared to define themselves very much in terms of their relationships. For high aspirers however, relationships appeared to be distinguished by a sense of equality and of supported autonomy, that is, parents trusted students to make decisions for themselves, whilst at the same time offering guidance and support. High aspirers therefore felt that parents acknowledged the student's ability to make informed choices and as a result, felt respected as an adult in her own right.

In many ways the role of parents, in terms of a student's perception, can be considered as another form of capital but one that is emotional/psychological. Just as with other capitals, the interactions of parents and daughters appear to impact and interact with educational aspirations because of their effects on levels of self-confidence and self-esteem. The idea that a capital can be linked to the emotional is relatively new and was first suggested by Nowotny (1981) (see also Bradford and Hey, 2007). For Nowotny, 'emotional capital' is a capital acquired by women in the private sphere and is invested in children, most notably in aspirations and strategies within education. Nowotny conceptualizes emotional capital to be non-transferable in economic terms, being limited to the private sphere, and is defined by a mother's knowledge, contacts and 'access to emotionally valued skills and assets' (1981: 148). Reay (2004b) develops this concept further to encompass emotional encouragement and support that, whilst not defined entirely by class, it is implicitly inferred that for the working class is limited by it. This is because, as Reay notes, 'middle-class mothers, in their pursuit of educational advantage for their children [do so] at the cost of their emotional well being, and working-class mothers, constrained in ways that mitigate against the acquisition of both emotional and cultural capital, are at risk of disadvantaging their children, albeit in different ways' (2004b: 71). Fundamental to current conceptualizations, however, is that emotional capital is the domain of mothers.

What was interesting in this study however was whilst students' mothers were indeed considered supportive several students also felt their fathers were both encouraging and ambitious for their daughters also. Thus emotional support (or emotional capital) is that perceived by students to be related to encouragement and support, as Reay (2004b) suggests, but also appears to be implicitly interconnected with promoting self-confidence and self-esteem as well as supporting student's self-reliance and independence. Whilst high-aspiring students lack positive role models for their career and educational ambitions, this does not seem to be detrimental to aspirations (of course this is not to suggest that the lack of a positive role model would not hinder achieving ambitions). Indeed, parental relationships that students feel were marked by encouragement, support and a sense of respect appear to be far more important because it also appears to create a sense of equality and autonomy within the family. Emotional capital then, when conceptualized to be emotional encouragement, support of ambition, confidence in daughters ability to achieve and interest, invested by of a least one significant kin member, appears to be a highly useful tool for exploring the aspirations of the students in this study. It perhaps permits an explanation as to why actual economic cost of different post-16 options are evaluated differently, that is, why for some families costs are less risky than for others and accounts for why some students aspire more highly than others, despite not always having the appropriate levels of educational attainment.

Developing this further, an investment of an 'emotional capital' appears relevant on two levels: first because it appears to promote self-confidence and self-esteem as well as encouraging students to develop a sense of personal efficacy and autonomy. As Li and Kerpelman (2007) note, daughters are better prepared to make their own choices 'when they experience explicit permission to do so' (2007: 113). Secondly, confidence, positive self-esteem and a sense of personal autonomy could be considered as translating into the classroom and may account, in part, for why some students appear to feel more confident in engaging with teachers and school and in taking some control of their own education, in terms of doing what they must to achieve.

Essentially then, I am suggesting that emotional capital as a concept appears to be of some use and has the potential to offer illumination for this study as to why some students of similar backgrounds aspire differently. Emotional support has the potential to be considered in terms of a capital because of a suggested link with aspirations, based on student perceptions. Aspirations that transfer into actual outcome will consequently impact on economic capital, in contrast to Nowotny position. Thus, if invested at the right level the transformation of aspirations into employment success is hopeful. Acknowledging the important role that the perception of emotional support plays in students' lives can also be highly important to parents who, aware of the deficits in their economic and cultural capital, can feel good about the positive contribution that they are able to make to their children's education. As Gillies (2005) notes, current educational policy tends to demonize the working class through a clear and direct target on their lacking middle-class values and skills. However, as she also adds, emotional capital is not about ensuring educational success, but is concerned with equipping children psychologically. For the high aspirers in this study this appeared to be important in shaping their ambitions for themselves. Despite the fact that I did not talk to parents and families first hand, students' perceptions of the role of parents suggest that there were differences in the emotional support of the different groups. In this study, differences appeared in the type of emotional support students perceived they had, in terms of supported decisions making. However, I reiterate that this is only tentative and, alongside with the need to explore what level of support is useful, would be a possible theme for further research.

Cultural Capital and Habitus

Cultural capital as a concept is useful in that it can account well for the aspirations of both the low and middle aspirers. However, drawing on Goldthorpe's (2007a) critique of Bourdieu's conceptualization and application of cultural capital, the fixed nature of cultural capital is not useful in explaining the aspirations of the high aspirers. This is because cultural capital, when conceptualized as something acquired from families, does not account for how students can acquire more for themselves within schools, as Halsey et al. (1980) show. This is evident in the high-aspiring students who recognize and actively strategize to build upon and enhance their own skills. Evidence suggests that students were able to acquire their own cultural capital and this was apparent on two levels: institutionally – higher set girls are challenged educationally and have greater expectations that push them to do what they must to achieve; and, individually – acquisition is apparent in the strategies high aspirers adopt to improve their chance of examination success and attractiveness to university admissions officers. That high aspirers attempt to accumulate greater levels of cultural capital for themselves, whilst low and middle aspirers did not, appears to be a response to their ambitions, with students appearing to rationalize, in terms of the costs and benefits, what they must do if they are to achieve their goals.

The importance of cultural capital also appears less significant than cultural reproduction theory suggests when considering the role that families play *within* their children's education. Whilst lacking in the skills to assist their daughters on a practical level, what appeared to be more important was the perception of parental interest and encouragement. In addition, the view that the value families place on their children's education results from class dispositions and habitus is also questionable, indeed is demeaning to the parents of the middle and high aspirers in this study who, despite lacking in experience of further and higher education do not appear to value it any less. The idea that the value that families place on education is largely determined by the experience of education is therefore not straightforward as it appears that a lack a further education that enables some parents (and I am by no means suggesting all parents) to recognize and value the opportunities that further education can provide for their daughters. Just as students do, parents appear to recognize the competitive nature of the labour market and share the view that educational qualifications offer the potential for future employment security. Indeed, this very fact may account well for the increasing numbers of mature students (myself included) now attending colleges and higher educational institutions.

In making the points that I do, I am not suggesting that cultural capital in education is not important. Indeed through carrying out this study, it was quite apparent that many students lacked linguistic knowledge and skills and knowledge more broadly, about the educational system. In terms of students' potential to achieve at GCSE and at A level, as well as successfully applying to various educational institutions, it was evident that many students were at a very distinct disadvantage. However, what this research indicates is that some students were able to recognize their deficits and attempted to compensate by asking for help and clarification, re-doing work and so forth. This suggests that in this study, the skills associated with class are not fixed and that students, as autonomous individuals, are able to generate cultural capital in their own right. This suggests an important consideration to both educators and policy makers who, whilst recognizing that habitus can be partially influenced through programmes such as the Aim Higher scheme, that is, by providing knowledge and experience of that which is unfamiliar, do not necessarily always appear to recognize that educational aspirations are about more than just knowledge.

Social Capital

Social capital within education is important as it appears to reinforce positive attitudes towards education as well as promoting a sense of individual autonomy. In this study I offer no clear empirical evidence of the role that parents' social capital (as conceptualized theoretically) has in shaping educational aspirations. However, evidence is offered that suggests that young people are able to accumulate social capital in their own right (based on current definitions) and do not rely solely on parents' social capital. This is consistent with Morrow's (1999) finding. Self-acquisition was demonstrated by high aspirers' keenness to be pro-active agents rather than passive recipients within their education. In explaining why this may be so, it is trust that appears significant. Students who appear to trust in school and the people within it are the students who express the most enthusiasm to participate within it. Trust is implicit in high aspirers' belief in meritocracy and is demonstrated in terms of student rationalization, that is, involving oneself will be worth it (e.g. see Chapter Five, Case Study 5.1 – The Trouser Protest). More broadly, trust may explain why civic engagement is so varied, that is, it explains why an individual may help out at school or at work but, not in their neighbourhood. I therefore suggest that, for this study, in conceptualizing social capital the causal relationship may be reversed. Theory suggests that social capital generates trust, willingness to share, civic engagement and so on. yet evidence presented appears to suggest that trust is a pre-requisite to being willing to participate in the first instance. Therefore, to some extent, it is trust that generates social capital rather than social capital that produces trust.

In determining why some students are more trusting than others, a combination of factors appear important and it would no doubt be pertinent to elaborate further as to what I mean by 'trust'. Using a standard defin-ition, trust is defined as the 'firm belief in the reliability, truth, ability, or strength of someone or something' (Online Oxford Dictionary, accessed 2007). For the students included here, trust in the educational context appears to relate to a students' ability to believe in the principles of merit-ocracy, that is, effort is worth relative to the rewards received. A student's ability to trust in school and the staff within as well as trusting in the value of educational credentials *per se* appears to be determined by a positive experience of schooling as well as confidence within school for example, in engaging in school and challenging, even if implicitly, what is perceived as unfair, for example, teacher evaluations and assessments. Trust then appears fundamental to a student's desire to involve herself in the political and organizational life of the school and appears to interact significantly with degrees of attachment (see section on 'Social Attachment').

From student's narrative it appears that students are individual beings and not simply dependents. Contrary to some current thinking, students are able to generate capital in their own right which they utilize to their own advantage. Unlike both Coleman (1987) and Putnam (2000), trust is presented as pre-requisite for acquiring and generating social capital and, contrary to Bourdieu's (1997) contention, social capital is not neces-sarily solely determined by factors associated with class for these students. Whilst connections and associations between individuals and organizations may well be limited to those within ones social landscape, trust in the first instance does not limit that landscape in social terms (particularly when considered within the educational context). Whilst parental social capital will undoubtedly have positive consequences for a student's education, a lack of social capital does not necessarily appear detrimental to student's educational values, attitudes and aspirations as theory appears to infer. Some students were able to create capital in their own right. Thus, in this study, a student's experience of school impacts on her ability to trust and it is this that appears to have consequences for a student's capacity to generate social capital (with all the positive influences on education that this appears to promote, for example, desire to engage in the civic life of the school).

Social Attachment

Granovetter (1973) discusses the importance of the strength of social ties within social life and posits that it is weak ties that are the most advanta-geous and strong ties the most inhibiting for example, in finding work.

In exploring these ideas within aspirations, social ties do emerge through my data as noteworthy and differing strength of attachment were noted amongst students with different aspirations. When social ties/attachment are conceptualized as relating to emotional dependency then, somewhat differently to Granovetter, it is loose and not weak ties that appear important.

In exploring the strength of ties (or attachment) to institutions, that is, school, family and friends, differences were noted amongst all three groups of students and these differences appeared to be an important explanatory factor behind different aspirations. Low-aspiring students expressed weak attachment to school and family home (demonstrated by their desire to leave both the education system and family home as soon as possible), whilst middle aspirers expressed a much stronger degree of attachment (demonstrated by their strongly articulated desire to remain both at their current school and family home). High aspirers, in contrast, were distinguished by much looser ties. The low aspirers' weak attachment to school is explained as the result of a student's sense of not belonging, not 'fitting in' at school; whilst a wish to move from the family home was articulated as a desire for independence or simply freedom because home life was not happy. The strong attachment of the middle aspirers however, reflects the opposite position in that strong attachment to family home and school appears to emerge as a response to the emotional needs of students, in terms of confidence, security and familiarity. Finally, high aspirers appear to express looser ties to both school and family home relating to their greater levels of self-confidence and independence. However, it is worth pointing out that a loose tie does not imply a lack of affection. For example, high aspirers who articulate a desire to move away from home desire to do so not because they are unhappy at home, like the low aspirers, but appear to continue the theme of independence being very much linked with higher educational aspirations. The same is true when understanding student's motivations for further educational study. A desire for new experiences and meeting new people, rationalized as beneficial to the student, is what underpins a students desire to leave her current school rather than remain.

In considering the three groups of students in terms of degree of attachment, differences in Granovetter's model are noted. The apparent weak ties of the low aspirers appear to offer one explanation as to why these students choose to remove themselves from environment to which they feel no attachment and explain also, why the strong bonds of the middle aspirers appear to hold them where they are. In contrast to Granovetter however, the weak ties of the low aspirers were just as disadvantageous, albeit in varying degrees as the strong ties he identifies. In this study it was the loose ties of the high aspirers that appeared to be the most profitable. In explaining why this may be so it could be inferred that it is levels of dependency that influence the degrees of students' attachment. To illustrate, low aspirers appear to lack attachment because of their negative perceptions and experiences of school, whilst the middle aspirers appear to be dependent on what is familiar. The high aspirers, in contrast, have much looser attachment to a particular school for example, because they appear to be more self-reliant and confident.

Social Attachment and Friendships

In terms of friendships, strong ties were noted amongst all students, although ties presented as somewhat looser amongst high aspirers. This is because, whilst friends were very important socially and emotionally for all students, they were less important to high aspirers with respect to future plans. High aspirers did not follow friends in terms of post-16 choices, that is, what and where to study and, unlike the middle and low aspirers, were keen that post-16 choices would provide opportunities for making new ones. For the low and middle aspirers however, friendships were much more important in that the choices of these students often reflected the choices of their friends. With respect to the middle aspirers, this appeared to be positive and students often followed friends to college, sixth form and onto specific courses, which they may not have done otherwise. For the low aspirers, however, it resulted in students following friends into the work place.

In their respective studies Hargreaves (1967) and Ball (1981) found that friendships matter and that within friendship groups, which tend to be contained with a band, pro- and anti-school cultures emerge dependent on setting. For example, within lower set groups sub-cultural values emerge, in opposition to the prevailing educational ethos, which impacts on students' attitudes and choices within education negatively. The results of this study support these findings, particularly as the closest friendships were often amongst students of the same academic set, despite mixed ability tutor groups. However, the social nature of school and friendships also appears important on an emotional level too. Having friends was important because friends were those who were trusted by the students and, implicitly, they appeared to matter to a student's sense of belonging.

It could be inferred then that the sense of belonging that having a good friend provides is significant to understanding a student's self-identity because of the feelings of security, self-esteem and confidence that being part of a group and therefore liked engenders. As Giddens (1991) notes, sentiments associated with friendships only tend to exist when they are useful and reciprocated. For students who are beginning to define their future identities through the choices that they make, friendships appear both useful and significant on an intrinsic level. The emotional support and, more importantly, acceptance of friends appears relevant in helping define who one is and who one might expect to be, (e.g. see Chapter Five, Case Study 5.2 – Stephanie). Being part of a group appears to offer a collective identity and implicitly suggests that having friends is a significant marker of your social acceptability that infers something about who one is. Whilst not articulated in these terms, the apparent reinforcement of social bonds was evident in the shared grooming, shared style of dress and displays of physical affection, for example, embracing. Friendship practices appear not just to confirm and reinforce shared social bonds but also, reiterate the social nature of self-identity via the self-reflective nature of friendships. Whilst friends are clearly important in the aspirations of some students, understanding friendships in terms of what they tell a student about themselves also appears relevant too.

Ethnicity

This study included a large number of students from ethnic minority backgrounds with a significant proportion of ethnic minority students to white students as aspirations went up. However, the higher proportion of ethnic minority students in Year 12 is likely to be reflective of parental/student preference for single sex schooling as well as the fact that very few white students remained in the sixth at 'Southwell'. In exploring some of the factors that may account for the educational aspirations of the ethnic minority groups included it is clear that, just as with other students, factors associated with practices, autonomy and trust appeared to matter to the same degree for ethnic minority students as did the role of self-identification however, some differences were noted and these are discussed below.

From observations and interviews in school it was apparent that clear distinctions operate in terms of friendship groupings. For example, friendships appeared to be differentiated along ethnic lines and between Asian and whites were almost exclusive, with some mixing with black students. Students were aware of these differences and explained it as the result of 'having nothing in common' with each other. In addition to social distinctions some students also referred to racism within school and, just as Basit (1996) found, some negative stereotyping of Asian students was indeed expressed by teachers. Differentiation of this nature is significant and likely to have an impact on how students situate themselves within school, in terms of self-identification. In addition, it has potential consequences in terms of the guidance and advice given to ethnic minority students and the type of aspirations and ambitions being encouraged. For the low aspirers it is possible then that a sense of having less status in school explains, to some degree, lower aspirations. Whilst a lack of status within school was also referred to by white low-aspiring students, it is possible that for ethnic minority students this is further compounded by a sense of discrimination. High expectations are fundamental to success, as Richardson and Wood (2004) note.

Although tentative, it is also possible that in this study differing educational aspirations amongst students from different ethnicities may be explained by differences in immigration status. Battu and Sloane (2004) found income returns for education differed between first generation and second generation immigrants. In this study, most (although not all) high-aspiring African students were first generation immigrants, whilst Pakistani students, whose aspirations were more mixed, were second generation. In this study most black-African students were quite optimistic about their chances of success and appeared to clearly embrace the ideals of meritocracy, the British equivalent of 'The American Dream' where effort brings rewards. Pakistani girls, having been in the UK longer and perhaps with the experiences of their families to draw on did not articulate the same confidence. In some ways the mixed aspirations of the ethnic minority girls in this study may reflect Platt's (2007) finding that Pakistani and Bangladeshi groups suffer an ethnic penalty in terms of level of attainment and potential for upward mobility. Whilst some Pakistani student's aspirations could therefore be considered as reflecting a resigned acceptance of potential future inequality, the high aspirations of other Pakistani girls could be understood as a challenge to that same inequality.

Whilst research shows that children from some ethnic minorities achieve lower levels of educational attainment than their White peers, research also suggests that 'some children with working class parents are more likely to end up in professional/managerial class families than white British people from similar origins' (Platt, 2005: 1). However, ethnic minority groups are at much greater risk of unemployment than their white counterparts. Considered in this light, the educational aspirations for higher education of the ethnic minority students included here could be considered as a risk aversive strategy, whereby educational credentials provide an indemnity to the possibility of unemployment whilst at the same time offering a route and opportunity for social mobility. As with the white students in this study, ethnic minority students viewed educational qualifications as linking with employability and job security and appeared to evaluate the risks and costs of different educational routes in these terms. However, unlike the white students, risk evaluations could also be considered as reflecting an understanding of race in the labour market, in terms of potential discrimination. As Rassool notes, some ethnic minority groups seek 'not only to challenge socio-cultural/political processes of domination but also to re-define their experiences, expectations and aspirations within everyday life and, ultimately, their position within society'(2004: 205). In this sense, the higher educational aspirations of some ethnic minority students could be considered as an individual's attempt to reflexively define their own future identity. However, whilst ethnic identities are clearly not static, it is possible that educational identities are still raced because of the implicit link between education, potential discrimination and future employment.

For the high aspirers then, education and particularly higher education was rationalized very much in terms of perceived employment benefits, that is, greater choice, better salaries and so forth. which appeared reflective of the very high value placed on education by many of the students and their families. Indeed, families were overwhelmingly cited as the main positive source of encouragement for student aspirations and for some were the site from where a sense of obligation to do well and make the most of educational opportunities was located. The findings from the ethnic minority students in this study appear to reflect the findings for white students in that a student's perception of her level of autonomy and trust within the home appears to link with self-confidence and aspirations. Whether differences in parenting practices can be explained as the result of liberal versus traditional interpretation of values, norms and expectations amongst different families of similar ethnic backgrounds (e.g. when to wear *Hijab* – see Chapter Four) is not clear. In addition, whether the cultural values and norms specific to different ethnic minority groups should be considered as ethnicized social capital as Dwyer et al. (2006) and Crozier and Davies (2006) (and implicit in Archer and Francis (2006)) suggest, is beyond the scope of this study. It is possible to speculate however, and consistent with white students, that the role of families could be considered in terms of the 'emotional capital' discussed earlier.

Whilst I would suggest that it is not always useful to dichotomize students in ethnic terms, just as it is not useful to consider aspirations in binary terms such as class, it is important nonetheless to consider the inequalities experienced by different social groups whilst, at the same time, attempting to avoid inferring normative cultural differences to explain outcomes. As this study shows, whilst some cultural disparity may explain some of the tensions within the experiences of education and differences in aspirations it does not appear to explain it all nor explain an individual's or family's interpretation of 'cultural values' for the students here. Whilst there is disparity in the educational attainment of some ethnic groups (with a possible explanation being that this is the result of a lack of skills and knowledge associated with class and social/cultural capital), that many ethnic minority students are achieving and have aspirations for higher education is clear (Modood, 2006). Understanding those aspirations however, is more complex. For example, Platt (2005) suggests that the reason that some ethnic minority students are achieving educationally and are achieving upward mobility could be the result of the downward mobility experienced by families on arrival to England. Therefore, that families may be classified now as 'working class' does not explain their aspirations and using class in the British context ignores how different backgrounds and life experience shape educational values and aspirations in the first instance. In the same way that significant disparity is evident in the levels of educational attainment of different ethnic minority groups, so difference is evident in the levels of educational aspirations within ethnic groups. It is possible that an ethnicized self-identification within the educational context explains some of the differences in the nature of aspirations of the students in this study. Research suggests that recognizing ethnic identities within schools and the curriculum has positive outcomes in raising levels of educational attainment and reducing disaffection (Mac an Ghaill, 1988; Richardson and Wood, 2004; The Runnymede Trust, no date). This would no doubt prove positive for educational aspirations also.

In light of the literature presented in Chapter Two, the findings from the students I met and spent time with appear to support, either explicitly or implicitly, the findings of other research. Discrimination, whilst not explored in any depth, does appear to matter and is consistent with the findings of Singh Ghuman (2001) and Shain (2003).Whilst not articulated in race terms, it is possible that ambitions and aspirations reflect these processes, with future plans a rationalized response. In considering the factors that impact on aspirations, for a significant proportion of ethnic minority students in this study, education and educational success is highly valued and highly prized. As Tyrer and Ahmed (2006) found, education is seen as the route for enhancing prospects and opening up choices and whilst different aspirations may be considered as reflecting individual choice resulting from a number of influences, it is possible that ethnicity is significant to these choices and that educational aspirations are a means by which, as Shain (2003) suggests, students strive to create, challenge or maintain their ethnic identities. Other ideas presented in also appear important to the aspirations of ethnic minority students such as trust, autonomy and belief in meritocracy. For example, whilst it is likely that aspirations are raced in terms of an understanding of potential future work place discrimination, perceptions of parenting might also have a bearing. Mac an Ghaill's (1988) study did not explore students' perceptions of the role of their families in his research but in this study perceptions of families appear to matter. This is because, whilst parenting practices of the Asian students did present as more protective, perceptions of trust within families still appears to matter to the same degree as for white students. Where difference is noted it is across groups and not ethnicity. Here at least, differences in students' perceptions of parental encouragement and trust appeared to differ amongst low-, mid- and high-aspiring groups rather than ethnic groups. This would support the view that it is important to understand inequality at a more micro level when seeking to understand complexity and differences in the experience of the individuals included.

Gender

Gender presented throughout as a relevant and important cornerstone of both aspirations and self-identification. Gendered ideas, in terms of the stereotypical norm of women as carers and nurturers, were predominant is both occupational choices and in terms of anticipated life course plans. Whether accepting and embracing these ideals or attempting to renegotiate, gender is clearly significant in understanding how a student's understanding of self influences and shapes aspirations and ambitions.

For the low aspirers, future identities were constructed to be ones in which children and steady relationships were predominant. For these students, self-identity appeared to be very much constructed with respect to others. For example, heterosexual relationships and being part of a couple appeared to offer an important bench mark for students' self-esteem, both in terms of how they see themselves but also, implicitly, in how they wish others to see them. For the low aspirers, traditional gendered roles appear to offer an identity to those students not achieving an educational one; for these students a gendered identity *is* attainable and implicitly appears to infer an element of social status because of its conformity to social norms. In terms of occupational aspirations, the choices of the low aspirers appear to reflect both a gendered and a classed identity, in that the occupational choices of these students reflect the typical low pay, low status employment types of working-class women, that is, child care and retail outlets.

For the middle aspirers, gender also appears just as significant to understanding aspirations because it features so predominantly in their future careers choices. For the middle aspirers, careers as nursery nurses, secretaries and hair and beauty technicians were most frequently aspired to. Future relationships also feature largely in the ambitions of middle aspirers and gendered ideas appear to underpin ideas of how their lives as adults will be. For example, whilst middle aspirers recognize their freedom to combine motherhood with a career (as opposed to remaining at home once children are produced), they also acknowledge that the responsibility of primary carer will remain theirs. Students articulated a belief that combining home and work will depend on their ability to juggle.

Finally, gender is also important for the high aspirers, albeit in different ways and is apparent in the desire of high-aspiring students to re-negotiate a future role of dependent within a relationship, to one of equality and economic independence. These views are reflected in students' aspirations for high status and high salaried occupations (which are very much associated with economic independence and greater choice) and is also explicitly demonstrated when students discuss their desire for self-reliance, that is, being able to provide for themselves. Marriage and children were also much more loosely linked to future life plans. Therefore, whilst attempting to renegotiate traditional gendered identities in future trajectories, gender remains a very powerful variable of influence in the high aspirers' aspirations because of the students' desire to challenge normative practices of gender.

For the girls I meet, gender clearly matters within student self-identification and ideas associated with gendered identities are explicitly expressed when considering the way that students present themselves. All the students in this study appeared to adopt a very feminized presentation of self and acts of grooming amongst students were common. In this sense, students appear to understand their identity as a gendered one confirmed through their external presentation of self. Bourdieu recognizes that gender is a form of social division and domination and his ideas of habitus were usefully adapted by Reay (1998b) to incorporate the idea that habitus is gendered as well as classed. When considering the aspirations of both the low and middle aspirers this concept works well in explaining why these students aspire to very gendered future identities. However, if habitus is both sub-conscious and fixed, then as a conceptual tool it does not work so well in explaining the high and middle aspirers' recognition of gender inequality, both in the public and private sphere. Beck's view that women recognize the need for self-reliance may be useful in explaining these students. Beck (1992) states that feminism has been very useful in emancipating women yet as bearers of children they will always be constrained in what they can actually achieve. This is because children pose a significant hurdle for women to overcome, in terms of their ability to compete in the labour market. Therefore, whilst greater equality in opportunities now exist for women, a lack of good, affordable child care and income disparity means that many women are not able to access the opportunities available. Whilst not articulated in these terms, these ideas do appear to underpin the aspirations of the high aspirers in that their desire for enjoyable, well paid employment permits greater freedom and independence. In relation to their views on children, it could be inferred that better occupations, with their better salaries, permit a student to pay for the good child care that will enable her to achieve this.

Class

Whilst understanding students' aspirations in class terms is clearly useful for making sense of macro patterns, this study (whilst small scale and qualitative) suggests that, for the students in this study, it is not so useful in explaining how attitudes and aspirations are shaped in the first instance. Theory of class culture and dispositions do not explain well the variation within class nor explain why some working-class girls in this study value education more highly than others. A more useful conceptualization of class would therefore be a model that considered the psychological alongside the social. This is because whilst it could be argued that considering the impact of psychological factors on attitudes and aspirations is problematic when exploring the role of social processes, I tentatively suggest that it is difficult to disengage the two. As Beck states, class as it stands is value laden yet what can classifying someone as working class really tell us? It may indicate what resources are available but not how future lives will evolve nor what individuals value. In this sense, class does appear to be a 'zombie category'. However, dismissing class as totally defunct would be to ignore the fact that social life is not equal; there is disparity in educational success, in access to resources and within gender and ethnicity. Therefore, it would possibly be more useful to consider class as a system of variability, that is, with inequality experienced individually.

In theoretical terms, the students in this study were observed to be decidedly rational in that they clearly evaluated options available to them. However, students' cost/benefit analysis appears to incorporate a psychological dimension, for example, whether it is advantageous to self-esteem or not, to continue education dependent on students' confidence they can make it as well as the inter-related link with desire for social mobility and status. In Goldthorpe's RAT model (1996) student evaluations do incorporate an analysis that considers the likelihood of success; however the affects of such assessments are less significant that the economic constraints students face. I would suggest then that integrating the psycho/social more explicitly into the RAT model would make it extremely useful for exploring and explaining aspirations. This is because it is my contention that it is this psycho/social component of evaluations that is most important, in the first instance, and that economic evaluations are of less relevance in evaluating future educational pathways. This is because whilst economic constraints may hinder the actual realization of higher educational aspirations in the final outcome, economic factors were not discussed, or were viewed as being of little importance, by the students wanting to go to university. What appeared significant to student's evaluations, in the first instance, was whether a student had confidence in her abilities to 'make it'.

As illustrated, for the students at 'Southwell', perceptions of the cultural landscape in terms of employment opportunities and labour market constraints means that post-16 options are now evaluated differently because costs, risks and employment opportunities have changed. In many respects, education and educational credentials appear to have become a new social and cultural norm. That students are evaluating education in this way is also supported in a large national survey of Year 7 students which found, quite significantly, that the majority of the young students included recognized the link between further educational qualifications and employment despite their young age (Croll et al., Continuum, 2009). What is significant therefore is, why some students evaluate the different options available to them differently, that is, higher education. Whilst it could be argued that a student's understanding of her academic ability may account for why a higher education is less risky for some than others, in terms of student's understanding of her chances of success, this was not true when considering the mixed attainment levels of some of the high-aspiring students in this study. Therefore, whilst undoubtedly relevant in choosing future educational pathways other factors identified appear as important as economic resources. For example, perceptions of parental influences (and the link with cultural and social capital) appears to be just as noteworthy as economic capital because encouragement and support appear to link significantly with self-confidence and goes some way to explaining why some students rationalize costs differently. At least in the context of this study, a desire for your children to do well, having ambitions for them or, at least, accepting and encouraging your children's ambition, appears to transcend the boundaries of class. Allowing autonomous decision making whilst keeping involved and supportive is not the preserve of specific groups and does not require money to provide it. It is perhaps here that parents with the least amount of available economic resources to invest in their children's education are able to make the greatest difference to the educational outcomes of their children; a sense of emotional encouragement and support as much as parents' cultural and social capital appears to influences aspirations, perhaps even more so. As illustrated, high-aspiring students were able to generate their own cultural and social resources, yet their ability to do this appears to depend, in part, on their perception of the emotional investment of parents.

That students appear able to recognize and compensate for deficits in cultural capital (I define cultural capital to be linguistic abilities and skills – because of the clear link between vocabulary and ability to both understand what is being taught and perform in formal examinations – as well as knowledge, for example, of the educational system) and can generate their own social capital is also important to discussions about the usefulness of class within education. This is because the idea that students can acquire more capitals in their own right is contrary to the collective nature of class posited by cultural reproduction theorists; a stance that presents young people as dependent on families for their skills, values and dispositions. That young people are able to recognize and then to strategize to maximize their cultural resources and thus their potential to do well diverges significantly from views of the nature of class based skills. Clearly, some students were pro-active in the creation of their own future identities and families appear to support them in their ambitions. A more important question would therefore be why is it that some students were able to recognize and were willing to do what they need to do to succeed whilst others do not? Ideas presented relating to practices may go some way in exploring this.

In some respects contextual differences may also be worth bearing in mind when explaining aspirations as it is possible that high aspirations reflect knowledge of the local labour market. For example, the labour market within the town in which the school is situated is distinguished by a variety and abundance of employment opportunities. How many students would have had aspirations for further or higher education if the school was situated in an area of high unemployment is not clear. However, statistics for the town relating to the number of school leavers not in employment, education or training (NEET) for April 2007 was 10 per cent. This is only slightly smaller than the national average of 10.3 per cent at the end of 2006 (Source: DfES) whilst the particular area in which the school is situated is in the top 5 per cent of areas most deprived nationally for education, skills and training (see Chapter Three).

While arguing against an over-reliance on explanatory terms such as class to explain the educational aspirations of the students included in this book, I should make it clear that I am not suggesting that social inequalities do not prohibit the achievement of ambitions. Indeed, unequal resources relating to, for example, economic capital, knowledge of the educational system and the skills necessary for educational success, were clearly evident. In addition, some of the students I met whose aspirations moved from mid to high where clearly at a disadvantage in that they lacked the skills base (although not the enthusiasm) to acquire the level of educational attainment necessary for ambitions to be met. One can only guess whether the potential for a different outcome would have been possible had higher aspirations emerged earlier in students' academic lives. To speculate more broadly, I would suggest that in achieving government targets on rates of higher education participation, it is aspirations that are significant and is what educational policy should be targeting much earlier. This is because, whilst policies and initiatives have the potential to be effective in helping students acquire the skills they lack and thus improve rates of attainment, without addressing the factors that appear to influence attitudes and aspirations, rates for participation in higher education are unlikely to change.

Chapter 7

Conclusion

At the beginning of this book I set out to understand and explain the factors that matter in the educational aspirations of the students included in this study. I wanted to know why some girls aspired to a higher education whilst others did not, even when they appeared to share so many things in common. To do this I sought to understand aspirations in terms of a student's structural situation, as well as exploring how her relationships and experiences of school shaped self-identification and consequently impacted on aspirations as well as attitudes to education. In exploring aspirations and what shapes them, several factors have been identified as relevant and whilst this research is a case study concerned with the educational aspirations of those included, as opposed to differential attainment, I tentatively suggest that several of the factors identified as important to aspirations could be important to attainment also.

In considering educational aspirations; it is perhaps self-identification that appears to be key; how a student identifies oneself within an educational context will have important consequences for how they then engage within it and their trust in meritocracy. Practices and relationships within school therefore matter because they reflect important messages to students regarding their suitability for different post-16 routes. Messages students receive within school appear to be reflected upon and rationalized in relationship to the broader social and cultural context, which students then appear to evaluate in relationship to their sense of their own abilities and likelihood of success.

In explaining the different educational and occupational aspirations of the high, middle and low aspirers, some research may suggest that aspirations reflect a student's structural location in terms of set placement within the school, with high aspirations being the result of high educational expectation from students in higher sets, whilst low aspirations reflect low expectations from students in lower set. However, this research suggests that this is not always so as some low aspirers achieved higher levels of educational attainment than high aspirers. Other factors discussed in this research interconnect and interrelate with structure to shape and reinforce educational identity, for example, perceptions of emotional support, trust and autonomy appear significant because of the apparent link with self-esteem, self-confidence and a student's desire to engage in the institutional life of the school. The psychological and social consequences of a student's perception of encouragement by parents in terms of emotional support, as well as trust and autonomy within the family, appear to relate to a student's educational values and attitudes and her belief in meritocracy. This appears to matter in terms of the evaluations she will then make of the future educational and career opportunities available to her.

In considering the relationship between class and aspirations of the students in this study, either cultural reproduction or rational action theory would readily explain the relationship between the class background and classed ambitions of the low and middle aspirers. However, neither theory appears to adequately explain the aspirations of the students who aim high. For these students, indeed all students included in this study, a slight adaptation of rational actor theory by Goldthorpe would be useful. This is because students clearly demonstrate an ability to calculate and evaluate the costs and benefits of the different options available to them. However, a student's analysis appears not determined completely on an economic basis but incorporates a psychological dimension that is shaped by social processes also. In line with Beck's assertion, students are clearly evaluating their choices reflectively and in relation to a much broader cultural landscape. In many ways, credentialization has emerged as a new social and cultural norm, with education now an important marker of identity and students recognize this. In understanding how students situate themselves within this context, it is the link between self-identity; how a student perceives oneself, and choice that appears to be important. The factors that influence a student understanding of self are fundamental to understanding a student's attitudes and what a student wants to be because it appears to impact on her ability and desire to accumulate cultural and social capital. In theoretical terms, this research suggests that educational aspirations appear to emerge through an interaction of structure and individual factors, which are reflected on individually by students. These factors shape attitudes and form a framework on which a student evaluates her suitability for the different options she could pursue. I suggest then, that whilst I do not, how class will impact on the actual realization of higher educational ambitions, in the shaping of aspirations, students included in this study appear to more individualized than classed because the practices that shape identities that then appear to influence aspirations appear to be experienced differently. However, this is not to suggest that inequality does not exert influence or is self-determined. As factors associated with ethnicity illustrate, this is clearly not so. For the ethnic minority students included in this study, ethnicity appeared to be implicitly important to their aspiration, suggesting that aspirations are raced even if not classed. That social divisions exist is also evident in the very structure of the school, the relationships within it and the ambitions and aspirations of some of the students. What I am suggesting however is that inequality for these students is contextual rather than collective and varies among individuals, in this case among individuals within the context of a school. As Savage notes, social identities are not classed identities but individual identities which 'operate relationally' (2000: 150) and in this study this appears to be the case.

In conclusion I suggest that whilst class is useful for explaining macro patterns it has less relevance as a variable for micro analysis in this research. Whilst undoubtedly complex, class as a term assumes to explain the values, norms, implicitly aspirations and consequently outcomes of particular groups. Yet in this study, class does not explain how individual biographies are experienced or how these individual experiences shape attitudes and aspirations. Therefore, whilst on an objective level class can usefully be employed to organize groups of individuals along economic lines, at the subjective level there are inherent problems when trying to make assumptions about how class may influences outcomes in terms of aspirations and ambitions. I suggest that the changing cultural context in which the young people in this study and their families live means that it is no longer possible to continue to use terms such as class for these students. This is because differences in the aspirations of the individuals included and the factors shaping them appear not to be readily explained by class. As the discussion on families influences demonstrates, that some families experience hardship appears to be a strong motivating factor behind the aspirations for social mobility of some of the students in this study. Thus, whilst class may indicate what economic resources a family has available it cannot tell us what values and aspirations a family or student has or whether ambitions and dreams will be realized. However, rejecting class to explain micro processes does not mean ignoring the social differences that result from social and economic inequality. Instead, I argue that whilst class is very powerful in explaining educational attainment, for this study understanding aspirations appears to be somewhat more complex. I suggest that the interplay of class alongside other equally important factors including for example, gender, ethnicity, levels of trust, self-confidence and self-identification has an important impact on shaping the attitudes and aspirations of the individuals included and appear to explain why some of the working-class girls believed in meritocracy and aspired more highly than others.

I conclude that in this research, whilst undeniably embedded in a social and economic context that appeared to be structured, this context is experienced individually and the degree of its impact appeared to be significantly influenced by a student's own biography. Therefore, whilst economic constraints might seriously hinder the aspirations of one student, paradoxically it compelled another to achieve. By focusing on the individual and their experiences, insight is offered that suggests that it is a student's understanding of self that offers the greatest insight into why some students in this study have aspirations for further and higher education whilst others do not. That inequality exists is without doubt and is inherent within every aspect of social life. Yet, for the students in this study, educational aspirations could not be accounted for simply by social background nor was attainment always a function of aspirations either.

Possible Implications for Schools

The following implications for schools are a response to the findings of this research:

1. Whilst a proposal to introduce personalized learning into schools is to be commended, I recommend that such a scheme encompass more than just one-to-one academic tutoring. Through my role as mentor in school what was very apparent was that some students, low aspirers particularly, required more than just educational support. Many of the girls I met (including those not part of this study) had issues that were external to school yet impacted on their capacity for learning. For some, having someone to talk to about worries and concerns became more important than the practical assistance I was there to offer. However, having someone to offer a listening ear had unintended consequences in that the students

most reticent about catching up with course work, with support, became more willing to try. Of course, such a level of support requires time and staff and raises an important question with regards to just how much we can realistically expect our schools and teachers to do. The answer to such a question would of course depend on whether the education system is about producing a future work force with the qualities and skills necessary for Britain's economy to compete in a global market, or whether education is about helping each individual achieve their maximum potential? If the answer is the latter, then it will be necessary for our educational system to expand its remit further to encompass a more holistic approach that encompasses the psycho/social as well as the intellectual needs of all its students. As the chapter on the low aspirers illustrates, there are many factors external to the school that have a bearing on a student's participation within it. A shift away from concern with league tables and achieving government and LA targets and a concentration on all individual students achieving their full potential would be profitable not just for students but also for teachers' job satisfaction. In the words of one teacher 'the GCSE league table doesn't show it all . . . it doesn't show the time I take to sit and listen to a girl who's had an argument at home or might be worried that she's pregnant . . . it doesn't show all the things we do that are just as important'. Whilst I acknowledge that it is far easier to introduce new practices than remove established ones, I would argue that a serious commitment to raising the aspirations of all children can only really ever be achieved by radical change.

2. In terms of raising aspirations, this research explicitly demonstrates the need for much earlier career advice and an overhaul of the system of work experience. That careers guidance and advice was unhelpful and not nuanced enough was almost unanimously stated by students. Many articulated a belief that careers advice, particularly with respect to making GCSE and further educational choices, was something that they would have liked to have begun thinking about much earlier in their school lives. As it stands, many of the students felt rushed and unsupported in the choices that they made. In addition, work experience placements were clearly ineffectual in providing students with an opportunity to acquire knowledge about the array of available employment opportunities. Whilst clearly enjoyed by all students, the limited type of placement offered had important consequences for some. As the chapter on the low aspirers shows, work experience placements were often a student's only access to 'careers advice'. For low aspirers with no one encouraging or promoting ambitions, important yet implicit messages are received in

terms of the type of work that these students are suitable for and should aspire to. That these jobs are predominantly low paid and low status work as nursery assistants and retail sales assistants is therefore unfortunate.

3. Practical assistance with finding out about entry requirements for college and university admissions as well as assistance with EMA eligibility and applications and the like would benefit many students. Several of the students I met where unsure of what grades were needed for example, to apply to college for a catering or child care course. In addition, some were not sure what EMA was or where to find out if they were eligible for it. Whilst information is displayed around the school, students are often uncertain and in need of directing. The same is also true for students undertaking the Universities and Colleges Admission Service (UCAS) application process. Whilst a designated member of teaching staff is available for help with application forms, students often told me that the teacher was unavailable or had little time due to many other commitments. This means that whilst students can get some feedback on Personal Statements for example, more practical help in terms of where and what to study is lacking. As illustrated in Chapter Five, many students made applications to higher education institutions that were doomed to fail. With greater support and direction it is possible that applications that better reflected both the interest and attainment of a student might have ensured that the aspirations did not falter and die.

4. In discussing some of the implications for school emerging from this research, I would like to point out that I am not criticizing the staff of 'Southwell'. During my time there it was apparent that the staff work exceptionally hard to provide as much help and support as possible to their students. As is usually the case, points two and three are therefore naturally linked to the need for greater funding and resource provision in school. If the government is seriously committed to raising both educational attainment and aspirations and see a significant rise in higher educational participation rates, then greater funding is essential.

Possible Avenues for Further Research

The following suggestions emerge from this book as potential areas for further research:

1. Emotional Capital – Emotional capital is an underused concept that has the potential to offer insights in to the role that families, particularly

parents, play in their children's education. The role of families in education is typically seen in terms of the 'hands on' practical assistance and involvement in schooling that families do or do not provide alongside the associated consequences that involvement has for educational attainment. However, this research suggests that perceptions of encouragement and support can be just as important, if not more so. In addition, research tends to focus on the significant role that mothers have in their children's schooling. This is because mothers are most often considered the primary carers of children. Yet this research suggests that student perceptions of the importance of fathers are overlooked. Future research that makes clear the conceptualization of emotional capital would make operationalizing it easier. Research with parents directly would also be both useful and interesting. The concept has potential to offer a much deeper exploration and understanding of the effect of the emotional investment of parents on students' educational outcomes.

2. Trust – The role that trust has to play, both in a student's willingness to engage in the institutional life of the school and in terms of her faith in meritocracy, would be useful to explore further. This research suggests, contrary to current conceptualizations, that trust is a pre-requisite to, rather than an outcome of, social capital. Exploring this further would be useful because of the possibilities that such an understanding would provide in the challenge to re-engage disaffected students within school.

3. Cultural Capital – It is undisputed that cultural capital matters within education. However what this research suggests is that, in line with the findings of some other work, students *are* able to generate and accumulate more cultural capital in their own right. Investigating how and why some students are able to recognize shortfalls and attempt to compensate for them, whilst others do not, would be useful. Exploring this further has practical implications for the drive to raise the GCSE attainment rates of lower achieving schools and individual students.

4. Work Experience and Career Advice – The impact that work experience and career advice had on the ambitions and aspirations of the low-aspiring students in this study was significant. I suggest then that this is an area for further research. From students' narratives, careers advice and work experience appeared to be both gendered and classed (when operationalized in terms of the skill and pay). Whether this finding is generalizable or not and whether it would apply to all or just some schools would be worth exploring, as would the link between careers

guidance, work experience placement and young people's future occupational aspirations. If future research findings were consistent with the findings of this research, the recommendation I make for an overhaul of the career guidance and work experience placement scheme would be much more justifiable.

Appendix 1

The Participants

I present here a list of some the key students in this study. Whilst I spent a lot of time with many students, the following are those for whom the most amount of background information was available (see Tables 1, 2 and 3).

Explanatory Notes to Tables 1, 2 and 3

1. Information on family occupational and educational background is based on student information.
2. Key stage 2 average points: This score is derived from compulsory SAT tests taken in Year 6 (primary school). Keystage 2 average score is thus a measure of attainment at point of entry to secondary school, in Year 7. For information, grade 4 is the level expected with grade 4b denoting the expected target, 4c slightly below the expected target and 4a slightly above the expected target. Grade 5 is an above average score. For students in Year 12 a single grade is given. Information was not available for all students.
3. Predicted number of GCSE grades at A–C is based on compulsory SAT tests taken in Year 9 (Keystage 3).
4. Success at GCSE is measured by a bench marker, with 5 grades at A–C for GCSE considered as successful. Actual GCSE attainment is not available for Year 12 students.
5. Aspirations reflect students' intention prior to actual GCSE or A/S attainment.

Table 1 Low aspirers – Year 10

Name	Set	Ethnicity	Parental occupation	Parents/ family educational background	Keystage 2 average points (Year 7)	Predicted number of A–C at GCSE – based on keystage 3 results – Year 10	Level of attainment at GCSE – Year 11	Post-16 outcome	Whether in receipt of EMA/FSM
Nicola	Three	White	Father: Lorry driver Step mother: Sales assistant at a retail outlet	No one who continued in further education	3a	5	3.5 A–C	Left school Whereabouts not known	N/A
Lilly	Four	Black-African	Lives with foster family Occupation unknown	N/K	Not available	4	No grades at A–C	NEET	N/A
Jennifer	Two	White	Mother: Unemployed	Did not continue	4c	8	7 A–C	Left to work in a shoe shop	N/A
Lauren	Four	White	Mother and step-father: Both part-time cleaners	No one who continued	4b	4	1 C	NEET	N/A
Leanne	Four	Mixed race	Mother: Does not work	N/K	4a	4	No grades at A–C	Left school Whereabouts unknown	N/A
Mary-Anne	One	White	Father and step family: Father: Building labourer M: Not known	Father did not continue Mother: N/K	4a	9	6 grades at A–C	Left school Whereabouts unknown	FSM
Samantha	Three	White	M: Secretary F: Delivery driver	No one who continued	4b	5	4 A–C	Left to work in retail outlet	FSM

Note. NEET: Not in education, employment or training; N/K: Not known; N/A: Not available.

Table 1 Summary

The table for low aspirers shows the set, ethnicity and parental background of the students grouped into this category. Whilst the majority of students are white, the family background of students, where known (in terms of parental occupation and education), are similar. As might be expected, the majority of these students are drawn from sets three and four, except for Mary-Anne who is in set one and Jennifer, set two. Whilst the predicted number of GCSE A–C grades of three of the students fall below the target level of five, this is not so for four students, two of whom were predicted to do well with targets of eight and nine and two predicted to achieve five GCSE A–C grades. In terms of actual grades achieved, the post-16 outcomes of Lilly, Leanne or Lauren might be as expected in that low achievement leads to low aspirations and outcomes. However, the grades of Jennifer, Mary-Anne and Samantha (as a border line) and post-16 outcome are not as might be predicted as these students left education despite achieving well (compared to middle and high aspirers). Neither Lilly nor Leanne achieved any grades at GCSE despite being predicted to achieve four. Lauren, also predicted to achieve four, managed only one.

Table 2 Middle aspirers

Name	Set	Ethnicity	Parental occupation	Parents/ family educational background	Keystage 2 average points (Year 7)	Predicted number of A–C at GCSE based on keystage 3 results – Year 10	Level of attainment GCSE or Advanced – Year 11 or 12/13	Post-16/18 outcome	Whether in receipt of EMA/FSM
Lisa	Year 12	White	Mother: community care assistant Father: Not known	Not known	4	4	Left	Working in pharmacy	EMA
Ruby	Year 12	White	Mother: Works in retail outlet in town centre	Mother did not continue. Rest of family not known	5	6	Left	Not known	EMA
Sandy	Year 12	Black-African	Mother: Cleaner	Older sister training as nurse	N/A	6	B,C, D at A2	Working for pharmacy assistant certificate	EMA
Seema	Year 12	Asian	Father: Taxi driver Mother: Does not work	No one in family continued	N/A	4	E, E, D at A2	Attended sixth form, moved to London with family	N/K

Rene	Year 12	White European	Neither parent works	No one who continued	N/A	4	B,B, C at A2	Believed to be working	FSM
Shazia (sister of Momena)	Year 12	Asian	Father: Taxi driver Mother: Housewife	Brother attended university	N/A	1	Left end of year 13 before taking exams	Attended sixth form, NEET	EMA
Momena (sister of Shazia)	Two	Asian	Father: Taxi driver Mother: Housewife	Brother attended university	N/A	4	1 C GCSE	Attending sixth form	N/K
Helen	Three	White	Not known	No one who continued	3a	1	2 A-C GCSE	Catering course at college	N/K
Raheela	Three	Asian	Father: Taxi driver Mother: House wife	No one who continued	N/A	6	3 A-C GCSE	Local college	N/K
Abby	Four	White	Mother: Housewife Father: Not known	Not known	3c	2	No grades at A-C	Hairdressing apprenticeship	N/K

Note: NEET: Not in education, employment or training; N/A: Not Available; N/K: Not known.

Table 2 Summary

The middle aspirers include students from Years 12/13 and 10/11. Set is not known for Year 12/13. Whilst parental occupation is similar to the low aspirers, three of the students included have some family knowledge of further education: the two sisters have an older brother who attended university (but has yet to find employment) whilst Sandy has an older sister training to be a nurse. Based on target grades at GCSE, three students were predicted to exceed the target of five A–Cs, seven to miss them. Where GCSE's achieved is known, post-16 outcome is not as expected when compared to low aspirers. This is because the three students who achieved low grades have remained in education. In addition, the outcomes of both Rene and Sandy are also not as might be expected given their success at A2 level (when compared to high aspirers).

Table 3 High aspirers

Name	Set	Ethnicity	Parental occupation	Parents/family educational background	Keystage 2 average points (Year 7)	Predicted number of A–C at GCSE – based on key stage 3 results – Year 10	Level of attainment GCSE or Advanced level – Year 11 or 12/13	Post-16/18 outcome	Whether in receipt of EMA/FSM
Wafa	Three	Asian	Father: Taxi driver Mother: Housewife	No one in family	4c	2	D, E, U at A/S	Stayed on at current school – applied to London university	N/K
Nasrat	Three	Asian	Father: Taxi driver Mother: Housewife	Older brother attending college	Not available	3	A, E, U at A/S	Stayed on at current school – applied to local university	FSM
Deborah	One	Mixed race	Father: Cleaner Mother: Cleaner	Neither parent continued education	4a	10	10 A–C GCSE	Moved to further education college some distance from home – Accepted Southampton	EMA
Emily	One	White	Father: Works with glass Mother: Quit smoking counsellor	Father: Did not continue Mother: Not known	4a	10	7 A–C GCSE	Moved to further education college some distance from home – Accepted to Brighton	N/K

Continued

Table 3 Continued

Name	Set	Ethnicity	Parental occupation	Parents/family educational background	Keystage 2 average points (Year 7)	Predicted number of A–C at GCSE – based on key stage 3 results – Year 10	Level of attainment GCSE or Advanced level – Year 11 or 12/13	Post-16/18 outcome	Whether in receipt of EMA/FSM
Stephanie	One	White	Brother: Builder	Brother did not continue Rest of family not known	4a	10	8 A–C GCSE	Further education some distance from home – Accepted to Brighton	N/K
Fatima	Four	Black-African	Mother: Does not work	Mother did not continue Uncle went to college	Not available	4	2 A–C GCSE E, U, U at A/S	Studied at current school – offer received for Twickenham university	EMA
Sahara	Year 12	Asian	Not known	Not known	4	8	A, B, B at A2	Attending local university	N/K
Lotte	Year 12	Mixed race	Not known	Father attending college in evenings with aim to go to university	5	8	D, D, D at A/S	Left to study at local college at end of Year 12	No

Note: N/K: Not known.

In addition,

Student A – Black-African, applied to Oxford, predicted four A–Cs at GCSE, E and U at A2. Application rejected, student left for employment.

Student B – Black-African, (joined sixth form) applied to Oxford, C, E and U at A/S. Application rejected, student left for employment.

Student C – Black-African (joined sixth form), applied to Oxford E, U and U at A/S. Application rejected, student left for employment.

Table 3 Summary

The high aspirers include students from Year 12/13 and 10/11 and share similar backgrounds to the low and middle aspirers. Of the high aspirers, two have family members who have experienced further education; one studying at evening class with the intention to go on into higher education. Whilst the aspirations for higher education might be as predicted for the students in set one and Year 12, based on target and actual grades, this is not true of three of the students included in this category. Wafa, Nasrat and Fatima were not predicted to do well at GCSE and did not achieve particularly well in their actual attainment at A/S. However, all three of these students have still applied to a university. The same is also true for the additional three students for whom family background information was not available.

Background Summary of the three groups of aspirers

In Chapters 3–5 data was presented for low, middle and high aspirers, defined by their educational intentions at 16 and 18. The purpose of this small scale qualitative study is to explore the perceptions of these particular students and to consider how these perspectives on family, school and so on may relate to aspirations. It is not intended to generalize to a population of young women with regard to explaining educational plans. Nevertheless, it is still important to consider other possible differences between the three group in terms of social characteristics and levels of attainment which may relate to differences in aspirations. The initial aim of the study was to look at differences in aspirations of girls from similar social backgrounds and educational attainments so the extent of similarity between the three groups needs to be examined. Data relevant to this are presented in Tables 1, 2 and 3.

The socio-economic status or social class of the families of the girls in the study are given in the tables where available. In nearly all cases, for all three groups, the parents are either in manual occupations or are unemployed. This is true for all but one of the low aspirers, all but one of the middle aspirers and all but one of the high aspirers. In no cases are families in clearly middle-class occupations. It seems fair to conclude that, in terms of occupationally defined social class, the three groups are similar.

A second issue is with regard to attainment. Aspirations may be the result of the experience of educational success or failure. The relationship though may be complex as having particular types of aspiration may influence attitude and effort in regard to school work. Aspirations may both influence attainment and be influenced by it. For this reason, two measures of attainment have been considered of particular relevance. The first is the Key stage 2 results, based on tests taken at the end of primary education. This is an attainment measure which cannot be influenced by experiences at the secondary school. The second is the school's prediction of likely GCSE outcomes. This gives an indication of how teacher view the students and does not reflect decisions the girls may take at the time of the examination, for example, not turning up or not trying, which in turn may be the result of aspirations. For the low aspirers, five had fours at Key stage 2 (the expected level) and one a three (below expected). For the middle aspirers one had a three, one a four and one a five. For the high aspirers, five had fours and one a five (above expected). In the case of predicted GCSEs, four out of seven low aspirers were predicted five at C and above, three out of nine middle aspirers were predicted this outcome and five out of eight high aspirers were predicted five C+s. Overall it seems that the three groups entered the school with very similar levels of achievement centred around level four at Key stage 2. The school's view of their academic performance somewhat favours the high aspirers in terms of predicted achievement but only to a small extent and, for example, four of the low aspirers were predicted to do better than three of the high aspirers. So, while attainment is relevant to aspiration, it does not determine it.

Data are also provided in the tables about the ethnicity of the girls in the three groups. With a small sample like this it is not possible to do justice to the complexities of ethnic identity. However, non-white pupils predominated in the high and middle aspirer groups (six out of eight and five out of nine respectively) while they were under-represented among the low aspirers with two out of seven. These are very small numbers and it is clear that White and non-white pupils are represented in all three groups and that the middle and high aspirers are very similar in their ethnic make up.

Appendix 2

Research Methodology

For those with an interest, I extend here the discussion of the research methods used and provide additional information relating to the school, research methods, how key concepts were operationalized as well as issues encountered.

The Case

In February 2005 the school underwent an OfSTED inspection. These inspections occur once every six to eight years and are carried out to assess the performance of a school under various criteria, for example, how high are the standards of education, how well is the school managed and so on. The results of the inspection deemed 'Southwell' to be unsatisfactory and failing, with problems identified of a severe enough nature to warrant it being placed on Special Measures.[1] Primarily, weaknesses were identified in teaching, educational attainment, effectiveness of the school management and having unacceptably high levels of absenteeism/truancy. However, the school was deemed as successful in its sixth form and for promoting racial and cultural tolerance and for acknowledging religious diversity. As part of the process of being placed on Special Measures, the school had to undergo many subsequent visits and the findings from these visits were published as Monitoring Letters. Whilst this period was undoubtedly stressful for both the staff and the students, this turbulent period in the school's life provided me with a good research opportunity, most notably in terms of watching the school transform. In June 2006 the school was removed from Special Measures, six months ahead of schedule.

Student Selection

Students were selected on the basis of their willingness to participate, following an address to each tutor group. Among these volunteers, I initially obtained a sample of 45 volunteer students (26 in Year 10 and 19 in Year 12). Some of the original volunteers were lost from the study after only one meeting, whilst many more new students who became aware of what I was doing through friends joined throughout the course of my time in school. In total, I meet or spoke with more than 60 students. From these students there was a core of 25 students with whom I met most regularly. These included students from across the four main streams in the school, with a broad mix of high and under achieving students. Core students were those students I spent a significant amount of time with. However, there were also many other students I also spent large amounts of time with. As I was not able to collect the same level of background information I have not counted these as core students nor used them in the key analysis. However, as I did know these students' intentions, comments drawn from focus groups discussions are still included to illustrate points raised.

Of those students included from Year 10 through 11: nine were white, four Pakistani Asian, two mixed race, two black-African and from Years 12 through 13: three were white, three were Pakistani-Asian, one mixed race and one Black-African. This sample of students is not statistically represen-tative and issues of student self-selection bias that arise are worth bearing in mind. For example, as my sampling approach was that of convenience sampling, that is, a sample drawn from those who were willing to participate amongst those to whom I had access (Cohen et al., 2001), then issues arise concerning potential differences between those students who were willing to participate and those who were not. Some of this bias, however, may have been countered by a connection I had with a student who was a member of my target year group, Year 10.[2] To illustrate, I entered one tutor group and explained my research and then asked if there were any volunteers. The silence was deafening. No one expressed an interest and the non-response was causing some amusement. Just as I was about to thank the class and leave, one student piped up 'hey, do you know Sarah?' When I replied that I did, the student put her hand up and said 'Okay, I'll be in it then, she said you was alright'. This student was soon followed by many more. In this instance, potential non-participation was countered by the fact that stu-dents had prior knowledge of me, provided by one of their peers.

Participant

In addition to my role as 'researcher' in school, I also acted as mentor to groups of Year 11 students, some of whom were included in my study.

The mentoring of students was one of a number of initiatives the school adopted to try and raise the aspirations of its students (e.g. inclusion in the Government Aim Higher scheme). Mentoring involved meeting with students and helping them with issues such as planning revision schedules, catching up with course work, going through college prospectuses, finding out information regarding EMA or, in some cases, just being someone to chat to. Involving myself in school in this way helped create a sense of reciprocity, that is, my role in school had a value in the eyes of teaching staff outside that of simply 'researcher'. I mentored for the duration of the study and have continued to do so even after my time in the field was formally over. Data from the mentoring session are included in the results but only for those students who were already involved in the study when they reached Year 11. Whilst for ethical reasons I have not included information from those students who were not participating, some of their comments were useful in terms of directing my own thinking. In addition to mentoring, I also ran some informal sociology revision classes for sixth form students and continue to support some of my original participants in this way.

Analysing the data

The relationship between social class or SES and various aspects of educational participation and attainment has been a central feature of the sociology of education. It is also an important aspect of the questions being considered in this book. As was shown earlier, the school being studied serves a relatively disadvantaged part of the town in which it is located, although the town overall is prosperous. It is therefore likely that the girls who are the subject of this study will themselves come from relatively less advantaged social and economic backgrounds. However, this cannot be simply assumed and it is important to establish empirically the socioeconomic circumstances of their families. As well as providing an overview of the class background of the sample as a whole, it is also important to consider possible socio-economic differences between the girls who have been placed in different categories, for analytical purposes, with regard to their educational aspirations.

There is a variety of approaches to classifying and measuring social class as discussed by, for example, Crompton (1998). She distinguishes between what she calls the 'common sense' schemes such as the Registrar General's based upon a hierarchy of rewards and status, subjective scales of occupational rankings and schemes such as that of John Goldthorpe's CASMIN scheme (Devine, 1997; Crompton, 1998) which attempt to address theoretical ideas in sociology (in particular those associated with Marx and Weber) and to incorporate notions of class relations. However, what all these schemes have in common is that they are based on occupation and that they incorporate a distinction between manual and non-manual occupations as one of the key dividing points in the scale. As Crompton puts it, occupational schemes generally '. . . assume that occupations involve a set of typical work activities which are then classified into . . . first, the level of skill and qualifications involved and second, the nature of the work activities . . . [despite changes] occupational class schemes used by government departments have remained remarkably similar . . . managerial and professional occupations at the top and unskilled workers at the bottom' (1998: 60). While non-manual occupations are sometimes sub-divided in class terms (including 'intermediate' classes and higher and lower managerial) (Crompton, 1998; Rose and Pevalin, 2002) manual occupations are normally described as 'working class' when class terminology is employed (e.g. Ball, 2003).

This basic distinction between manual and non-manual occupations was followed in the present study and for the purpose of classifying the social economic background of the students in this research students were grouped broadly into those from manual and non-manual occupations. This approach follows the division common to most socio-economic classifications and is consistent with official figures cited in this study and elsewhere. The approach also recognizes that in a small scale study like this, focusing on relatively few students, it was not possible to address issues of different class fractions or the complexity of some of the more recent socio-economic classifications (e.g. Rose and Pevalin, 2002). For this reason, students from non-manual backgrounds were excluded from the study on the basis that there were too few of them for meaningful comparison with other students to be made (three students were excluded in this way whose parents were a teacher, an engineer and a GP).

Details of the occupations of parents of girls in the study are given in the appendix (Tables 1–3). The data presented are based on the reports of the girls themselves and are, of course, dependent on the girls knowing the occupations of their parents. There are a few instances where the occupations are unknown. The data also reflect some of the issues with using classification schemes, for example, with the complexity of classifying women into these schemes. The 'traditional' view (e.g. Goldthorpe 1983; Roberts, 2001) that the social class of a family is determined by the occupation of the (male) head of household has been widely challenged (Roberts, 2001). Where the occupations of partners differ, families have sometimes been characterized as 'cross class' (Heath and Britten, 1984). A common approach is to use the 'dominance' approach where the family is categorized according to the occupation of the partner in the more advantaged situation (Rose and Pevalin, 2002). Of course, this has the consequence of shifting upwards the proportions of families in particular socio-economic situations.

The present study is on a small enough scale for exact occupations to be reported for the parents of the girls in the study and this is done in Tables 1–3 in Appendix 1. For the reasons given above, girls whose families were clearly not in manual occupations have been excluded. The situations of those whose parents had occupations which may have led to a different classification and those whose parents did not work are discussed below.

To a limited extent, other data related to socio-economic circumstances is also available. Being in receipt of EMA[3] or Free School Meals (FSM) is also a useful measure of social deprivation. Unfortunately in this study ability to attain this information was largely dependent on what a student was willing to share. As the school was reluctant to divulge personal information as to which students were in receipt of FSM (and because of potential sensitivity around the question) data on FSM[4] was only obtained from four students. In this study I am therefore unable to utilize EMA or FSM in my basic classification of the SES of students due to the incomplete data available. However, where data is available it is used to check and support the classification of students.

Categorizing Students

A key analytical category used in the study is that of aspirations, especially aspirations applied to education. In the three substantive chapters, the girls studied have been categorized as 'low', 'middle' and 'high' aspirers. The notion of aspiration is intertwined with a complex of other responses to education and other aspects of their lives including attitudes to school and aims for careers and family. These in turn were, at least potentially, related to ideas about gender and ethnicity and to family relationships. In order to make sense of the emerging interview and other material, data was analysed both theoretically and empirically and was explored in terms of patterns. Adopting this approach was extremely useful as, after initially organizing students along the lines of how they felt about school, clear themes and similarities began to emerge in other ideas referred to, for example, around gender and future careers, as well as in future intentions. For example, those that felt most negative about school also intended to leave at 16, whilst those that were most positive also intended to go to university. However, whilst in general a coherent set of responses emerged in terms of patterns in attitudes and ideas, there was also a complexity of responses and attitudes, intentions and so on, that did not always fit together neatly. For example, not all students wanting to leave school at 16 were negative about education, whilst not all students intending a higher education were positive about school. Moreover, many aspects of responses should be seen as a continuum rather than a clear categorization. Students varied in their levels of response to school rather than being in pro- and anti-school groups.

The one dimension on which girls could be clearly distinguished into groups was with regard to educational intentions at 16 and then at 18. Consequently, students were classified into groups of 'low aspirers', 'middle aspirers' and 'high aspirers' on the basis of planning to leave at 16, planning to leave at 18 and planning to go on into higher education. Whilst students could have been organized into groups labelled in a variety of ways, classifying students based on their intentions seemed the most appropriate approach, despite the complexity, because of the very clear differences amongst students that was evident in terms of what they actually intended to do. Yet, whilst categories clearly represent aspirations, they also reflect the attitudes and ideas within groups more generally. For example, most of the students classified as 'low aspirers' made direct negative references to education as: 'pointless', 'useless', or 'not important'. Other more implicit indicators that related to issues around self-esteem and so on also demonstrate patterns. However as already noted, despite similarities, some variations were noted in ideas and attitudes, and attitudes are undoubtedly complex. Thus, whilst aspirations are clearly reflective of intentions, the attitudes of students within groups should not be considered as very clear and distinct groups. Naturally the approach I have taken relies on researcher judgement. However, the approach of 'analytic induction' is what enabled my categories to emerge, confirming the usefulness of the three way classification and these proved extremely useful for the theoretical analysis and presentation of my data where, within these groups, aspirations and variations are then explored in more depth.

Research Issues

Foster et al. (2000) caution against using case studies as a means for making evaluative and/or value judgements on the basis of assumed consensus[5] and this is something I have tried to take into account throughout. However invariably they are issues that, given the nature of the study, arise and some of these I address here.

Participant and Observer

The biggest issue I encountered initially was, surprisingly, with me. As a 'mature' white woman studying at university, as far as was apparent to most of the students, all we shared in common was our gender. For example, that my age might be a problem was never expressed explicitly but was inferred indirectly, for example, through deference or, by stating things such as 'it's harder when you're older [going back to education] . . . oh! no disrespect to you miss'. Largely, however, it appeared most apparently in students' difficulty and reluctance to call me simply 'Carol'. (In the end we did achieve it!) I believed that building relationships was an important aspect for any in-depth qualitative research and to do this, participants and researchers need to be able to connect with one another on some intrinsic level. I realized then that, if I was going to be able to achieve this, I would need to share something of myself in order for students to feel some sense of commonality with me. Sharing of oneself has a certain vulnerability attached to it; however, the decision proved to be the correct one and significantly enhanced the connections I made with the students. For example, students were incredulous when I informed them that my own experience of secondary schooling was one of disengagement and dissatisfaction, with 'but you're really clever miss, 'cause you're at university, what did you do? How come you're at university now?' This knowledge was particularly useful for those students categorized as 'low aspirers' because it enabled them to be less self-conscious and more open when they described their own attitudes and experiences. The fact that I had shared their feelings at one time primarily facilitated a sense for students that 'I understood'. Conversely, the fact that I was at university was also useful with the high aspirers too. I was someone who was perceived as sharing the same values and aspirations as themselves, that is, in terms of higher education and, having grown up in the same neighbourhood, I was an example of someone who was realizing their ambitions. However, the information I shared that had the biggest impact on students' abilities to relate to me was the knowledge that I too had been a student at their school.[6]

In terms of my age and ethnicity, these factors remained beyond my control. In fact my age did became a source of fun and students would appear to take pleasure in educating me, for example, through exploring with me the relative merits of Tupac versus Snoop Doggy Dog or, by explaining what a 'chav'[7] was, whilst differences in ethnicity meant that I was perceived as being open to learning. For example, students would assume I would not understand their culture and thus would explain it to me. Whilst researcher symmetry is useful, as Vincent and Warren note (2001), in creating 'sameness' between researcher and researched, asymmetry proved to be just as useful in that by retaining an element of 'the stranger within' (2001: 44), deeper exploration was possible. Whilst I endeavoured to connect to the students in my study, an important difference was always present, that is, I was an adult. Despite this, I came to learn that it was my interest in the student that appeared to matter most: my attention, my concern and my ability to listen. However, it is this that also created another important issue for me.

Letting Go

Whilst spending a reasonable period of time in the field is useful for observing changes in attitudes and behaviour and so on over time, it also means that relationships of affection are more likely to occur. Time encourages familiarity and invariably, whilst you wrestle to retain an element of objectivity, you do come to care for your respondents. I have lost count of the number of times I have gone home and lain awake at night wondering whether X was alright or, whether Y had performed well in her exam. However, learning when to let go or stand back was what I found hardest. An example of this was when I discovered that Lilly had been thrown out of her foster carer's home (see Chapter Three), my instinct had been to offer her a home. I knew, however, that this was not realistic for either Lilly or myself yet my anxiety for her was overwhelming. Another example relates to students behind on GCSE course work. To avoid their getting in to trouble for non-completion, my instinct was to do more than I should to help them. Whilst I was largely able to refrain from doing so, there were occasions when I know I did more than I should have, that is, buying materials and equipment, providing guidance and advice on what to write and so on. The hardest point in the research came, however, when it was time to say goodbye. Whilst for many of those in my study this was not a problem, some expressed anxiety at not seeing me any more. Some of these students took my email address and some my mobile number and have remained in infrequent contact with me. Others who were moving on in to the sixth form sought reassurance that I would still come and visit them there. This I agreed to do. My agreement came from a genuine desire to retain contact but also from a sense of moral obligation. To spend a long time building relationships with people in a quest for knowledge and then simply abandon them when one has what one wants is plainly wrong.

The Outsider

One of the difficulties I experienced during the course of my time in school was the sense I often had of 'being on the outside'. Whilst this was never an issue for me when I spent time with students, it was something I often felt quite acutely when in the staff room. Having been formally introduced during a staff meeting, most staff were fully aware of why I was in school and thus, as a consequence, I felt I was often viewed with suspicion. For example, staff would be talking but would cease when I sat down or when they were alerted to the fact I was there. This meant that I often felt very hesitant about asking questions or doing anything other than observation. With time and familiarity however, attitudes towards me did thaw and, in some cases, became positively friendly. This resulted in staff becoming more open with me and less guarded. With time to reflect I have come to feel that whilst it may have been perfectly natural for staff to feel suspicious of someone doing research in school, the teachers at 'Southwell' may have had more justification for feeling so as they were already under pressure of public scrutiny due to the OfSTED inspection and subsequent monitoring visits.

Being an outsider in research has its advantages in that it helps to retain objectivity; however, moving closer has its rewards for research also. In this research, becoming participant through my role as mentor was fundamental to my tentative acceptance by staff into school. Becoming a participant in this way, by supporting and liaising with staff meant that my role in school became meaningful and gained legitimacy. Staff would express gratitude when I supported students to complete work for their classes and moving from observer to participant had the added advantage of allowing me to explore to some small degree the enormous pressure staff are under. For example, heavy curriculum demands mean that staff have very little time to do more than teach in the first instance. Whilst assistance is there for students that fall behind, it appears that there is little staff can do for students who require more one to one support (for any number of reasons) to get them back up to date (for an example, see Leanne, Chapter Three). The usefulness of becoming participant in case study research is clearly evident, where my mentoring of Leanne altered the expected outcome for her in terms of her GCSE child care course, that is, she went from non-attendance in class and no course work completed to handing it all in, apologizing to the teacher for her past behaviour and getting a letter of praise sent home. Participation in this way afforded me an opportunity to see both perspectives, that is, the pressure the teacher was under in terms of 'getting it all done'; the pressure the student felt which led to a break down in their relationship and her self-imposed opting out;[8] and the all round relief both felt when her work was completed. Being a participant as well as an observer in research thus allows a greater depth to data but it also facilitates a tentative acceptance of those that are important to your research because they allow you to be there.

A Note about Ethics

This research was subject to approval of both the head and my liaison teacher within the school and the University Ethics committee. Research was carried out only with those students who had volunteered to take part and, in addition, parental consent was sought for those students under the age of 16. All participants were given an information sheet to retain for themselves and were periodically reminded that they were free to withdraw at any time. This point was made particularly clear to those students whom I also mentored, whom I frequently reassured of my continued assistance should they choose to leave the study.

As trust is an important element of any research I consciously decided, during the course of my study, to avoid sensitive issues or topics that may have required, ethically and morally, that I report a student. Issues of drug use, under-age sexual relationships and drinking were therefore avoided during interviews and focus groups. When these issues were touched on, it was at the instigation of the student. However, as students either referred to these topics in relationship to others or spoke of past incidents, for example of getting drunk, no particular ethical issues were raised. When concerns regarding students did arise, I did not hesitate in immediately informing the appropriate member of staff (the student concerned would also be informed that I would be doing so). For an example of one such incident see Lauren in Chapter Three. Finally, prior to field work commencing and at my own instigation, I obtained Disclosure[9] clearance and provided the school with a copy for their records.

Notes

1 Being placed on 'Special Measures' has important consequences for schools in that should they fail to make significant improvement within a two year time frame, they can be closed.

2 Due to ethical issues, this student was not included in my study.

3 EMA is not a perfect measure due to variation in income eligibility and the impact this then has on the award received.

4 For Hobbes and Vignoles (2007) using FSM as a measure of SES is inherently difficult. This is because 'FSM is a measure of claiming FSM rather than eligibility for FSM' (Hobbes and Vignoles, 2007: 3) and is therefore considered an unreliable measure of low income.

5 Foster, Gomm and Hammersley illustrate an application of value evaluations within the study of educational inequality. They state that the term is often used to refer to either a fact or a difference. Typically though, it is used negatively. Foster, Gomm and Hammersley argue that it is false to assume that all inequality is unjust/negative. For example, they illustrate that the policy for equal opportunities for pupils with special educational needs requires extra funding per head than for other children of the same age. They argue that 'equality in one sense is achieved only at the expense of inequality in others' (2000: 217). Therefore, they caution against the use of descriptive words laden with value messages.

6 I believe that it was the fact that I was a past student at the school when the current head taught as a maths teacher that facilitated my access. The head believed that I would serve as a role model to students and this would be a positive thing with an OfSTED inspection looming. I am not sure that I would have been so fortunate in my access without this connection and past history.

7 Chav or Charv/Charver *('ch' pronounced as in chair)* is a mainly derogatory slang term in the United Kingdom for a sub-cultural stereotype fixated on fashions such as gold jewellery and 'designer' clothing. They are generally considered to have no respect for society, and be ignorant or unintelligent. (Source: http://en. wikipedia.org/wiki/Chav accessed April 2007.)

8 Non-completion was a common response of low-aspiring students who often felt overwhelmed with the amount of work they had to do. This was then exacerbated by confusion and uncertainty about what actually was expected. 'Not wanting to look stupid' was often implied as a reason why support was not sought by the students. This then creates a vicious cycle that sees students getting further and further behind.

9 'Disclosure' is the process whereby a person's criminal history is checked with the Criminal Records Bureau. Following several high profile cases of convicted sex offenders gaining work in schools, it is now a legal requirement that all staff (and volunteers) have police clearance.

Bibliography

Ahmed, F. (2001), Modern Traditions? British Muslim Women and Academic Achievement. *Gender and Education,* Vol. 13, No. 2.

Archer, L. and Francis, B. (2006), Challenging Classes? Exploring the Role of Social Class within the Identities and Achievement of British Chinese Pupils. *Sociology,* Vol. 40, No. 4.

Archer, L. and Hutchings, M. (2000), 'Bettering Yourself'? Discourse of Risk, Cost and Benefit in Ethnically Diverse, Young, Working Class Non-participants' Constructions of Higher Education. *British Journal of Sociology of Education,* Vol. 21, No. 4.

Arnot, M., David, M. and Weiner, G. (1999), *Closing the Gender Gap: Post-war Education and Social Change.* Cambridge: Polity Press.

Atkinson, W. (2007), Beck, Individualisation and the Death of Class: A Critique. *The British Journal of Sociology,* Vol. 58, No. 3.

Attwood, G. and Croll, P. (2006), Truancy in Secondary School Pupils: Prevalence, Trajectories and Pupil Perspectives. *Research Papers in Education,* Vol. 21, No. 4 (December).

Ball, S. J. (1981), *Beachside Comprehensive: A Case Study of Secondary Schooling.* Cambridge: Cambridge University Press.

Ball, S. J. (1990), *Politics and Policy Making in Education.* London: Routledge.

Ball, S. J. (2003), *Class Strategies and the Education Market: The Middle Classes and Social Advantage.* London: Routledge Falmer

Bandura, A., Barbaranelli, C., Caprara, G.V. and Pastorelli, C. (2001), Self-Efficacy Beliefs as Shapers of Children's Aspirations and Career Trajectories. *Child Development,* Vol. 72, No. 1.

Basit, T. N. (1996), 'I'd Hate to be just a Housewife': Career Aspirations of British Muslim Girls. *British Journal of Guidance and Counselling,* Vol. 24, No. 2.

Basit, T. N. (1997), 'I want more Freedom, but Not Too Much': British Muslim Girls and the Dynamism of Family Values. *Gender and Education,* Vol. 9, No. 4.

Battu, H. and Sloane, P. J. (2004), Over-Education and Ethnic Minorities in Britain. *The Manchester School,* Vol. 72, No. 4.

Beck, U. (1992), *Risk Society: Towards a New Modernity.* London, Thousand Oaks and New Delhi: Sage Publications.

Beck, U. and Beck-Gernsheim, E. (2001), *Individualization.* London, Thousand Oaks and New Delhi: Sage Publications.

BERA, (2007), *Research Uncovers Social-Class Bias in School Setting Decisions.* Press Release, September.

Berger, P. L., Berger, B. and Kellner, H. (1973), *The Homeless Mind.* London: Penguin Books.

Bernstein, B. (1971), *Class, Codes and Control*. London: Paladin.

Bhavnani, R. (2006), *Ahead of the Game: The Changing Aspirations of Young Ethnic Minority Women*. United Kingdom: Equal Opportunities Commission.

Biggart, A. (2002), Attainment, Gender and Minimum-aged School Leavers' Early Routes in the Labour Market. *Journal of Education and Work*, Vol. 15, No. 2.

Boeck, T. (2007), *Young People, Social Capital and the Navigation of the Life Course*. London: DfES Youth Strategy Review.

Bogenschnieder, K. (1997), Parental Involvement in Adolescent Schooling: A Proximal Process with Transcontextual Validity. *Journal of Marriage and Family*, Vol. 59, No. 3 (August).

Boudon, R. (1974), *Education, Opportunity, and Social Inequality: Changing Prospects in Western Society*. New York, London, Sydney and Toronto: John Wiley and Sons.

Bourdieu, P. (1977), *Outline of a Theory of Practise*. Cambridge: Cambridge University Press.

Bourdieu, P. (1997), In: *Education, Culture, Economy, Society*, (Halsey, A. H., Lauder, H., Brown, P. and Stuart Wells, eds), The Forms of Social Capital. Oxford: Oxford University Press.

Bourdieu, P. (1998), *Practical Reason*. Stanford: California Stanford University Press.

Bradford, S. and Hey, V. (2007), Successful Subjectivities? The Successification of Class, Ethnic and Gender Positions. *Journal of Educational Policy*, Vol. 22, No. 6.

Cohen, L., Manion, L. and Morrison, K. (2001), *Research Methods in Education, Fifth Edition*. London: Routledge Falmer.

Coleman, J. S. (1987), Families and Schools. *Educational Researcher*, Vol. 16, No. 6.

Coleman, J. S. (1988), Social Capital in the Creation of Human Capital. *The American Journal of Sociology*, Vol. 94, (Suppl.: Organisations and Institutions: Sociological and Economic Approaches to the Analysis of Social Structure).

Connor, H., Tyers, C., Modood, T. and Hillage, J. (2004), *Why the Difference? A Closer Look at Higher Education Minority Ethnic Students and Graduates*, Research Brief RB552, Department for Education and Skills.

Connell, R. W. (1987), *Gender and Power*. Cambridge: Cambridge: Polity Press.

Connel, R. W., Ashenden, D. J., Kessler, S. and Dowsett, G. W. (1982), *Making the Difference: Schools, Families and Social Division*, George Allen and Unwin.

Cooley, C. (1922), *Human Nature and the Social Order*. New York: Charles Scribner's Sons.

Croll, P. (2004), Families, Social Capital and Educational Outcomes. *British Journal of Educational Studies*, Vol. 52, No. 4 (December).

Croll, P. (2006), *Occupational Choice, Socio-economic Status and Gender: A Study of Secondary School Pupils in Great Britain*. Paper presented at the European Conference on Educational Research, University of Geneva, September.

Croll, P. and Attwood, G. (2005) Truancy in Secondary School Pupils: Prevalence, Trajectories and Pupil Perspectives (with Paul Croll). *Research Papers in Education*, Vol. 21, No. 4 (December).

Croll, P., Attwood, G. and Fuller, C. (forthcoming), *Children's Futures: Early Orientations to Education and Careers*, London: Continuum.

Croll, P. and Moses, D. (2005), *The Formation and Transmission of Educational Values and Orientations.* Final Report to the ESRC, Ref R000239963.

Crompton, R. (1998), *Class and Stratification: An Introduction to Current Debates, Second Edition.* Cambridge: Polity Press.

Crozier, G. and Davies, J. (2006), Family Matters: A Discussion of the Bangladeshi and Pakistani Extended Family and Community in Supporting Children's Education. *The Sociological Review,* Vol. 54, No. 4.

Dale, A., Shaheen, N., Kalra, V. and Fieldhouse, E. (2002), Routes into Education and Employment for Young Pakistani and Bangladeshi Women in the UK. *Ethnic and Racial Studies,* Vol. 25, No. 6.

Demie, F. (2001), Short Report: Ethnic and Gender Differences in Educational Achievement and Implications for School Improvement Strategies. *Educational Research,* Vol. 43, No. 1.

DfES. (1997), Excellence in Schools. HM Government.

DfES. (2003), *Every Child Matters: Change for Children in Schools.* HM Government.

DfES. (2004), *Widening Participation in Higher Education.* HM Government.

DfES. (2005), *Extended Schools: Building On Experience.* HM Government.

DfES. (2006), *Education and Skills, Widening Participation in Higher Education.* HM Government.

DfES. (2007), *NEET Statistics: Quarterly Brief.* HM Government

Devine, F. (1997), *Social Class in America and Britain.* Edinburgh: Edinburgh University Press.

Devine, F. (1998), Class Analysis and the Stability of Class Relations. *Sociology,* Vol. 32, No. 1.

Devine, F. (2004), *Class Practices: How Parents Help Their Children Get Good Jobs.* Cambridge: Cambridge University Press.

DiMaggio, P. (1982), Cultural Capital and School Success: The Impact of Status Culture Participation on the Grades of U.S. High School Students. *American Sociological Review,* Vol. 47, No. 2.

Du Bois-Reymond, M. (1998), 'I Don't Want to Commit Myself Yet': Young People's Life Concepts. *Journal of Youth Studies,* Vol. 1, No. 1.

Dwyer, C., Modood, T., Sanghera, G., Shah, B. and Thapar-Bjorkert, S. (2006), Ethnicity as Social Capital? Explaining the Differential Educational Achievements of Young British Pakistani Men and Women. Paper presented at the Ethnicity, Mobility and Society, Leverhulme Programme Conference, University of Bristol, 16–17 March 2006.

Edwards, B. and Foley, M. W. (2001), Review: Much Ado about Social Capital. *Contemporary Sociology,* Vol. 30, No. 3.

Francis, B., Hutchings, M., Archer, L. and Melling, L. (2003), Subject Choice and Occupational Aspirations among Pupils at Girls' Schools. *Pedagogy, Culture, Society,* Vol. 11, No. 3.

Gallie, D. (1996), In: *Changing Forms of Employment: Organisations, Skills and Gender,* (Crompton, R., Gallie, D. and Purcell, K., eds) Skill, Gender and the Quality of Employment. London and New York: Routledge.

Gambetta, D. (1987), *Where They Pushed or Did They Jump?* Cambridge: Cambridge University Press.

Gaine, C. and George, R. (1999), *Gender, 'Race' and Schooling: A New Introduction.* London: Falmer Press.

Gewirtz, S., Dickson, M., Power, S., Halpin, D. and Whitty, G. (2005), The Deployment of social Capital Theory in Educational Policy and Provision: The Case of Educational Action Zones in England. *British Educational Research Journal,* Vol. 31, No. 6 (December).

Giddens, A. (1991), *Modernity and Self-Identity: Self and Society in the Late Modern Age.* California: Polity Press.

Gillborn, D. and Mirza, H. S. (2000), *Educational Inequality: Mapping Race, Class and Gender: A Synthesis of Research Evidence.* Office for Standards in Education.

Gillies, V. (2005), Raising the 'Meritocracy': Parenting and the Individualization of Social Class. *Sociology,* Vol. 39, No. 5.

Goldthorpe, J. H. (1983), Women and Class Analysis: In defence of the conventional view. *Sociology,* Vol. 17.

Goldthorpe, J. H. (1996), Class Analysis and the Re-orientation of Class Theory: The Case of Persisting Differentials in Educational Attainment*. *British Journal of Sociology,* Vol. 47, No. 3 (September).

Goldthorpe, J. H. (2007a), 'Cultural Capital': Some Critical Observations. *Sociologica,* No. 2.

Goldthorpe, J. H. (2007b), 'Cultural Capital': A Response to the Comments, *Sociologica,* No. 2.

Goldthorpe, J. H. (2007c), *On Sociology, Second Edition, Volume Two: Illustration and Retrospect.* California: Stanford University Press.

Goldthorpe, J. H. and Breen, R. (2000), In *On Sociology: Numbers, Narratives, and the Integration of Research and Theory,* Explaining Educational Differentials: Towards a Formal Rational Action Theory. Oxford: Oxford University Press.

Granovetter, M. S. (1973), The Strength of Weak Ties. *The American Journal of Sociology,* Vol. 78, No. 6.

Grenfell, M., James, D., Hodkinson, P., Reay, D. and Robbins, D. (1997), Acts *of Practical Theory: Bourdieu and Education.* London: Falmer Press.

Girl Guiding UK. (2007), *Gender Bias Still Blights School Careers Advice.* Press Release.

Hallam, S. and Ireson, J. (2006), Secondary School Pupils' Preferences for Different Types of Structured Grouping Practices. *British Educational Research Journal,* Vol. 32, No. 4 (August).

Halsey, A. H., Heath, A. F. and Ridge, J. M. (1980), *Origins and Destinations: Families, Class, and Education in Modern Britain.* Oxford: Clarendon Press.

Hargreaves, D. H. (1967), Social *Relations in a Secondary School.* London: Routledge and Kegan Paul.

Heath, A. and Britten, N. (1984), Women's Jobs do make a Difference. *Sociology,* Vol. 18.

Hey, V. (1997), *The Company She Keeps: An Ethnography of Girls' Friendship.* Buckingham: Open University Press.

Hillage, J., Kodz, J. and Pike, G. (2001), *Pre-16 Work Experience Practice in England: An Evaluation.* Research Report No. 263, Department of Education and Employment.

Hobbs, G. and Vignoles, A. (2007), *Is Free School Meal Status a Valid Proxy for Socio-economic Status (in schools research)? London: Centre for the Economics of Education.* London School of Economics.

Hodkinson, P. and Sparkes, A. C. (1997), Careership: A Sociological Theory of Career Decision Making. *British Journal of Sociology of Education,* Vol. 18, No. 1.

Hubbard, L. (2005), The Role of Gender in Academic Achievement. *International Journal of Qualitative Studies in Education,* Vol. 18, No. 5 (September–October).

Hutchings, M. and Archer, L. (2001), 'Higher than Einstein': Constructions of Going to University among Working Class Non-Participants. *Research Papers in Education,* Vol. 16, No. 1.

Ireland, E. and O'Donnell, L. (2004), Post-16 and Post-18 Transitions: Initial Findings, *Excellence in Cities Evaluation Consortium.*

Jary, D. and Jary, J. (2000), *Collins Internet Linked Dictionary of Sociology,* Collins.

Jenkins, R. (1992), *Pierre Bourdieu,* Revised Edition, London and New York: Routledege.

Joseph Rowntree Foundation. (2006), *Findings: Informing Change.* Ref: 0336.

Joseph Rowntree Foundation Findings Report. (2006), *Planned Teenage Pregnancy: Views and Experiences of Young People from Poor and Disadvantaged Backgrounds.* Bristol: The Policy Press.

Khattab, N. (2003), Explaining Educational Aspirations of Minority Students: The Role of Social Capital and Students' Perceptions. *Social Psychology of Education,* Vol. 32, No. 2 (uncorrected proof).

Lareau, A. (1997), In: *Education, Culture, Economy, Society,* (Halsey, A. H., Lauder, H., Brown, P. and Stuart Wells, A. eds) Social-Class Differences in Family-School Relationships: The Importance of Cultural Capital. Oxford: Oxford University Press.

Li, C. and Kerpelman, J. (2007), Parental Influences on Young Women's Certainty about Their Career Aspirations. *Sex Roles,* Vol. 56.

Lucey, H., Melody, J. and Walkerdine, V. (2003), Uneasy Hybrids: Pyschosocial Aspects of becoming Educationally Successful for Working-Class Young Women, *Gender and Education,* Vol. 15, No. 3.

Lutterell, W. (1989), Working Class Women's Ways of Knowing: The Effects of Gender, Race and Class. *Sociology of Education,* Vol. 62, No. 1 (Special Edition on Gender and Education, January).

Lyndsey, G., Pather, S. and Starnd, S. (2006), *Special Educational Needs and Ethnicity: Issues of Over and Under Representations.* Department of Education and Skills, Research Report, RR757.

Mac an Ghaill, M. (1988), *Young, Gifted and Black.* Milton Keynes and Philadelphia: Open University Press.

McRobbie, A. (1978), *Women Take Issue: Aspects of Women's Subordination.* Women's Study Group, London: Hutchinson.

Mercia Research and Strategy (2005), *Skills, Employment and Learning in #### [1]: A Labour Market Assessment.* Worcester.

Merton, R. K. (1938), Social Structure and Anomie. *American Sociological Review,* Vol. 3, No. 5 (October).

Miriam, D. E., Ball, S. J., Davies, J. and Reay, D. (2003), Gender Issues in Parental Involvement in Student Choices of Higher Education. *Gender and Education,* Vol. 15, No. 1.

Modood, T. (2006), Ethnicity, Muslims and Higher Education Entry in Britain. *Teaching in Higher Education,* Vol. 11, No. 2 (April).

Modood, T. (2004), Capitals, Ethnic Identity and Educational Qualifications. *Cultural Trends,* Vol. 13(2), No. 50 (June).

Modood, T., Berthoud, R., Lakey, J., Nazroo, J., Smith, P., Virdee, S. and Beishon, S. (1999), *Ethnic Minorities in Britain, London.* London: Policy Studies Institute.

Morris, M. and Golden, S. (2005), *Evaluation of Aimhigher: Excellence Challenge Interim Report.* Slough: National Foundation for Educational Research.

Morrow, V. (1999), Conceptualising Social Capital in Relation to the Well Being of Children and Young People: A Critical Review. *The Sociological Review,* Vol. 44, No. 7.

Nowotny, H. (1981), In: *Access to Power: Cross-National Studies of Women and Elites,* (Fuchs Epstein, C. and Laub Coser, R., eds) Women in Public Life in Austria. London: George Allen and Unwin.

O'Connor, P. (2006), Young People's Constructions of the Self: Late Modern Elements and Gender Differences. *Sociology,* Vol. 40, No. 1.

Office for National Statistics (2006), *Education: Chinese Pupils have best GCSE Results.*

OfSTED. (2005), Special Measures: Monitoring Inspection of 'Southwell' Girls School, December.

Osgood, J., Francis, B. and Archer, L. (2006) Gendered Identities and Work Placement: Why Don't Boys Care? *Journal of Education Policy,* Vol. 21, No. 3.

Osler, A. and Vincent, K. (2003), *Girls and Exclusion: Rethinking the Agenda.* London and New York: Routledge Falmer.

Pahl, R. (2006), In: *Porcupines in Winter: The Pleasures and Pains of Living Together in Modern Britain,* (Buonfino, A. and Mulgan, G., eds) On Respect: The Social Strains of Social Change. London: The Young Foundation.

Pakulski, J. and Waters, M. (1996), *The Death of Class.* London: Sage.

Phillips, T. and Western, M. (2005), In: *Rethinking Class: Culture, Identities and Lifestyle,* (Devine, F., Savage, M., Scott, J. and Crompton, R., eds) *Social* Change and Social Identity: Postmodernity, Reflexive Modernisation and the Transformation of Social Identities in Australia. Basingstoke: Palgrave MacMillan.

Platt, L. (2005), Migration and Social Mobility: The Life Chances of Britain's Ethnic Minority Communities. Bristol: Joseph Rowntree Foundation, the Policy Press.

Platt, L. (2007), Making Education Count: The Effects of Ethnicity and Qualifications on Intergenerational Social Class Mobility. *The Sociological Review,* Vol. 55, No. 3.

Putman, R. (2000), *Bowling Alone: The Collapse and Revival of American Community.* New York and London: Simon and Schuster.

Rassool, N. (2004), Sustaining Linguistic Diversity Within the Global Cultural Economy: Issues of Language Rights and Linguistic Possibilities. *Comparative Education,* Vol. 40, No. 2.

Reay, D. (1998a), 'Always Knowing' and 'Never Being Sure': Familial and Institutional Habituses and Higher Education Choice. *Journal of Education Policy,* Vol. 13, No. 4.

Reay, D. (1998b), In: *Acts of Practical Theory: Bourdieu and Education,* (Greenfell, M., James, D., et al., eds) Cultural Reproduction: Mother's Involvement in Their Children's Primary Schooling. London: Falmer Press.

Reay, D. (2004a), Education and Cultural Capital: The Implications of Changing Trends in Education Policies. *Cultural Trends*, Vol. 13(2), No. 50 (June).

Reay, D. (2004b), Gendering Bourdieu's Concepts of Capitals? Emotional Capital, Women and Social Class. *Sociological Review*, Vol. 52, No. 18 (suppl. 2), pp. 57–74.

Reay, D. (2005), Doing the Dirty Work of Social Class? Mothers' Work in Support of their Children's Schooling. *Sociological Review*, Vol. 53, No. 2, pp. 104–115.

Reay, D. (2006), The Zombie Stalking English Schools: Social Class and Educational Inequality. *British Journal of Educational Studies*, Vol. 54, No. 3 (September).

Reay, D. and Wiliam, D. (1999), 'I'll be a Nothing': Structure, Agency and The Construction of Identity Through Assessment [1]. *British Educational Research Journal*, Vol. 25, No. 3.

Richardson, R. and Wood, A. (2004), *The Achievements of British Pakistani Learners RAISE Project 2002–04*. Stoke-on-Trent: Trentham Books.

Roberts, K. (2001), *Class in Modern Britain*. Basingstoke: Palgrave.

Rose, D. and Pevalin, D. (2002), In: *A Researchers Guide to the National Statistics Socio-economic Classification* (Rose, D. and Pevalin, D., eds) The NS-SEC described. London: Sage.

Savage, M. (2000), *Class Analysis and Social Transformation*. Buckingham, Philadelphia: Open University Press.

Schneider, S. and Stevenson, D. (1999), *The Ambitious Generation: America's Teenagers. Motivated but Directionless*. New Haven and London: Yale University Press.

Shain, F. (2000), Culture, Survival and Resistance: Theorizing, Young Asian Women's Experience and Strategies in Contemporary British Schooling and Society. *Discourse: Studies in the Cultural Politics of Education*, Vol. 21, No. 2.

Shain, F. (2003), *The Schooling and Identity of Asian Girls*. Stoke-on-Trent: Trentham Books.

Shotts, P. (2007), Report by the Director of Education and Children's Services: 14–19 Strategy for Education in ####.[2]

Siann, G. (1996), Motivation and Attribution at Secondary School: The Role of Ethnic Group and Gender. *Gender and Education*, Vol. 8, No. 3.

Singh Ghuman, P. A. (2001), Asian Girls in Secondary School: A British Perspective. *Intercultural Education*, Vol. 12, No. 2 (July).

Sullivan, A. (2001), Cultural Capital and Educational Attainment. *Sociology*, Vol. 35, No. 4.

Swartz, D. (1997), *Culture and Power: The Sociology of Pierre Bourdieu*. Chicago and London: The University of Chicago Press.

Swidler. A. (1986), Culture in Action: Symbols and Strategies. *American Sociological Review*, Vol. 51, No. 2 (April).

The Runnymede Trust (no date given), *Black and Ethnic Minority Young People and Educational Disadvantage*.

Tinklin, T., Croxford, L., Ducklin, A. and Frame, B. (2005), Gender and Attitudes to Work and Family Roles: The Views of Young People at the Millennium. *Gender and Education*, Vol. 17, No. 2 (May).

Tyrer, D. and Ahmed, F. (2006), *Muslim Women and Higher Education: Identities, Experiences and Prospects. A Summary Report*. Liverpool: John Moores University and European Social Fund.

Van de Werfhorst, H. G. and Hofstede, S. (2007), Cultural Capital or Relative Risk Aversion? Two Mechanisms for Educational Inequality Explore. *The British Journal of Sociology*, Vol. 58, No. 3.

Vincent, C. and Warren, S. (2001), 'This Won't Take Long . . .' Interviewing, Ethics and Diversity. *Qualitative Studies in Education,* Vol. 14, No. 1.

Warmington, P. (2003), 'You Need A Qualification for Everything These Days'. The Impact of Work, Welfare and Disaffection upon the Aspirations of Access to Higher Education. *Students*, Vol. 24, No. 1.

Willis, P. (1977), *Learning to Labor: How Working Class Kids Get Working Class Jobs.* New York: Columbia University Press.

Wright, C., Weekes, D. and McGlaughlin, A. (1999), Gender-blind Racism in the Experience of Schooling and Identity Formation. *International Journal of Inclusive Education*, Vol. 3, No. 4.

Online Resources

Office for National Statistics, http://www.statistics.gov.uk/cci/nugget.asp?id=1003 (accessed November 2006).

The Standards Site, Department for Children, Schools and Families, Home School Arrangement: Parental Involvement http://www.standards.dfes.gov.uk/parentalinvolvement/hsa/ (accessed September 2007)

UCAS data, http://www.ucas.com/figures/ucasdata/socio/index.html#analyse (accessed January 2007).

Indicators of deprivation for use in school funding: September draft of notice to authorities: http://www.teachernet.gov.uk/_doc/10254/Technical%20Review%20of%20Deprivation%20Indicators%20(Sept%2006)%20Full%20draft.doc

Notes

[1] The name of the place included in the title of this report is deliberately excluded to protect the anonymity of both the school and its students.

[2] The name of the place included in the title of this report is deliberately excluded to protect the anonymity of both the school and its students.

Index

Note: Page numbers in italics denote tables.

9 781441 152077